D0596212

BORDERS on STAGE

Plays Produced by Teatro Bravo

Edited by Trino Sandoval

with contributions by
Daniel Enrique Pérez and
Guillermo Reyes

The Lion & The Seagoat, LLC
Phoenix, Arizona

THE WOMEN OF JUAREZ

By concentrating on the fate of one young factory worker, writer-director Ruben Amavizca places those murders in a strikingly human context, pulling no punches when it comes to placing blame – particularly on the corrupt Mexican officials who have botched the case from the beginning. Amavizca seldom sensationalizes his subject matter, but the statistics are nonetheless overwhelming. At least 261 women have been slain since 1993, according to the Mexican attorney general's office. Their families now clamor for justice, and Amavizca lends an effective voice to that outcry.

— Los Angeles Times, 9/11/03

...is a necessary mirror in today's politically complicated society;...the reflection of a world in dire need of poetic juctice.

— Polly J. Hodge, Chapman University, Gestos, 11/05

BOXCAR/EL VAGÓN

Based on the hundreds stories of Latinos who risk their lives each year to enter the United States through southern deserts, *Boxcar*, by Silvia Gonzalez, is the tale of five men crossing the border in a sweltering freight train. The drama roused so much political discussion that the Repertorio Español recently transformed the stage into a political forum.

— Backstage, 9/20/07

14

...it's only natural after seeing a play like *14* to wonder if the cocky vaquero striding down Broadway, or the weathered abuelita hawking frutas, or the father windowshopping with his wife and children, or their friends or members of their familia have ever attempted their own border crossing. And then you're struck by a realization: The border isn't 100 miles to the south. It's right here. Right now.

— Orange County Weekly, 3/6/08

MISS CONSUELO

The audience had best buckle up lest they laugh themselves clear out of their chairs when playwright Guillermo Reyes' undaunted heroine faces off with forces determined to mold her into their expectations of Latin women.

— Daily Record, 10/31/97

No comedy this year has more laughs in it.

— Star Ledger, 11/5/07

Miss Consuelo scores some direct hits on the funny bone---especially when the playwright is taking on pretentious writing teachers, academic politics and minority political correctness.

— Arizona Republic, 3/26/02

PLACES TO TOUCH HIM

A captivating theatrical journey...Guillermo Reyes' *Places to Touch Him,* in its premiere production (at) Teatro Bravo, is the playwright's most fully realized, most expertly crafted story in recent years.

— Phoenix New Times, 9/26/02

Places to Touch Him finds Reyes moving in the right direction of a landmark, definitive work.

— Get Out, Tribune, 9/15/02

ISBN 978-1-4276-3222-7

Editor-in-chief: Virginia Betz
Executive Managing Editor: Trino Sandoval
Editorial/production supervision and graphic design: Guadalupe
Candanedo
Cover Art Director: Guadalupe Candanedo

This book was set in Times New Roman PS 10/11.5

 Copyright © 2008 by The Lion & The Seagoat

All rights reserved. No part of this book may be reproduced, in
any form or by any means, without permission in writing from
the publisher. Requests for permission should be addressed to:
The Lion and the Seagoat at lionandseagoat@gmail.com.

Cover photographs courtesy of the following:

The Women of Juarez – Carlos Ramirez
El vagón – Teatro Bravo
Places to Touch Him – Sean Kapera

For Victor Esteban Briones Sandoval

Contents

Preface

By the 1990s, Phoenix, Arizona, was already one of the top ten most populated cities in the country and by the end of that decade the Hispanic population in the city reached 34 percent (U.S. Census Bureau, 2000). Despite these striking statistics, Phoenix did not have an established theater company that produced Latino-themed plays even though there were occasional attempts by local Latino artists to stage productions. There were also traveling theater troupes that brought productions to Phoenix and in some instances, mainstream theater companies produced a token Latino-themed play.

Motivated by the demographic statistics and the lack of Latino theatrical productions in Phoenix, in the summer of 2000, Guillermo Reyes, Daniel Enrique Pérez and I, launched the first season of Teatro Bravo, a bilingual theater company. The mission of Teatro Bravo would be to produce quality Latino-themed plays in English and Spanish. We wanted to promote the complex portrait of the Latin American populations in United States and to entertain and enlighten with diverse, unpredictable, sometimes confrontational, but always caring and engaged theater. We wanted to reach audiences of all ages and all cultures, and to invite audiences to learn about the triumphs and troubles of Latin American culture through theater. It was also of prime importance for us to develop and showcase the much needed talents of Latino actors, directors, playwrights, choreographers and designers. Our personal and educational backgrounds, our community involvement, and our professional experiences proved to be the perfect combination for a successful launching of Teatro Bravo!

Guillermo, a Chilean-born playwright and Arizona State University professor of Playwriting, had a culturally inclusive and innovative vision as our artistic director. Daniel Enrique, a Phoenix native, now a professor of Chicana/o and Latina/o studies at University of Nevada, Reno, with a background in U.S. Latino culture, became our managing director. I, a native-born Mexican with a California upbringing, and a professor of Spanish at Phoenix College with an educational background in Mexican and Latin American culture took on the role of executive producer. Seven years later, we had produced more than twenty plays and readings.

Our productions have included classics, such as the Pablo Neruda's translation of *Romeo and Juliet* and Mexican playwright Miguel Sabido's *Juana la loca (Juana, Mad Queen of Spain)*, some more commercial presentations such as *Entre mujeres (Among Women)* by Santiago Moncada from Spain and *Sexo, pudor y lágrimas (Sex, Shame and Tears)* by Mexican playwright Antonio Serrano. The productions of the Chicano comedic troupe, Culture Clash, *A Bowl of Beings* and *The Mission* proved to be favorites with our Chicano community, as did the witty comedies of Guillermo Reyes' *Miss Consuelo* and *The Hispanick Zone*. We also ventured into a perilous zone by producing plays that a certain segment of our community still considers taboo, such as the gay-themed plays *Places to Touch Him* and *Men on the Verge II,* both by Guillermo Reyes, and the Spanish translation of Eve Ensler's

The Vagina Monologues. This sample of Teatro Bravo productions is proof of our commitment to produce plays that are diverse and engaging. At the same time, the most significant aspect of the work that we do is the production of plays that address the most pressing social and political issues facing our community today: Latina/o identities, racism, discrimination, feminicide and immigration.

The topic of immigration, highlighting the plight of all of those individuals who leave their home country to enter the United States and the often vicious anti-immigrant sentiment they face at the turn of the millennium has caught the attention of Latina and Latino playwrights. At Teatro Bravo, we believe it was, and is, our moral responsibility and obligation to bring to the stage these sensitive and sometimes confrontational issues. It is important to note that Arizona is on the frontlines of the immigration debates. Arizona has been one of the states in the Union that has made national and international headlines for its hard-line and uncompassionate attitude towards immigrants. Many times, this attitude stems from the reactionary conservative sector of the community. During the last few years, much anti-immigrant legislation has been approved by the Republican-controlled legislature and by the voters. The urgency of the emotionally-charged immigrant issue in our Latino community and the community-at-large has received our collective attention and is one of the reasons that all of the plays included in this anthology deal with this subject matter. It is our intention that the content of these plays provide the immigrants' perspective to the dialogue on this issue. Most importantly, all of the plays included in this anthology consider the human element of the immigration debate in a sensitive, civil and compassionate manner.

This anthology includes five plays produced by Teatro Bravo with introductory notes on each production by Guillermo Reyes and an essay on the plays by Dr. Daniel Enrique Pérez. The order of the plays in the anthology is arranged in such a way that it connotes the physical movement across the U.S.-Mexico border, starting with the powerful and moving play by Los Angeles-based Ruben Amavizca Murua, *The Women of Juarez*, in which he depicts the tragic disappearances and deaths of young women, many of them from southern Mexico, in the border city of Juarez, Chihuahua, Mexico. The second play, *El vagón* by Silvia Gonzales S., is based on the heart wrenching true story of a group of men fatally trapped in a boxcar as they try to cross the border from Mexico into the United States. The subsequent plays, *14* by José Casas and Guillermo Reyes' *Miss Consuelo* and *Places to Touch Him*, deal with the wide-ranging socio-economic and political issues impacting the lives of Latin American immigrants in the United States.

I would like to acknowledge the hard work of all the actors, directors, writers, technicians, choreographers and designers who have generously contributed their time and talent to bring to fruition all of Teatro Bravo productions. I especially would like to thank all the volunteers: Guadalupe Candanedo and Dr. Virginia Betz, the Teatro Bravo Board of Directors, and Board of Advisors for their support.

Finally, thank you all of our individual supporters, the Phoenix Art Commission and the Arizona Commission on the Arts who have made it possible for us to produce these plays through their financial contributions.

Trino Sandoval
Phoenix, Arizona
June 2008

Note: We are aware that Spanish orthography may vary from play to play. We have left this at the discretion of the authors, who have somewhat different ideas and styles about how to represent Spanish and/or Spanglish in the printed text. Some writers use an accent on their names and others do not. For the most part, if the text is in English, no accents are used but if the text is in Spanish we italicize and use accents.

Teatro Bravo
Board of Directors 2007-2010

Guillermo Reyes .... Arizona State University
Artistic Director

Trino Sandoval, Ph.D. .... Phoenix College
Executive Producer
and Board President

Mónica Castañeda .... Maricopa Community Colleges
Secretary and Treasurer

Rosa Elena Amavisca .... Community Member

Anthony H. Chambers, Ph.D. .... Arizona State University

José Antonio (Tony) Colón, Esq. .... Maricopa County
Public Defender's Office

Heidi García, Ph.D. .... North High School

Marcos Najera .... KJZZ radio 91.5 FM

Cecilia Rosales-Torres, Ph.D. ...... Latino Perspectives Magazine

Sylvia Russell .... North High School

Carmen Urioste, Ph.D. .... Arizona State University

Board of Advisors

David W. Foster, Ph.D. .... Arizona State University

Jorge Huerta, Ph.D. .... University of California, San Diego

Juana Suárez, Ph.D. .... University of Kentucky, Lexington

Pam Sterling, Ph.D. .... Arizona State University

Dramatizing the Borderlands: Staging Chicana/o and Latina/o Lives and Deaths

A borderland is a vague and undetermined place created by the emotional residue of an unnatural boundary. It is a constant state of transition. The prohibited and forbidden are its inhabitants.
— Gloria Anzaldúa

Staging the border(ed) is undoubtedly one of the most important political acts in which one can engage, especially during a period in the United States that has experienced one of the most heated and controversial debates regarding borders and migrants. Besides creating and contributing to a dialogue on such issues, the stage becomes a transgressive and transformative space where outcomes are often unpredictable. In staging the border(ed), people become geopolitical subjects whose lives materialize in tangible ways and every individual who is present during any performance participates in this transformation, including the cast, crew and public. By border(ed), I am referring to both physical and metaphorical borders as well as to the people who have crossed or been crossed by them. The plays selected for this collection center on such spaces and experiences. *Places to Touch Him* and *Miss Consuelo* by Guillermo Reyes, *Las mujeres de Juárez/The Women of Juarez* by Rubén Amavizca, *Boxcar/El vagón* by Silvia González S. and *14* by José Casas are just a few of the plays produced between 2002 and 2006 by Teatro Bravo. Producing these plays required dealing with real borderland issues, both on and off stage. In this essay I will discuss the realities of staging Chicana/o and Latina/o lives and deaths, especially as they relate to issues of (im)migration, sexuality, violence and Latinidad. I am particularly interested in showing how performances on the border and of the bordered can create social change and transform communities.

When each of the plays mentioned above was presented, the border(ed) materialized in tangible ways: people who had never been to the theater before found themselves transfixed by a new artistic medium, some saw themselves or their families represented on stage for the first time, others learned about historical figures and current events that they did not know much, if anything, about, and many experienced a consciousness-raising that inspired them to take action. What sets these plays apart from the average theater-going experience is that the lives on stage are rarely seen in theaters, especially in communities that have not had the privilege of seeing teatro Chicana/o-Latina/o. Characters that range from gay Chicano politicians to young Mexican women who disappear take the stage to another dimension, where Chicanas/os and Latinas/os are not gang bangers, gardeners or housekeepers. Instead, their lives are presented in their full complexity, with issues that are poignant and relevant. In this way, teatro Chicana/o-Latina/o becomes an artistic medium that documents actual lives and addresses the sociopolitical issues that affect them.

Luis Valdez has taught us that Chicano theater is first and foremost a reaffirmation of life and, secondly, that it is "particularly our own, not another imitation of the *gabacho*." He also emphasized that in order to act as an instrument of change, it "must be revolutionary in technique as well as content"(7). To him, the politics of doing theater was as important as the art form itself. Whereas many artists produce art to entertain or aesthetically please their audience, Chicana/o and Latina/o artists have demonstrated overwhelmingly that they have a strong political agenda with a commitment to enact change, while also paying attention to aesthetic values.

In his seminal book, *Chicano Theater: Themes and Forms* (1982), Jorge Huerta contends that Luis Valdez's Teatro Campesino "became the symbol of the Chicano's theatrical expression, inspiring Chicanos all over the country to form other *teatros* dedicated to exposing the sociopolitical conditions of the Mexican-American community"(1). Huerta also underscores the important role that *Teatro Campesino* served in educating the Chicano community. Besides its effort to expose injustices, enact change and educate—all of which remain essential aspects of this particular art form—teatro chicana/o-latina/o has evolved in order to reflect the diversity of Chicana/o and Latina/o people in the United States and on el otro lado. Whereas sometimes this means staging the lives and circumstances of people who actually exist, at other times it can include imagining Chicana/o and Latina/o people in new roles in society, realms that remain to be inhabited and appropriated.

(Re)Imagining the Border(ed)

A number of Guillermo Reyes's plays do a particularly good job of imagining new possibilities for Chicanas/os and Latinas/os. His characters are unique and complex. They are also strong, intelligent and multi-faceted, almost always challenging categories of race, class, gender and sexuality. Although many of his characters are loosely based on real people, they are often imbued with additional traits that reconfigure notions of Latinidad.

For example, in Reyes's *Places to Touch Him*, a politically astute gay Chicano lawyer named César runs for public office. The fact that Reyes has created such a character for the stage requires that César materialize every night his character is performed, wherever he might appear. One possible result is that this imagined character will influence others who might identify with him and produce a real-life César who runs for office and does things for la comunidad. In fact, during the production of *Places to Touch Him*, a gay Chicano ran for a seat in the House of Representatives for the first time in the state of Arizona and won. Naturally, fantasy influences reality in the same way that reality influences fantasy. The inevitable mapping of identities that occurs when people see others who are like them on stage or in the media is extremely powerful. This makes creating new and positive portrayals of Chicana/o and Latina/o people all the more important, especially when there is a dearth of such representation in the media. Throughout the history of Teatro Bravo, we have had audience members thank us for portraying what they perceived to be their lives or people with whom they can identify on stage. The possible outcomes after undergoing such a process of self-identification are endless. These reconfigured notions of self can move people in new directions. They can inspire those who have not perceived themselves in certain roles to delve into new social locations.

As Rosaura Sánchez suggests in her essay, "On a Critical Realist Theory of Identity," "positionality" allows one to assess social conditions and locations; it can also be a "politically productive" site where counter-discourses and a "critical assessment of hegemonic ideologies" can take place (39). Furthermore, she contends that through identification (or disidentification) one can create new social locations where multiple elements of identity politics can be (re)considered. The main characters in *Places to Touch Him* undergo a similar process. They constantly evaluate their conditions in order to establish new social locations that ultimately reshape their careers and their lives.

In the play, César meets and becomes enamored by a young, very attractive, working-class Chicano named Domingo who distracts César from his campaign. Whereas César must portray a clean-cut and mainstream persona to potential voters, Domingo is the embodiment of a hypersexual gay macho clone. The relationship between the two is tinged by an array of taboos Domingo brings to the table, including his job as a part-time stripper at a local gay nightclub and the three-way he coordinates between him, César and a waiter at the same nightclub. The nightclub itself is the target of local officials who run a sting operation to uncover a prostitution ring in it. When Matt, César's campaign manager, discovers César's extracurricular activities, he is placed in the position of trying to protect his client from serious repercussions.

While César recognizes that his constituents are largely heterocentric and ethnocentric, he also longs for intimacy with another man and a connection to his cultural background—both become aspects of his identity that he must either conceal or reject in some way. His polished English, his law degree, the affluent circles he inhabits, and the lonely, uneventful single life he leads become locations where he risks losing his sense of Latinidad and queerness. However, César's positionality *vis-à-vis* a heteronormative Anglo society facilitates his identification with Domingo—the idealized version of the queer Chicano macho. Domingo represents everything that César can't openly be: Chicano and hyper-homoerotic. Domingo has the freedom to participate in gay spaces and is the epitome of the gay macho clone, with his handsome face, chiseled body, and sexually active lifestyle. He speaks in Spanglish and has close ties to his family. What's more, Domingo's primary role model, his father, is uneducated, working-class and in a precarious, life-threatening situation: "My old man did what he could, but he was undocumented and worked as a dishwasher until he retired. I can't blame el jefito for his poverty. He's back in Sonora, with cancer" (183). While Domingo must deal with the immediate needs of his father, he also aspires to finish a college degree and obviously admires César. Domingo is undergoing an identification process similar to that of César. He recognizes some of the privileges César enjoys, like having friends in the legal profession who can help Domingo's father in a time of need. For these two characters, being queer and Chicano requires a constant negotiation of sexual and identity politics. The two find themselves uncontrollably and inexplicably attracted to one another. Domingo must focus on his education to transcend his working-class background, which requires a less demanding social and sexually active lifestyle. César wants to be with someone who can satisfy his erotic desire and help him get in touch with his cultural roots, while not compromising his political aspirations. Both trajectories require that the characters imagine themselves in a new social location where queerness and Latinidad can coexist peacefully. While this proves to be a challenge for both characters, the process permits an identification—even if it's merely temporarily—with the desired outcome.

Similarly, in his play *Miss Consuelo*, Reyes is at the forefront of identity politics. Here, he also obfuscates the lines that are typically drawn between fiction and reality. Miss Consuelo, a working-class Mexican immigrant turned novelista is engaged in writing a fictitious romance novel where the characters she creates come to life on stage and act out what she conceptualizes in her mind and on paper. As Reyes explains in his notes for the play:

> Consuelo is a real woman with an accent. Not a TV stereotype of the accented Latina, but the real thing. If I've provided a few hints about her accent by spelling some of her dialogue such as 'foorious pashions,' it's not meant to box in an actress and a director into pronouncing it that way. I'm more interested in the real, lively, somewhat eccentric, but always grounded human being that Consuelo is. The accent is not the most important element of her speech, and a hint of it is better than a thick mess of sounds that prevent the actress from creating a true character (132).

Therefore, Miss Consuelo is absolutely not intended to be the stereotypical Latina that permeates Hollywood films and prime time English-language television. Instead, Reyes is interested in creating a Latina who challenges and interrogates such stereotypical representations. As the narrator suggests at the beginning of the play, *Miss Consuelo* is "a tale by Miss Consuelo as narrated by Miss Consuelo's characters in Miss Consuelo's imagination" (133). Miss Consuelo wants to write romance novels, but not typical American romance novels nor the Mexican telenovela type. As she explains to one of her characters, she is "the only romance writer in the world devoted to hot, passionate, but clean romance" (135). As Miss Consuelo writes her novel and creates her characters, the same characters shape her own life. She engages in conversations with them and they challenge the circumstances in which she places them. As a result, each character she creates becomes an extension of herself, her life and her desires. Neither the characters nor Miss Consuelo remain in fixed social locations. As in the case of *Places to Touch Him*, their positionality also facilitates a process of identification that transforms their existence.

Miss Consuelo's creative writing teacher at the local community college, Mr. Caldwell, tries to get Miss Consuelo to write a stereotypical Latina novel based on what he imagines to be her immigrant background. After reading her manuscript,

"Romance of the Guacamoles," he tells her that he does not feel she is close enough to the script and accuses her of attempting to write about something that is unfamiliar to her. In his view, the script lacks what he expected to see in a Latina novel: the plight of undocumented immigrants, border issues, colonization, etc. He encourages her to write about something that is "close to the essence of [her] minimal existence, of [her] angst-ridden soul, of [her] agonizing sense of immigrant selflessness" (137). Although Miss Consuelo migrated to the U.S. legally and has acculturated in many ways, Mr. Caldwell's misidentification of her as an "angst-ridden" undocumented immigrant leads to a constant, identity-politics battle between the two. Miss Consuelo identifies as Miss Consuelo, the one-of-a-kind romance novelista who employs a unique use of English and Spanish grammar in her writing. She recognizes that her "Englich" is what makes her Miss Consuelo Chavez, la novelista. Ironically, Mr. Caldwell harasses her about improving her English grammar, but tries to get her to make the contents of her writing a little more Latina—in a stereotypical way, of course. Miss Consuelo rejects both of Mr. Caldwell's suggestions. Instead, she engages in a process of identification with other realms that fosters her personal and creative agency.

As border(ed) subjects, Miss Consuelo, Cesar and Domingo represent new social locations for Chicana/o and Latina/o people. These fictitious characters inhabit and negotiate spaces that have not traditionally been accessible to members of this ethnic group. In some way, they are able to convert their borderland state to a place where they are not only legitimized, but where they possess the autonomy and the skills to pursue their dreams.

Staging Migrant Lives and Deaths

As a theater of the oppressed, teatro chicana/o-latina/o is always concerned with the politics of representation as well as the representation of politics. Dealing with issues related to identity politics and State politics is necessary when staging Chicana/o and Latina/o lives. As Suzanne Oboler suggests in *Ethnic Labels, Latino Lives: Identity and the Politics of (Re)Presentation in the United States*, engaging in politics is one way an ethnic or minority group moves toward inclusion in the larger community, especially when it experiences antagonism: "the continued struggle for full citizenship, equal rights, and social and cultural inclusion in the 'national community' requires that Latinos and other minorities affirm group rights and interest in political terms when confronted by nativist attacks" (98).

All of the plays included in this collection confront State and identity politics with zeal and gusto. As regards the politics of representation and the representation of politics, Rubén Amavizca Murúa's *Las mujeres de Juárez/Women of Juarez* (originally written in Spanish), Sylvia González S.'s *Boxcar/El vagón* (originally written in English) and José Casas's *14* (bilingual, English and Spanish, in its original form) are particularly concerned with engaging in timely political debates. These plays were based on real incidents that involved, and continue to involve, violent deaths: the brutal rapes and murders of hundreds of women in Juarez and the tragic deaths of migrants who attempt to enter the United States in pursuit of the American dream. Through staging the lives and deaths of people who live on the border, across the border and everywhere in between, these plays participate in a discourse on U.S.-Mexico economic and immigration politics while honoring the lives and affirming the rights of bordered people.

Las mujeres de Juárez is just one of several cultural texts that have emerged as a response to the Juarez murders in Mexico. Other texts include: Lourdes Portillo's documentary *Señorita extraviada*, Alicia Gaspar de Alba's (2005) *Desert Blood: The Juarez Murders* and Gregory Nava's *Bordertown* (2006). Teatro Bravo staged the Spanish version of Amavizca's *Las mujeres de Juárez* in Phoenix in 2005 and the production traveled to Reno that same year. In 2007 Teatro Bravo staged the English version in Phoenix and the play seems to have taken on a life of its own. We continue to receive requests and invitations to take the play to various institutions and communities. Of all of the plays Teatro Bravo has produced since its inception, *Las mujeres de Juárez* has to be the most compelling. It has grabbed audience members unexpectedly and moved people emotionally and politically. Even the cast and crew were deeply affected by participating in this production. They often expressed inexplicable phenomenon, like sensing the presence of some of the women who had been murdered.

These very deep emotional reactions were transferred on stage and profound messages came across to audience members. For some, it was the first time they had heard about the disappearances and murders of women in Juarez and, for many who knew something about the subject beforehand, it raised new issues and questions. For example, one audience member commented that she thought she knew what to expect, but she did not expect to be moved so deeply or learn so much about what was happening in Juarez. The same audience member said the play raised many questions for her regarding gender issues, corruption, and the role of the U.S. with regard to the issue. Her comments were precisely the type of critical thinking in which I hoped audience members would engage when seeing the play. The young lady, Liliana Diaz, happened to be one of my brightest students at the University of Nevada, Reno, and an aspiring lawyer. She was taking one of my courses at the time and I had promoted the play and discussed the issue in class. Overall, we used the play as a way of educating the community about an important subject. We put together a bilingual fact sheet with general information and a section, titled "What Can You Do to Help?," and we handed it out at the play. The sheet included the names and contact information of associations that were addressing the issue. We also order several copies of the UCLA Chicano Studies Research Center *Latino Policy & Issues Brief,* titled "The Maquiladora Murders, or, Who is Killing the Women of Juarez, Mexico?" (Gaspar de Alba, 2003) and had them available at each performance. Finally, we had an English synopsis available for those who did not know Spanish well. After seeing the play, one of my graduate students, Rachel Tillotson, was so inspired to learn and do more, that she did her Master's thesis, titled "Borderland Women: Cultural Production on the Women of Juarez," on the subject, which she completed in 2006.

The play positions young Mexican women—represented by Maritza—at the center of a debate surrounding the maquiladora industry, globalization, and women's rights. While the audience has an opportunity to get to know and empathize with a struggling Mexican family, the text is imbued with politics, largely transmitted through the use of various narrative voices that comment on the sociopolitical conditions of the area. The narrators provide alarming statistics, call on the multinational corporations to take responsibility for the safety of their workers, and provide possible leads in an attempt to solve the disappearances and murders of the women. All of these tools are used to move, educate, and incite the public.

One of the most rewarding experiences in the years we have spent producing teatro Chicana/o-Latina/o in the community has been witnessing how diverse the audiences have been. The fact that most of the people involved in Teatro Bravo have had close ties with community colleges and universities has helped to diversify the audience even more. For *Las mujeres de Juárez* in particular, the demographic composition of the audience was unique. We had people who did not know a word of Spanish but who were very interested in the subject matter mixed with students who were learning Spanish sitting next to native Spanish speakers and people from the community from a wide variety of socioeconomic backgrounds. It was truly a unique way to bridge communities that are often divided by the borders created by the institutions in which we participate. As Nicolás Kanellos has suggested in *Mexican American Theater* (1987), it is important to take into account the nature of the audiences and the social, political and cultural environment in which the performances take place. For Kanellos, Latino theater serves the "social and political purposes of the community" (117). This can involve everything from grass roots organizing to providing a form of cultural entertainment. Furthermore, in *A History of Hispanic Theatre in the United States* (1990), he contends that some of the characteristics that are prevalent in the trajectory of "Hispanic" theater in the U.S. are: "the ability to create art even under the most trying of circumstances, social and cultural cohesiveness and national pride in the face of racial and class pressures, cultural continuity and adaptability in a foreign land" (xv). Certainly, these characteristics continue to shape Chicana/o and Latina/o theatrical productions and the communities they are often intended to serve. The challenges associated with dramatizing the borderlands are countless, but so are the rewards. Dealing with border issues on stage also requires taking on the responsibility of participating in the debate, educating people, overcoming a series of unexpected obstacles and preparing yourself emotionally. As Gloria Anzaldúa has taught us, the borderlands is a space that is constantly in transition and those who inhabit it are "los atravesados"—the "prohibited and forbidden" (3). Borderland people were involved in all aspects of the production of these plays, as were real borderland problems.

By staging Sylvia Gonzalez S.'s *Boxcar/El vagón*, we were able to engage in a timely political debate. In 2006, during an intense period of debates regarding immigration and the status of approximately twelve million undocumented immigrants in the U.S., Teatro Bravo staged this in Phoenix in Spanish and the production traveled to Reno once again. Whereas *The Women of Juarez* centers on mujeres, *Boxcar/El vagón*, with its all-male cast, gave us an opportunity to focus on migrant hombres.

As regards the politics of representation, one of the strongest messages *Boxcar/El vagón* sends to audience members is that migrants are first and foremost human beings. Whereas the rhetoric in the media during this period focused on the "wave" or "flood" of "illegal aliens," the play highlights the personal (hi)stories of five men who stowaway in a boxcar to get to the United States in pursuit of the American dream. The play is based on the real-life tragedy that occurred in Harlingen, Texas, in 1987 where 18 immigrants suffocated to death in the trailer of an 18-wheeler, they were being transported by human smugglers. By limiting the number of migrants in her play to five, Gonzalez S. was able to create a play where the audience has the opportunity to get to know each character well. Throughout the play we learn about their dreams and aspirations, we get to know their families and loved ones, and we have the opportunity to hear them sing and laugh. We also witness the inevitable, their tragic deaths. While on this journey, *Boxcar/El vagón* raises many social, political, and economic issues: push/pull factors, discrimination, and gender roles, just to name a few.

As regards borderland issues and the representation of politics, staging *Boxcar/El vagón* involved a number of challenges. Clearly, immigration issues were always present. As one might imagine, undocumented immigrants were eager to participate in this production, as has been the case with other plays Teatro Bravo has produced. Naturally, when staging a production that will be traveling within or out of the country, the cast and crew must have documents, at the very least a government-issued identification to fly domestically. Ironically, we were unable to cast undocumented individuals who sensed a strong connection with the play. While many felt it was a play that told their stories or reflected their lives or the lives of people they knew intimately, we felt a responsibility to avoid placing anyone in a situation where they might be deported. The opening night of *Boxcar/El vagón* in Reno, April 28, 2006, happened to take place shortly after El Día de Acción (April 10, 2006) when hundreds of thousands of people participated in immigrant rights rallies and marches across the U.S. In Reno, the successful march and rally did result in some negative consequences, as was the case in many other cities. A series of rumors, raids and scare tactics ensued in what was perceived to be an attempt to quell the immigrant rights fervor. On the Friday of the opening night, the local Spanish-language radio stations were warning undocumented immigrants not to go to work or leave their homes. They spread news and rumors that INS officers had set up checkpoints at certain locations on the highway and that there were undercover INS officers arresting immigrants at a local Wal-Mart. I received calls from several people that day who said they would not be able to attend the show because they were afraid to leave their homes. Months before we staged *Boxcar/El vagón* we had no idea we would be dealing with so many real borderland issues first-hand.

What makes these plays so unique is that they provide a public forum where highly marginalized people—namely, working-class Mexican women and undocumented migrants—are not only represented, but they can express their views as regards their specific social location or positionality and, ultimately, espouse a political agenda using an agent's voice. What's more, the fact that both of these plays can be, and have been, produced in Spanish and English, not only makes the play accessible to more people, but contributes to a debate on language and identity politics. The immigration debate in the U.S. has been largely shaped by a discourse on the use of Spanish. Suzanne Oboler claims that English language use is increasingly being used as a way to measure one's assimilation and integration into U.S. society, which, in effect, de-ethnicizes American nationalism: "since the 1960s, there has been what might be called a significant increase in linguistic discrimination through the gradual politicization of language" (93). For Oboler, this is "key to understanding the ongoing social and power *repositioning* of who might be considered an 'acceptable American'" (92). In the two plays, one important result of the "repositioning" of historically marginalized subjects (speaking Spanish, English or Spanglish) to the center is their legitimation, if not as "acceptable Americans," then, at the very least, as human beings who deserve to be treated with respect and dignity.

Language issues are at the center of José Casas's *14*, another politically charged piece that tackles ethnocentrism, xenophobia and racism. Casas creates a rich dialogue on these issues by creating a variety of voices, expressed primarily in the form of a series of monologues, where each voice raises and responds to particular issues and circumstances that have shaped race and immigration debates in the United States. Scenes take place in multiple cities and towns in Arizona, some on the border and others that may appear to be culturally far removed from it, like Scottsdale and Flagstaff. In this way, Casas is able to cover a large demographic that shapes the politics of the entire state and, in many ways, reflects the politics of the United States. The play is based on an actual incident that took place in 2001 near Yuma, Arizona, where fourteen immigrants perished trying to get to the United States. Again, real people, real lives, and tragic deaths take center stage. The play astutely engages the audience in an array of debates, with Anglo, Chicano/Latino and immigrant voices juxtaposed—some in English and a couple in Spanish. The voices Casas includes in his piece allow a debate between people that does not normally take place in mainstream media. More importantly, he gives voice to those who typically do not get a chance to express their views in a public forum.

By writing the plays included in this collection, among others, the playwrights themselves engage directly with a form of artistic and social activism that produces artistic and social transformation. In many ways, teatro will never be the same and neither will our communities. It is clear that these dramaturgos have a social and political agenda that comes with the territory, so to speak. In "Theater beyond borders: Reconfiguring the artist's relationship to community in the twenty-first century—moving beyond *Bantustans*," Thulani Davis insists that it is up to those of us who live on the margins of society to create a space where we can be seen and heard:

> The challenge is to make theater a public space where many private
> worlds can be seen and heard; to make a public space where the fictional
> boundaries of the past can be our metaphors, rather than our prisons.
> American theater is the natural public space for a society no longer able
> to keep its fictional fences standing (23).

For Davis, the people who live on the margins are precisely those who engage
in the act of crossing borders: "People living at the periphery of society are the
translators, the boundary crossers, moving back and forth from main to margin,
making autonomy in the shadows" (23).

The plays included in this collection are ultimately concerned with representing
autonomous human beings. By remaining steadfast and resilient, the bordered
subjects that inhabit the Chicana/o and Latina/o stage bring new meaning to
the borderlands. They are no longer forbidden or silenced, but legitimized and
empowered.

By staging all of these plays in multiple cities, institutions and creative spaces, Teatro
Bravo has continued one of Luis Valdez's traditions, that of taking theater on the
road. As Valdez asserts: "If the raza will not come to the theatre, then the theatre
must go to the *raza*" (10). I recall the year Trino Sandoval, Guillermo Reyes and
I were trying to come up with the financial means to begin the theater company.
We knew there was a void in the arts community in Phoenix that had to be filled.
We got many of our friends to volunteer to attend a fundraiser we put together at
a Mexican restaurant in south Phoenix, in the barrio known as Las Cuatro Milpas.
We found actors to perform scenes from some of the plays we wanted to stage and
we were able to raise enough money for our first show in 2000: Culture Clash's *A
Bowl of Beings*. Since then, we have continued to attract the raza to the theater and
take teatro to la raza. These plays and scenes from these plays have been performed
in community theaters, on university and community college campuses, and in
backyards, literally.

Clearly, Teatro Bravo has taken on Luis Valdez's challenge for "Chicanos to become
involved in the art, the lifestyle, the political and religious act of doing *teatro*" (10).
The journey has been rewarding; the results, priceless. Through engaging in the
production of these plays, we have transformed lives many times over, incited
change, moved people literally and figuratively, given thousands a chance to see
their lives reflected on the stage, and given hundreds of Chicana/o-Latina/o theater
professionals an opportunity to develop and practice their craft. By putting together
this anthology, we hope others will do the same. ¡Qué viva el teatro!

> Daniel Enrique Pérez
> Reno, Nevada
> December 2007

Bibliography

A Bowl of Beings. By Culture Clash. Dir. Guillermo Reyes. Teatro Bravo, Phoenix. Sept. 2000.

Anzaldúa, Gloria. *Borderlands/La Frontera: The New Mestiza*. San Francisco: Aunt Lute Books, 1987.

Bordertown. Dir. Gregory Nava. Mobius Entertainment, Ltd., 2006.

Davis, Thulani. "Theater Beyond Borders: Reconfiguring the Artist's Relationship to Community in the Twenty-First Century—Moving Beyond Bantustans." *The Color of Theater: Race Culture, and Contemporary Performance*. Roberta Uno and Lucy Mae San Pablo Burns, eds. London: Continuum International Publishing, 2002. 21-26.

14. By José Casas. Dir. Christina Marín. Teatro Bravo. Phoenix, Sept. 2003.

Gaspar de Alba, Alicia. *Desert Blood: The Juarez Murders*. Houston: Arte Público Press, 2005.

---. "The Maquiladora Murders, or, Who is Killing the Women of Juarez, Mexico?" *UCLA Chicano Studies Research Center Latino Policy and Issues Brief* 7 (2003).

Huerta, Jorge A. *Chicano Theater: Themes and Forms*. Michigan: Bilingual Press/Editorial Bilingüe, 1982.

Kanellos, Nicolás. *A History of Hispanic Theatre in the United Status: Origins to 1940*. Austin: U of Texas P, 1990.

---. *Mexican American Theater: Legacy and Reality*. Pittsburgh: Latin American Literary Review Press, 1987.

Las mujeres de Juárez. By Rubén Amavizca Murúa. Dir. Christina Marín. Teatro Bravo. Phoenix, 4-13 Mar. 2005 and Reno, 8-10 Apr. 2005.

Miss Consuelo. By Guillermo Reyes. Dir. Joseph Megel. Teatro Bravo, Phoenix. Mar. 2002.

Oboler, Suzanne. *Ethnic Labels, Latino Lives: Identity and the Politics of (Re)Presentation in the United States*. Minneapolis: U of Minnesota P, 1995.

Places to Touch Him. By Guillermo Reyes. Dir. Guillermo Reyes. Teatro Bravo, Phoenix. Sept. 2002.

Sánchez, Rosaura. "On a Critical Realist Theory of Identity." *Identity Politics Reconsidered*. Linda Martín Alcoff, Michael Hames-García, Satya P. Mohanty, Paula M.L. Moya, eds. New York: Palgrave Macmillan, 2006. 31-52.

Señorita extraviada. Dir. Lourdes Portillo. 2001.

Tillotson, Rachel F. "Borderland Women: Cultural Production on the Women of Juarez." Master's Thesis. Department of Foreign Language and Literature, University of Nevada, Reno, 2006.

El vagón. By Sylvia González S. Dir. Guillermo Reyes. Teatro Bravo, Phoenix, 17-26 Mar. 2006 and Reno, 28-29 Apr. 2006.

Valdez, Luis. *Luis Valdez—Early Works: Actos, Bernabé and Pensamiento Serpentino*. Houston: Arte Público Press, 1990.

THE WOMEN of JUAREZ

by Ruben Amavizca Murua
English translation by Eve Muller and Liane Schirmer

Author's biography

Ruben is a survivor of more than 120 theatrical productions and over 4,000 performances, working in such diverse fields as directing, choreography, acting, designing sets, sound, production, publicity, teaching, etc. The son of a seamstress and a farm worker, as a young man Ruben labored in a *maquiladora* in his hometown of Mexicali. He also worked as a journalist before devoting his life to the theater. He is a graduate of the National School of Theatre Arts in Mexico and Los Angeles City College. He has authored several original works for the theater, among them: *Frida Kahlo*, *The Night of Cuauhtemoc*, *Che*, *MacBato*, *The Women of Juarez*, and *Pancho Villa*. Since 1993, he has held the position of Artistic Director for both Grupo de Teatro Sinergia and Teatro Frida Kahlo.

The Women of Juarez was born out of his commitment to socially conscious theater and to honor the families of the victims. "Their struggle, undying love and commitment was humbling and offered hope for a solution to this feminicide. Each name tells the story of a life that was lost - one that all of us must hold sacred in the search for justice."

Introduction

Some plays make a subtle impression, cause a slight commotion and maybe even stir a quaint sense of satisfaction like a fine finish in a delicate wine, but others wring tears and outrage, and provoke a stampede at the box office. Ruben Amavizca Murua's play, *The Women of Juarez*, swept onto our stage like a category five storm, and continues to create an outcry whenever we revive it. We produced the original Spanish version in 2005, directed by Christina Marin, and then staged the encore in English directed by Pam Sterling, just as equally successful in Fall of 2007. In either language, the play stirs the public to ask questions about why genocide against women continues unabated on our doorstep in the border city of Juarez.

In 2004, as we planned the future season, I began to entertain the idea of producing *The Women of Juarez*. I had heard about the play's success from the ongoing e-mail blasts I receive from the Frida Kahlo Theater in Los Angeles. I lost count of the many times the author had brought the play back, a similar phenomenon to Ruben's other hit play, *Frida Kahlo*, which Teatro Bravo produced in Fall of 2001. I asked Ruben for a copy of the script and, upon reading it, sensed it could do well with local audiences here in Phoenix. We scheduled it for the Spring of 2005.

Local actress Margarita Villa played the working class mother who searches for her missing daughter in Juarez, only to find authorities disrespectful and hostile. Margarita, a Mexican-American actress, brought a convincing vulnerability to this role, and anchored it in the plain anguish we continue to experience whenever we hear of brutality against the women in Juarez. Her graceful presence on stage reminded me of why we do Latino plays in Phoenix: it's apparently an act of provocation altogether in Arizona. Latinos are rarely if ever seen on local stages, let alone to play working-class Mexican mothers. There is an unspoken assumption that one perceives from the local theaters that Latino plays will not appeal to "mainstream" audiences. An actual Mexican-born actress on stage speaking Spanish must seem like a foreign world to these audiences, but, no, this dramatic event is playing right down the block and people are coming to see it in droves. The use of Spanish isn't particularly controversial to us at Teatro Bravo. It's part of our mission, in fact, to work with both English and Spanish. This particular incident of genocide of women, or feminicide, also isn't a distant event. It isn't happening in Darfur, it's still happening a few hours' drive on our border with Mexico. If anything, the play reminds us of the cultural distance we must constantly travel to see ourselves represented on stage. The mainstream people's theater resides in London or New York. The stories they tell each other nostalgically appeal to the concept of a bygone era – older established plays that once shone on Broadway or the West End, or newer plays that are sanctified by a prestigious award, as a reminder that culture must be imposed by critics far away from our city. *The Women of Juarez* is penned by a Mexican author living in Los Angeles. That's it. No Pulitzers are involved, no Tonys, no New York Critics' Awards, just the plain audacity of portraying the reality of our lives here in the borderland. Basically, what we've got here is a local author with plenty to say. What must irk the mainstream critics most, I believe, is that there should be authors living right here in our midst who deserve to be seen on the local stages dealing with issues not sanctified elsewhere.

The Women of Juarez became our most successful production in the two permutations we have staged thus far, and it simply confirmed our suspicion that an audience exists for plays that portray urgent matters pertinent to our lives. It is the most local of plays, I believe, in the best sense of the word. It's live performance with a message, a fervent didacticism that says: "Here it is; deal with it." And we do. It forces us to look nowhere else but to our lives, and it requires people to do something about it, such as a letter to a congressman or the U.S. companies based in Juarez, to abet the process of securing the actual women of Juarez a safe, prosperous life. "Is that too much to ask?" the Mother in the play asks in her final haunting line, and we dare believe it is not. The play deserves to be seen and performed everywhere in this country. We're glad to be able to publish it.

> Guillermo Reyes
> Phoenix, AZ
> December 2007

Production History

The Women of Juarez by Ruben Amavizca Murua premiered at the Frida Kahlo Theater in Los Angeles, California, in August 29, 2003, directed by Ruben Amavizca Murua with the following cast:

> MOTHER... Ingrid Marquez
> FATHER....................Pedro J. Ortiz and Miguel Angel Miranda
> MARITZA .... Arely Lorena Araniva
> CHAYO.................................... Juanita Devis and Renee Duron
> NARRATOR 1 ....Carlos Albert
> NARRATOR 2 .... Laura P. Vega
> JUAN CARLOS..................Adalberto Lujan and Hector Muñoz
> POLICEMAN ....Roman Phillips and Juan Glezz

The Women of Juarez was produced by Teatro Bravo in its original Spanish version in March, 2005, at the John Paul Theater of Phoenix College in Phoenix, Arizona, directed by Christina Marin with the following cast:

> MOTHER...Margarita Villa
> FATHER.. Juan Gomez
> MARITZA.. Eunice Bravo
> CHAYO..Blanca Reyna
> JUAN CARLOS..Jonathan Estrada
> LAWYER... Isabel Sans
> CITY ATTORNEY and ENSEMBLE .... Ricardo Chilaca
> POLICEMAN and ENSEMBLE ....Luis Avila
> NEWSCASTER and ENSEMBLE ....Miguel Calvillo
> UNDERSTUDY...Nuvia Enriquez

The play was remounted in the English translation written by Eve Muller and Liane Schirmer in September, 2007, at the John Paul Theater of Phoenix College in Phoenix, Arizona, directed by Pam Sterling, along with assistant director Nestor Bravo with the following cast:

MOTHER..Rosa Linda Duron
FATHER... Masavi Perea
MARITZA.. Flory Mares
CHAYO..Perla Frias
JUAN CARLOS.. Carlos Ramirez
LAWYER 1 and ENSEMBLE......................................June Valk
LAWYER 2 and ENSEMBLE........................... Mario Mendoza
CITY ATTORNEY...Marcelo Dietrich
POLICEMAN and ENSEMBLE .... Mitch Menchaca
POLICEWOMAN and ENSEMBLE.....Johanna Bustos-Salmon
NEWSCASTER and ENSEMBLE........................... Arturo Martinez
ENSEMBLE... Juan Gomez
ENSEMBLE... Greta Skelly
SINGER.. Obed Hurtado

For performance rights, contact Ruben Amavizca Murua at avytrop@yahoo.com.

The Women of Juarez
FIRST ACT - SCENE 1

(In the dark, we hear noises. The light comes up slowly. Upstage left, a one-room house, with dirt floor, and two doors with mosquito nets: one on the right to the street; and one on the left to a porch. On the porch, there is a ratty table with an old metal tub, a washboard and a bucket. Backstage, we see clotheslines and a latrine. Everything is old, bought in third-hand stores. Next to the street door there are two girls sleeping on a single bed. Next to the bed, there is a dresser, a gas stove, a wooden table with four mismatched chairs, an ice chest and two plastic buckets. On the floor, by the bed, the Mother and the Father sleep on a cobija [= "blanket"]. The parents look older than their mid-thirties. The Mother sits up and yawns. The Father wakes up. Maritza, 17, the oldest daughter wakes up, breathes deeply trying to wake up. She gets up humming a song.)

MOTHER: Maritza, are you going to take a bath?
MARITZA: In a minute!
MOTHER: You want me to heat up some water for you?
MARITZA: No, thanks, *mami!* I'll just use cold.

(When the Mother turns away, Maritza, with a pillow, hits the other person on the bed. We hear some noise and Maritza exits.)

MOTHER: *Viejo* [= "old man"]! Get up! You need to go get some water. We almost ran out last night.
FATHER: All right.

(The Father stretches and sits. He takes his shoes, puts them on, takes the buckets and exits. The Mother prepares the family breakfast and sets the table. She talks and moves incessantly. Chayo, 15, her youngest daughter sleeps, ignoring Mother. Maritza, on the porch, takes the tub backstage.)

MOTHER: Chayo! Get up, you're going to be late! You'll miss the bus and then you'll have to wait another hour.
CHAYO: Let me sleep a little longer. It's only five in the morning.
MOTHER: But you take forever getting dressed and then you skip breakfast. You have to catch the 6 o'clock bus if you want to get to the factory by 8.
CHAYO: Just five more minutes!
MOTHER: Well, then don't complain later. In a few months, God-willing, we'll have saved up enough to move closer to the factory, so it won't take you three buses and two hours to get to work. But then, if we move closer to the factory, Maritza will be farther away from school. But I sure would like to move somewhere with electricity, running water and paved roads. I wish I had a water heater, so I wouldn't have to heat water on the stove. And if we had plumbing, all we'd have to do is turn on the faucet and we'd have hot water and we wouldn't have to take bird baths, or lug around buckets. Look, if we all pool our money together and save up, with the money you two make and whatever your

father makes at the market, along with what I make at the diner, we'd have enough by the end of the year to rent a little house and get out of this dump. I don't even know why we left the *rancho*; we're no better off. No running water, no electricity, no plumbing. At least I had my *comadres* [= "female friends"], back there. But there was no work, nothing for your father, and even less for us women. No matter where you go, it's always something.

SCENE 2

MARITZA: *(Returns and sits at the table on the porch. She writes on a small notebook.)* Dear diary: I woke up with a burning desire to fill these pages. My name is Maritza Martinez Lopez. I was born on January 24, 1984, under the sign of Aquarius. My hair is dark brown but I dye it auburn. I have dark brown eyes but I wear violet contacts. I'm a nursing student. My parents are Maria Rosario Lopez and Jesus Martinez, and I love them with all my heart. I have a younger sister, Chayo. Argh! I have so many dreams. I love to sing and dance around the house. My favorite songs are: *"Antología,"* by Shakira, *"Lo dejaría todo,"* by Chayanne and all of Selena's songs. *(Pause.)* I need to write, to go on living, or to be remembered after I'm gone. Today, I woke up afraid. Come to think of it, not afraid. It's more of a feeling…like I'm about to discover something. I got to run, otherwise I will miss my bus and I don't want to be late for school. *(She exits.)*

SCENE 3

(The light on the house comes up. The Mother keeps on with her morning routine.)

MOTHER: Maritza! Hurry up; you're going to be late. Chayo! Get up!
CHAYO: *Mamá*, let me sleep.
MOTHER: You should learn from your sister. She gets up early and is always cheerful, singing. She works and studies, and all you ever want to do is lie around. *(She sits on the bed and speaks sweetly.)* Why don't you go to school, hm? You finished junior high school. You could learn to be a secretary or a receptionist. It's better than working in a factory or being a cook like me. You girls have more opportunities than we did. Take advantage of them.

(Chayo doesn't pay attention. Upset, the Mother hits her once.)

CHAYO: *Amá!* [= "mom"]!
MOTHER: Hm! It's like talking to a wall. Goes in one ear and out the other. Look, here comes your father. Give him a hand with the water.

(Chayo extends her leg, opens the door and goes back to sleep. The Father enters, crosses backstage with the buckets of water.)

MOTHER: Breakfast is almost ready, *viejo. (Maritza sings backstage. Her singing is interrupted by her body's reaction to the cold water.)* Maritza! Hurry up, food's getting cold. One of these days you're going to catch pneumonia from all that cold water this early in the morning. But that'll be a thing of the past once we get a house. *(The Father comes back.)* Sit down, *viejo.* Breakfast is ready. Chayo! Did you go back to bed? Aren't you going to take a bath?

(The Father sits at the table.)

CHAYO: I took a bath yesterday.

MOTHER: Don't tell me you're going to go to work without taking a bath? A young lady should bathe every day. It's best first thing in the morning, so you can start the day nice and fresh. *(Chayo covers her head with a pillow.)* If you're not going to take a bath, then come to the table. Breakfast is ready. More coffee, dear?

FATHER: Ahem! Move it, Chayo. Come to the table, you're going to be late.

MOTHER: Maybe she'll listen to you, because she ignores me when I try to talk to her. Not Maritza. She's a good daughter and she does what I say.

CHAYO: *(Gets up, goes to the table and puts her hair in a ponytail.)* Maritza! Maritza! Always Maritza. I know she's your favorite.

FATHER: That's not true, Chayo. But your mother is right. You have to think of the future, or do you plan to work in the factory your whole life? You're almost sixteen. Don't you want to go to college?

CHAYO: Yeah, right. I'll go to medical school and meet Luis Miguel, and then we'll get married. Then I'll divorce him and marry Tony Mottola. That'll be the day.

FATHER: I'm serious, Chayo. Take a look at Maritza. She's going to nursing school.

CHAYO: Oh, *papá.* I don't know what to do. I'll probably just get married and let my husband support me.

FATHER: But the only men you ever meet are the guys from around here or the ones who work at the factory. How are you ever going to meet a different kind of man who'll take you out of this dump if you don't do something to better yourself?

MOTHER: Maritza! Breakfast is ready.

MARITZA: Coming. *(Enters drying her hair. She wears a nurse's uniform.)*

MOTHER: Is Juan Carlos picking you up? *(Chayo laughs.)* What are you laughing at?

CHAYO: Nothing.

MARITZA: *(Pulling Chayo's ponytail.)* You little brat…you're just jealous!

CHAYO: Leave me alone! You know what, I don't want to hear about your crappy life ever again! You drive me crazy! You're always pretending to be such a goody-goody but it's all just an act.

(The sisters argue loudly. We can't make out what they're saying.)

MOTHER: Chayo! That's enough!

FATHER: *(Hitting the table, he screams.)* Be quiet, both of you! You're acting like little girls! Hurry up and eat; we have to leave soon.

(Maritza sits down.)

CHAYO: She started it. Why don't you say anything to her?

FATHER: I said, "Both of you." You behave like cats and dogs, not sisters.

(The family eats in silence for a few seconds. Maritza hums Selena's "Bidi bidi bam bam." Under the table, Maritza kicks Chayo.)

CHAYO: *Papi!*

FATHER: Why can't we eat quietly for once?

(Maritza sticks her tongue at Chayo, mockingly.)

CHAYO: Leave me alone, you stupid cow!

MARITZA: Your grandma is the stupid cow!

FATHER: Hey! Show some respect for my mother-in-law!

(Mother reacts. Father and Maritza laugh heartily. Chayo, upset, gets up, grabs her plate, goes to the chest of drawers, takes some clothes and exits. Maritza hums again, but stops when Mother looks at her. Under the table, Maritza moves her feet, first slowly, then faster. The rhythm creeps up her legs, her hip and shoulders.)

MOTHER: Maritza!

FATHER: Stop it! You're going to break the chair!

(Maritza calms down and eats. She gets up, leaving her plate on the table. The Father does the same. He gets up and puts a shirt on. From the table, the Mother looks at them. Upset, she gets up, complaining unintelligibly. The Father looks at her; he's about to say something, but stops. The Mother exits backstage, with the plates. Chayo comes back wearing a skin-tight short dress. Maritza whistles a strip-tease tune.)

FATHER: You're going out dressed like that? More like undressed. You're practically naked.

CHAYO: Oh, *papá*. Don't start again. This is how all the girls dress around here. We're not in the *rancho* anymore, and it's not like I'm going to church or anything.

FATHER: But the men around here might get the wrong idea.

CHAYO: Well, personally…I don't care. Let them think whatever they want.

FATHER: But they could hurt you, or think that you're one of those…

MARITZA: Prostitutes?

FATHER: *(Turning to Maritza.)* Quiet! You be quiet! *(To Chayo.)*…a loose woman or something.

CHAYO: Don't worry, *papi*. I can take care of myself. *(Chayo playfully kisses him on the cheek.)*

MOTHER: *(Coming back.)* Viejo, call the gas delivery guy to bring another tank? It's almost gone.

FATHER: What time are you leaving?

MOTHER: In a little bit! I'm just going to clean up and get more water. The truck should be here any minute with fresh water and it's best to get there early before they run out or it gets dirty. Maritza, are you coming for lunch?

MARITZA: Yes. I got some homework and I need to study for tomorrow's exam. Juan Carlos is going to come by and walk me to the bus stop.

MOTHER: Chayo, when you get home, go get some water, we need to do the laundry.

CHAYO: Yes, *mamá*.

(The Mother pulls down Chayo's dress. Chayo pulls it up and the action is repeated.)

MOTHER: And, *m'ija* [= "daughter"], be very careful when you are on the bus because there are some creepy men that hang out over there. Don't talk to any of them or go anywhere with them. Come straight home after work.

CHAYO: Yes, *ma'*.

MARITZA: *(Mocking her sister.)* Yes, *ma'!*

CHAYO: Drop dead, bitch!

MARITZA: Don't worry, honey, one of these days you just may get your wish. Ha, ha!

CHAYO: Well, I hope it's really soon, because I'm sick and tired of you!

(The sisters argue again.)

FATHER: That's enough! Cut it out, you two or I'll…And don't you think I won't. I still can do it, you know!

MOTHER: May God and the Virgin of Guadalupe bless you and keep you safe along the way.

MARITZA: Bidi bidi stupid!

CHAYO: *(With Shakira's song melody.)* Ciega, sorda y rependeja ya me tienes rete harta!

FATHER: Shut up! Both of you shut up!

(Quietly, the Father and the girls leave.)

SCENE 4

(The Mother breathes with relief and leans against the door, then goes to the chest of drawers and turns on the battery-operated radio. We hear Las Hermanas Nuñez' *"Cuando te vayas." The Mother sings along while cleaning the table, stove and floor. The song is interrupted by the news jingle.)*

NEWSCASTER: The slaughter of young women continues in Juarez. Since 1993 over 150 women have been murdered and more than 300 are missing. Despite the fact that violence and impunity are on the rise, no concrete actions are being taken in order to put an end to the situation. Police reports indicate that the victims were prostitutes, drug addicts, or strippers who worked in nightclubs around the city. In response to the rumors that the suspect is a serial killer, the city attorney made the following statement:

CITY
ATTORNEY: This is not the work of a serial killer. The *modus operandi* is not the same, the bodies are left in different places and the victims are distinct from one another. It would be premature and irresponsible to say that this is the work of a serial killer.

MOTHER: *(Picking up her purse, turns the radio off and leaves while talking.)* It must be horrible to disappear, just like that, as if the desert had swallowed them up. Well, there must be some reason this is happening to them. They're probably out wandering the streets, going out with men. Thank God my daughters are good girls, both of them work and Maritza goes to school. Sometimes I wonder about Chayo, but deep down she's a good girl.

(Blackout.)

SCENE 5

(The lights come up on the house. It's almost 2 PM. Maritza comes in carrying a can of paint. She throws her purse on the table and drops the can by the chest of drawers. She hums "Bidi bidi bam bam," goes to the radio and turns it on, really loud. We hear Amanda Miguel's "El me mintió." Maritza sings along wildly, shedding her uniform with highly sexual movements. She caresses her legs, her waist, and her breasts. She grabs some jeans and a red blouse and puts them on. She goes to the table, sits, and opens a book. Still singing, she takes two pencils and "plays" the drums. The Mother comes in, stops at the door, and looks at her daughter. The mother goes to the radio and turns it off. Maritza reacts startled, looks at her Mother and smiles.)

SCENE 6

MOTHER: How did it go, dear?
MARITZA: Fine, *mami*. I'll finish my homework and I'm off to the factory.
MOTHER: I just came home to finish the washing and I'm headed back to the diner.
MARITZA: Juan Carlos is coming over on his lunch break. *(Takes an envelope and hands it to the mother.)* I cashed my paycheck. They finally paid me my overtime. And I bought more paint to finish painting the house.

MOTHER: How much do you want me to leave you?

MARITZA: Just enough to pay for bus fare to and from work, a soda and a sandwich.

MOTHER: Thanks, dear. *(Puts some bills on her daughter's purse.)* What's that?

MARITZA: Homework. "Proper procedures for cleaning deep wounds to prevent infection."

MOTHER: Oh, disgusting. Doesn't all that blood scare you, *m'ija*?

MARITZA: No, not at all. Actually, I love it when kids come in to the clinic, and to watch how they calm down while we bandage their wounds, and the happy smiles on their faces when they walk out the door. I love to help people.

MOTHER: Well, I'd pass out for sure if I saw a wound like that.

MARITZA: The other day a girl came in who had been severely hurt in an accident and Maricruz, that blonde girl in my class, fainted and fell and hit her chin, so we got to practice on her, too. *(Both women laugh.)* Juan Carlos is late. He said he'd be here before two.

MOTHER: Rest for a while. Sometimes I'm afraid you're going to get sick. Always on the go. Running from here to school, then back here again, studying, grabbing a quick bite and then off to the factory. You get home so late, you barely get any sleep, and then you start all over again.

MARITZA: If I work hard, someday I'll be somebody, *mamá*.

MOTHER: I sure wish Chayo would think like you, but you know how she is!

SCENE 7

(Juan Carlos, 18, comes to the door. He hides a guitar behind him and knocks.)

MOTHER: How are you, Juan Carlitos? Come on in! How have you been? Maritza told me that you finally found a job. I'm glad to hear that.

JUAN CARLOS: Yes, ma'am. And I want to save up for school, too.

MARITZA: Give me a minute. I just want to finish this chapter.

JUAN CARLOS: No rush.

MOTHER: Want some water? I think I still have some lemonade.

JUAN CARLOS: No, ma'am. Thanks anyway.

MOTHER: Won't you come in? Don't be shy. Oh, silly. Make yourself at home.

JUAN CARLOS: Thank you, *doña* [= "ma'am"].

(A long uncomfortable pause. Maritza looks at Juan Carlos, who looks at Mother, who looks at both. Mother understands they want to be alone.)

MOTHER: Well, I'm going to finish the laundry. Let me know when you're leaving, Maritza. *(She exits to the porch, pours water into the tub and washes on the board.)*

MARITZA: Yes, *mamá.*

JUAN CARLOS: Look, I brought you a present. *(Takes the guitar and shows it to her.)*

MARITZA: It's beautiful! *(She jumps into his arms, kissing him.)* Thank you so much, Juan Carlos!

JUAN CARLOS: *(Takes magazines from his pocket.)* And I also bought you these books that teach you how to play.

MARITZA: You must have spent a fortune and you just got your first paycheck.

JUAN CARLOS: Don't worry. I got a good deal on the guitar and I found the books in *don* [= "mister"] Manuel's used bookstore. And look at this: Selena's songs in *Guitar Made Easy!*

MARITZA: Thank you, thanks so much! *(She hugs him and kisses him.)*

JUAN CARLOS: I felt so bad not buying you a birthday present.

MARITZA: I told you not to worry about it. I understand. We're in the same boat.

JUAN CARLOS: I know, but I still wanted to buy you something.

MARITZA: It's the best present I've ever gotten. You know I've always wanted to play the guitar.

JUAN CARLOS: Well, now you have no excuse!

(They kiss passionately and fall to the bed. They forget they're not alone and make out. The Mother stops her washing to listen. She pretends to sing. Maritza and Juan Carlos stop and sit at the edge of the bed, embarrassed.)

MARITZA: Oh…my mom! *(Takes the guitar and plays something, but nothing musical comes out.)*

JUAN CARLOS: You're really good!

MARITZA: *(Flirtatious.)* With the guitar? *(Both laugh.)*

JUAN CARLOS: *(Doubts, gets up, sits back.)* I talked to my brother. He said that if I go to El Paso, he'd help me get a job and let me stay with him and his wife. I just have to find a way to get across, or save up enough to pay a *coyote* [= "human smuggler"]. But if I go, I'm going to miss you so much.

MARITZA: *(Handing the guitar back to him.)* Well, then, why go?

JUAN CARLOS: You know why. You can make more money over there.

MARITZA: That's exactly what they told us about Juarez, and look, it took me over a month to get a job at the factory. The night shift is so exhausting but I can go to school in the morning. Chayo got in because of me. But my parents had a really hard time finding work and we're barely getting by on the salary the four of us take home. It's no different here or there. What really matters is an education, so you can get ahead.

JUAN CARLOS: *(Hanging the guitar on a nail on the wall.)* I know, but it's hard. By the time I leave the shop, I'm so tired that I have no time or energy left to study. And on what I make I can barely make ends meet, much less pay for school and books.

MARITZA: Don't you think I get tired? But you just have to keep on going.

JUAN CARLOS: You know I want to marry you, and if I stay here, I'll never be
               able to save up enough to give you a decent life. I want us to
               live somewhere nice.
MARITZA: Listen, if I go with you across the border, I won't be able to go
               to school. I won't get any credit for my studies here. I'd have
               to start all over again and without papers it's going to be much
               more difficult.

(She sits at the table. Juan Carlos follows her.)

JUAN CARLOS: Once we're there, it's much easier. It's easy. We're gonna make
               it.
MARITZA: Let's wait a while. We're still too young to get married.
JUAN CARLOS: Don't you want to?
MARITZA: *(Screaming.)* Don't be ridiculous! I already said yes, but there's
               no reason to rush. I want to do things right. *(Juan Carlos looks
               at the floor. There is a long pause. Maritza calms down.)*
               Who knows, maybe I'll learn to play the guitar really well and
               become a famous singer – a star like Thalia.
JUAN CARLOS: *(Not wanting to fight.)* You know you're my star.

*(He kneels before her and tries to kiss her. Maritza offers her cheek. Juan Carlos
places his head on her lap. Silence.)*

MOTHER: Maritza! Bring me some water. There's none left.
JUAN CARLOS: I'll get the water, *doña.*
MOTHER: Oh, thank you, Juan Carlos! The buckets are next to the icebox.

(Juan Carlos takes the buckets. Before he reaches the door, Maritza stops him.)

MARITZA: Juan Carlos.
JUAN CARLOS: *(He stops without looking at her.)* What?
MARITZA: Nothing.

*(He exits. The Mother goes backstage to hang the wash. Maritza is alone on stage.
Long pause. She gets her diary from her purse and writes.)*

SCENE 8

MARITZA: "Dear diary: I'm a hopeless romantic and I dream of meeting
               the love of my life. I'll know he's 'the one' when he hands me
               a rose and serenades me. We'll get married, and we'll live in a
               nice little house, with two beautiful children, a boy and a girl.
               My ideal man has long, wavy hair, blue eyes, fair skin; he's
               about 6 ft. tall, nice, and not too muscular. He has a car and a
               bank account with over 100,000 *pesos* in it. Just kidding. All I
               really want is a kind man who loves me."

(Long pause. Closes the diary and hides it behind the bed. The Mother returns.)

SCENE 9

MOTHER: Maritza! It's almost 2 o'clock! *(Maritza is playing with a teddy bear and doesn't react. The mother observes her in silence.)* Are you going out tomorrow? To the dance?

MARITZA: *(Quiet.)* No! It gets so crowded and then you can't even hear the music!

MOTHER: Why don't you go for a little while? Just to get out. Have some fun.

MARITZA: I have a lot of homework, and I need to study for finals.

MOTHER: Are you tired?

MARITZA: No, *'ma? (A long pause.)* I care about him, but I'm just not sure he's the love of my life.

(Juan Carlos comes back with the water.)

SCENE 10

JUAN CARLOS: Here's the water, *señora.*

MOTHER: *(Getting up, the Mother opens the door for him to come in.)* Thank you, Juan Carlos. Dump it in the big container over there.

MARITZA: Juan Carlos, let's go!

JUAN CARLOS: Coming!

MARITZA: Juan Carlos, it's late!

JUAN CARLOS: I'm coming!

MARITZA: Juan Carlos, hurry up!

JUAN CARLOS: Quit bossing me around! See you later, *señora.*

MOTHER: May God and the Virgin of Guadalupe bless you and keep you safe along the way.

(The Mother does the sign of the cross on her daughter and goes back to her wash. Maritza and Juan Carlos turn away. Maritza stops, gives her purse to Juan Carlos, runs to Mother and gives her the teddy bear, a hug and a big kiss. The Mother looks at her. Maritza turns around and leaves. She reaches Juan Carlos, who's standing with his back to the door. Maritza pinches his behind and runs away, laughing. Juan Carlos jumps and chases Maritza. The Mother goes back to her chores. Suddenly, she stops. She's breathing heavy. She holds onto the wall, almost fainting. She turns to the street door and runs. The Mother crosses the house and screams at the door.)

MOTHER: Maritza! Be careful and don't be too late. If you're going to work overtime, call Chayo on her cell. You got yours? Maritza! *(Silence. She leans against the door, breathing heavily. She shakes her head up.)* The things I think of! No doubt about it, I'm getting old.

(Blackout.)

SCENE 11

(Two spots shine on downstage, one to the right, one to the left. The NARRATORS, both in their late 30s/early 40s, walk into these lights. Narrator 1 wears a glamorized Tarahumaran Indian costume as Miss Chihuahua usually does. Narrator 2 wears a "cowboy" outfit with boots, hat and a fringed leather jacket.)

NARRATOR 1:   Ciudad Juarez is located in a valley along the Rio Grande, bordering El Paso, north of the state capital of Chihuahua, 11 meters above sea level and enjoys a hot, arid climate.

NARRATOR 2:   Situated in the middle of the desert, Ciudad Juarez, a really big city, is surrounded by beautiful scenery that illustrates the living geological history of northern Mexico and the transformation of an area that formed part of the ocean thousands of years ago.

NARRATOR 1:   In 1658 the Spaniards occupied the territory of New Mexico and claimed that land for Spain, including the metropolis known today as Ciudad Juarez, a really big city.

NARRATOR 2:   In 1659 the town of Nuestra Señora de Guadalupe del Paso del Rio del Norte, was founded.

(Maritza walks at the end of the stage to wait for her bus. She takes out her Walkman and turns it on. While the narrators talk, the following scene takes place. Two men, the Rapists, come behind Maritza. They whisper to each other and walk to her. Maritza hums a song, the men repeat after her. Maritza discovers their presence, puts away her Walkman, and takes out her cellular. One of the men whispers something to her. She tries to walk away, but the other stands in front of her. Maritza pushes Rapist 1 trying to escape. He grabs her arm and slaps her hard. She falls to the ground, losing her purse. She tries to grab her purse and her cellular. The rapists kick her. Maritza doesn't move. The men stop. Rapist 1 kneels in front of her, pulls down his pants ready to rape her. Maritza opens her eyes and pushes the man to the side. She gets up and meets Rapist 2's fist on her face. She falls back unconscious. Rapist 2 pulls down her pants, tears her panties and throws them at his partner. Rapist 2 pulls down his pants and rapes Maritza violently. Rapist 1 moves to her head, grabs her purse and strangles her with the strap. Maritza wakes up and fights to free herself. Rapist 2 keeps raping her. Maritza loses consciousness. At a signal from Rapist 2, Rapist 1 takes out a knife and stabs Maritza on the chest. Rapist 2 arches his back, and rolls to his side. Rapist 1 takes his partner's place, grabs Maritza's legs and turns her around. He pulls down his pants and rapes Maritza even more furiously than Rapist 2, who moves to her head. At a signal from his partner, Rapist 1 stabs Maritza on the back. Rapist 1 convulses, collapses on Maritza's side, and slowly pulls his pants up. His partner helps him up. They take Maritza's things. One of them puts on the Walkman, turns it on and begins to hum Maritza's song. His partner joins him and both exit by the time the Narrator talks about the raceway.)

NARRATOR 1:   Between 1680 and 1693, Ciudad Juarez served as the capital of New Mexico becoming a border town by virtue of the Treaty of Guadalupe Hidalgo.

NARRATOR 2:   In 1865, president *don* Benito Juarez established the federal government in Paso del Norte, during the struggle against French imperialist intervention. In 1888 it became a city and was given the new name of Juarez.

NARRATOR 1:   Ciudad Juarez came into its own following World War II. Its proximity to the U.S. boosted its economy as a supplier of goods and services and a profitable tourist destination.

NARRATOR 2:   Its horse and dog tracks are the highlights of its tourist trade. It also boasts an international airport.

NARRATOR 1:   During the '50s and '60s, a large segment of the population works in factories, consumer goods and trade exchange. By the mid '60s, it is the most vibrant city in the state thanks to the industrial boom generated by large multinational corporations.

NARRATOR 2:   In 1965, the Border Industry Program supports the establishment of assembly factories, or *maquiladoras*, which transform the economy and foster the growth of the local and regional market, considerably increasing the female labor force.

NARRATOR 1:   Today, Juarez produces a television set every three seconds and a computer every seven.

NARRATOR 2:   Thanks to the *maquiladora* industry, tourism and the indomitable Juarez spirit, we have the lowest national unemployment rate, point-six percent, and the highest per capita income on the northern border. *Ajúa* [= "Yeeha"]!

NARRATOR 1:   The high quality of manual labor, as well as established international training and certification programs, attract worldwide industrial giants. This aspect is indubitably the cornerstone of the excellent business climate of the city and of the state.

NARRATOR 2:   Ciudad Juarez offers industrial parks adjacent to factories, among which are Yassaki, Delphi, Phillips, Thompson Consumer Electronics, and UTA, among others.

NARRATOR 1:   Really big fun in Ciudad Juarez!

NARRATOR 2:   Year after year, the locals enjoy the blessings of a sunny climate with outdoor activities, such as sports events, the traditional Expo Fair and the unparalleled spectacle of the bull fights brimming with magic and romance.

NARRATOR 1:   Rodeo has become a national sport due to the skill and courage it requires.

NARRATOR 2:   And if it's excitement you're after, the Juarez raceway is an adventure, filled with thrills and chills. You will marvel at race cars revving their engines as they try and speed past their competitors.

BOTH: We welcome you to visit our city steeped in history and tradition, Juarez. A really big city!

NARRATOR 1:   For more information regarding *maquiladoras* and industrial parks in Ciudad Juarez, feel free call the *Maquiladora* Association (AMAC) Tel.: 01(16)382-8133.

(Black out. The Narrators stay on stage. We hear the voice of the Rapist humming Maritza's song.)

SCENE 12

MOTHER: *(Waking up.) Viejo*, it's Maritza. Get the door.
FATHER: *(He wakes up, gets up and goes to the door. He opens but no one is there. He goes back to sleep.)* It wasn't her. It was *don* Manuel's daughter, Maribel.
MOTHER: It's late. It's after two and she's still not home.
FATHER: Don't worry, honey. She's probably working overtime.
MOTHER: Yes, but she always calls Chayo's cell to let me know.
FATHER: She probably missed the bus. She'll be home soon.
MOTHER: Oh, I don't know. I had a horrible feeling when she went to work today. She gave me a big hug and kiss right before she left. I noticed something – she had a strange look in her eyes.
FATHER: It's just your imagination, woman. Go to sleep. She'll be home any minute. If she had a problem, she would call Chayo from her cell. Did she take it with her?
MOTHER: I think so!
FATHER: See, nothing's happened to her. She probably just missed the bus. She'll be home soon.

(He goes back to sleep. The Mother gets up, covers her husband with the blanket, goes to the table and lights the candle. She cleans, but cannot concentrate on the task. The light for the Narrators comes back.)

SCENE 13

NARRATOR 2:   Life goes on despite the fear. In the poorest areas, not only are there no streetlights, there's no security. Since the roads aren't paved, the police cars won't drive by on patrol.
NARRATOR 1:   The majority of women work and are the driving force behind the *maquiladora* industry. Unemployment is a thing of the past. The *maquiladora* industry is in full swing.
NARRATOR 2:   People come from all over to stay here, or to cross the border, to improve their lives. Drug trafficking represents a valid way to defy the laws imposed by indifferent authorities.
NARRATOR 1:   The nightlife is the hottest in the country, and some say it's a reflection of the city's prosperity.
NARRATOR 2:   They are always gazing across the border. Geography engulfs them and buries them in a dizzying world of technology and productivity, commerce, exploitation, survival and hope.
NARRATOR 1:   Oblivious of what lies ahead – a grotesque world, full of horror, drug trafficking, police and political corruption, misogyny, *Santería* and pseudo-satanic rituals.

SCENE 14

MOTHER: *(We hear Maritza's song again. The mother goes to the door.)* Maritza! Is that you? *(Silence.)* Dear God! It's almost four in the morning; she's not home and she hasn't called. *(Waking her husband up.)* Viejo! Maritza's not home yet and it's so late.

FATHER: What?

MOTHER: Maritza's not back yet! Now I'm really worried. She's never, ever this late.

FATHER: Did you try the cell?

MOTHER: I don't know how to use that thing, and Chayo is sound asleep.

FATHER: Just wake her up!

MOTHER: *Ay, Virgencita de Guadalupe*, please don't let anything happen to her!

FATHER: *(Gets up.)* Chayo, m'ija! Call Maritza on her cell. It's 4 o'clock and she's still not home.

CHAYO: *(Half asleep.)* She probably ran off with Juan Carlos.

MOTHER: Don't say that. She wouldn't have done that…eloped…without letting me know.

CHAYO: *(Speed dials her phone.)* No answer. I'm telling you, she's probably with Juan Carlos.

FATHER: I'll go ask him. *(Exits.)*

MOTHER: Be careful. *(Closes the door and turns to Chayo.)* Chayo! How can you just go back to sleep like that?

CHAYO: 'má! You'll see, she's with Juan Carlos. Let me sleep.

(The Narrators' lights come up. A candle dimly lights the house.)

SCENE 15

NARRATOR 1: Life in Juarez is dangerous for women. Still, they struggle in poverty-stricken, hostile surroundings. The poorer neighborhoods are overrun with gangs and drug addicts.

NARRATOR 2: The majority of the victims are workers, attacked on the way home from work, or vice versa. That is, in public places.

NARRATOR 1: Various local organizations have requested that this border be declared to be in a "State of Emergency."

SCENE 16

(The Father comes running, followed by Juan Carlos. The Mother opens the door.)

MOTHER: Oh, no, no, no! No! *Ay*, my God, I'm worried sick.

FATHER: Calm down, *mujer* [= "woman"]! Chayo! Try your sister again. *(He runs and pours water in a cup, handing it to his wife.)* Chayo! Hurry up, girl!

MOTHER: I'm going out of my mind, *viejo*. Dear God, what could've

happened to her? She never comes home late without letting me
know and it's been more than four hours.

JUAN CARLOS: I walked her to the bus stop and she went to work. Chayo! Don't
you know any of her friends' phone numbers?

CHAYO: No! She never tells me a thing. What time is it?

MOTHER: Almost five.

FATHER: Let's go look for her.

CHAYO: There's nothing but desert out there, and it's pitch black.

FATHER: So what? She probably fell down somewhere in the dark and got
hurt. Chayo! You and Juan Carlos go to the bus stop and your
mom and I will head in the other direction.

*(They take flashlights and exit. The Narrators' lights come up. In the back we see
the flashlights cutting the dark.)*

SCENE 17

NARRATOR 1: The desert surrounding us is a vast emptiness. Nothingness.

JUAN CARLOS: Maritza!

NARRATOR 2: You look side to side and you feel and see nothing.

MOTHER: Maritza!

NARRATOR 1: In this infinite sea of sand and dust, our lives mean nothing.

CHAYO: Maritza!

NARRATOR 2: Our voices are lost and become nothing.

FATHER: Maritza!

NARRATOR 1: Our dreams are nothing.

MOTHER: Maritza!

NARRATOR 2: Thousands come and thousands go.

JUAN CARLOS: Maritza!

NARRATOR 1: The desert, the emptiness, the nothingness tells them they've
arrived at the Promised Land:

NARRATOR 2: "Ciudad Juarez…

NARRATOR 1: "Mexico's finest frontier"

CHAYO: Maritza!

FATHER: Maritza!

JUAN CARLOS: Maritza!

MOTHER: Maritza!

ALL: Maritza!

SCENE 18

*(The house is now fully lit. Juan Carlos and Chayo return. She crosses to the patio
looking for her sister. He stays in the middle of the room, thinking. Chayo returns.
She negates with a gesture. He reacts angrily, pacing up and down the place.)*

CHAYO: What time is it?

JUAN CARLOS: Six. *(Chayo speed dials again. No answer. She closes the phone)*
I'll ask Chava to lend me his car to go to the Red Cross. *(Exit.)*

CHAYO: Call my cell if you find her.

(She stays alone on stage, walks backwards to the bed and sits frozen for a moment. She runs to lock the patio door and then the front door. She falls back onto the bed and cries. She hears something and wipes her tears. Opens the door. The parents come back.)

MOTHER: Didn't you find her?

CHAYO: No.

FATHER: Where's Juan Carlos?

CHAYO: He went to borrow Chava's car, to go to the Red Cross.

FATHER: I'll go with him. Call work and tell them I'm going to be late. *(Exits.)*

CHAYO: Yes, *papá.*

(Long pause. No one dares to talk. Mother and daughter avoid looking at each other. The Mother gets up and tries to control herself. She walks to the stove.)

MOTHER: You hungry? Want me to make you some breakfast?

CHAYO: No, *mamá,* thank you.

(The Mother cannot stand it anymore and hits the stove. She screams and cries. Chayo runs to her and hugs her. Mother and daughter cry. The light on the house goes off. The Narrators' lights come up.)

SCENE 19

NARRATOR 2: The victims work for multinational corporations that pay no taxes in Mexico. Seventy percent of Fortune 500 companies utilize *maquiladoras* and they are increasing over 10 percent each year.

NARRATOR 1: There are more than 3000 companies employing over a million workers, with an annual product volume of $40 billion dollars.

NARRATOR 2: Ninety-eight percent are for the American market. Ninety percent of the *maquiladoras* are situated along the northern border, and a third are in Ciudad Juarez.

NARRATOR 1: These multinational corporations offer no security for their employees, the majority of which are women who must often come and go late at night.

NARRATOR 2: These corporations that earn millions from the city should subsidize public safety programs and assist government and civic organizations in putting an end to these murders once and for all.

(Both exit.)

SCENE 20

(The Mother and Juan Carlos walk up to the Policeman, sitting at a desk.)

MOTHER: *Señor!* Help us, please! My daughter didn't come home last night and we're really worried.

POLICEMAN: *Señora!* You must wait two days before filing a missing person's report.

MOTHER: What do you mean, two days?

POLICEMAN: That's right. Did you check with her friends?

MOTHER: No. She never would've stayed anywhere without letting us know.

POLICEMAN: Well, I'm sorry, ma'am. We have to wait 48 hours before filling out any report.

MOTHER: Please, sir. Don't be cruel!

POLICEMAN: Did you check the Red Cross?

JUAN CARLOS: Yes, and we went to the local hospital and the police station, and she hasn't been arrested or anything.

POLICEMAN: Well, I can't help you right now. You have to wait 48 hours.

JUAN CARLOS: We're not waiting. *Señora!* Let's go look for her at the school. Maybe one of her friends knows something.

(They exit talking and over the line lights fade out.)

MOTHER: Yes, *m'ijo* [= "son"]. And if not, then we'll go to the factory. Chayo went and said she'd talk to the girls that work the night shift, to see if anyone has heard anything.

SCENE 21

(The lights come up. The Policeman is sitting in the same spot. The Mother comes in running, followed by Chayo.)

MOTHER: *Señor*, please help me. My daughter hasn't been home in almost two days.

POLICEMAN: *Señora*, I already told you that we couldn't file a report until it's been at least 48 hours. She probably went somewhere with her boyfriend.

MOTHER: No, her boyfriend is looking for her too. She got off work at the factory and never came home. We've looked everywhere for her and she hasn't turned up. It's been almost 48 hours. What's the big deal if it's a little earlier? Please, look for her. For your mother's sake, please, *señor*.

POLICEMAN: Okay, okay. *(He takes a piece of paper from a drawer and a pen.)* All right then! Name?

MOTHER: Maritza Martinez Lopez.

POLICEMAN: Age?

MOTHER: 17.

POLICEMAN: Build?

MOTHER: Average.
POLICEMAN: Height?
MOTHER: Short, five feet, five inches.
POLICEMAN: Any scars or birthmarks?
MOTHER: None.
POLICEMAN: What was she wearing the last time you saw her?
MOTHER: Jeans and a red blouse.
POLICEMAN: Were the pants tight?
MOTHER: A little.
POLICEMAN: Hm! Had she been drinking?
MOTHER: No!
POLICEMAN: Any drugs?
MOTHER: No! My daughter is a good girl. She goes to school and works.
POLICEMAN: *(Malicious.)* Did she hang out with the wrong crowd?
MOTHER: No! She leaves school, comes home and from there goes to the factory, gets off late, but comes straight home.
POLICEMAN: Are you sure she didn't have any other boyfriends?
CHAYO: What's wrong with you, sir? My sister's been missing two days and you're doing nothing to help us. And now you're insinuating that she was a whore and a drug addict.
POLICEMAN: Shut your trap, you brat!
MOTHER: How dare you! Have you no feelings, no decency! Who do you think you are!
POLICEMAN: Watch it, *señora*! You're insulting an officer of the law!
MOTHER: And you're insulting me, and my daughter!
POLICEMAN: This happens because they're out on the streets. Why don't you stay home and watch your children?
MOTHER: We may be poor, but we're honest. You have no right to treat us like this.
POLICEMAN: Look, ma'am, don't give us any attitude or we won't look for your daughter.
CHAYO: But you have an obligation to help us.
POLICEMAN: She probably ran off with some guy. That's what a lot of them do. They leave and come back sooner or later, sometimes pregnant.
MOTHER: No, she's not like that. Don't talk about her that way.
POLICEMAN: Listen, stop making a scene, or we won't look for your daughter. Why waste our time? I bet she took off with some guy.
CHAYO: You have no right, you jerk!
POLICEMAN: *(Throws the file in the drawer.)* Shut the fuck up, you fucking cunt!
MOTHER: How dare you! You son of a bitch! Motherfucking idiot!

(She jumps to slap the Policeman. Before she does it, Chayo grabs her and drags her out of the place. The Mother and the Policeman keep screaming insults at each other.)

POLICEMAN: You'd better shut your trap, you old hag, or I'll throw you in jail.
CHAYO: Let's get out of here, *mama*. These pigs have no compassion. *(The Policeman sits down. Pause. Determined, Chayo returns by herself, stops center stage, and screams to the cop.)* Chinga *tu madre, pinche policía culero* [= "go fuck yourself, mother-fucking pig"]!

(The Policeman gets up. Chayo runs off stage. Blackout.)

Intermission

SECOND ACT - SCENE 22

(The Narrators are sitting at the family table with the Mother. Chayo pretends to sweep.)

NARRATOR 2: Don't worry, *señora*. We're going to help you here, but I'll be honest. *(Pause.)*
NARRATOR 1: The majority of these cases don't turn out well. *(Pause.)* Have you heard about all the murdered young women?
MOTHER: I think so.
NARRATOR 2: From what you've told me, your daughter might be one of those cases.
MOTHER: Impossible! My daughter wasn't one of those…God forbid!
NARRATOR 1: What do you mean?
MOTHER: Well, on the radio, the police and government say that those women were prostitutes, strippers and drug addicts. My daughter is a good girl. She works and goes to school.
NARRATOR 2: That's what the police want people to think, so they won't be pressured into conducting a thorough investigation.
NARRATOR 1: The truth is that, in the majority of cases, the victims were young women, factory workers. Just like your daughter.
NARRATOR 1: Look at these pictures. *(From her briefcase, she pulls out a photo album. Chayo gets closer to the table.)* They're photos of over 100 missing girls.
MOTHER: I can see my daughter's face in every one of them, every one of these girls. The black, black eyes, the black, black hair…as if she were a part of all of them. But my daughter can't be dead. She never hurt anyone.
NARRATOR 1: None of them were to blame. They weren't loose women, drug addicts or prostitutes.
MOTHER: But why?
NARRATOR 2: The police aren't interested because the victims were poor and often lived alone or in out-of-the-way places, like you do.

MOTHER: But who's to blame?

NARRATOR 2:   We don't know. All we know is that Juarez is the perfect place to murder women, because of the impunity. The failure of the police to resolve these crimes has turned Juarez into a paradise for maniacs, murderers. Throw in some drug smuggling, heroin and cocaine dealing, and this city has turned into one of the most dangerous places in the world.

MOTHER: So they have no idea who's responsible for all of this?

NARRATOR 2:   There are a number of theories out there explaining this mass murder of young women, including gangs of young, rich kids, assisted by bodyguards or the police. Other theories include the making of snuff films...

MOTHER: What's that?

NARRATOR 2:   Those are videos where the girls are murdered and their deaths are videotaped.

NARRATOR 1:   Other theories talk about drug dealers' perverse orgies, ritual homicide related to Satanism, organ trafficking. It might even be a social epidemic, or copycats, where other people recreate an established pattern, and in doing so, try to hide acts of domestic violence or sexual abuse of minors.

MOTHER: So then, what can we do to get them to look for my daughter?

NARRATOR 1:   Tomorrow we are going with you to the police and demand a copy of the file.

NARRATOR 2:   When was the last time you saw your daughter?

(The Narrators gather their stuff.)

MOTHER: It's been ten days.

NARRATOR 1:   *(Giving the Mother a card.)* You can also contact this organization, "May Our Daughters Come Home." It's an organization formed by families in your situation who are fighting to find their daughters. They can help you make flyers and hand them out in the streets. The group can help you in many ways, but, above all, it's a matter of moral support.

MOTHER: Well, what else can we do? The police won't help us at all. All they do is make filthy insinuations about my daughter. And she was a good girl. Why are they doing this? Why won't anyone at the factory do anything?

(The Narrators do not answer and exit. The Mother closes the door and leans against it. On the other side Narrator 1 leans against the door. Narrator 2 observes quietly and takes his partner's briefcase. They look at each other and exit. Pause. Chayo, who tried to conceal her nausea, runs off to the patio. The Mother follows her. Fade out.)

SCENE 23

(Maritza's voice is heard in the dark singing her song. Lights fade in. The Mother comes running from the patio, crosses the room and stands at the door.)

MOTHER: Maritza! Is that you? Maritza?

(Pause. It was just her imagination. She controls her tears, goes inside, takes clothes from the bed and goes to the patio. Slowly, Juan Carlos enters, with a backpack, and goes to the door. He is about to knock, but stops, looks inside through the mosquito net, turns around and exits. The Mother comes back, looks at Juan Carlos, rushes to the door and tries to say goodbye. Nothing happens. Juan Carlos leaves. The Mother changes the sheet on the bed and feels something under the bed. She pulls out Maritza's diary and opens it. The Mother recognizes the writing, in shock; she exits towards the patio and sits next to the metal tub. She cries, holding the diary against her chest. Pause.)

MOTHER: I look for you everywhere. I see your face in the faces of others. I hear your voice in every person I meet. I know you'll come home, saying, "Look, *mami*, what a beautiful day!" I know that you'll come home. That's why I stand at the door, waiting for you. You'll be back, you'll come home to talk to me, to sing, to tell me your thoughts, to share your laughter and smile with me. I have faith that you'll just show up, saying that it was all a joke. That you stayed with a friend, that you were mad at Chayo or Juan Carlos…

(Catatonic, the Mother stays sitting. The rest of the scene is slow and in silence, in contrast with the first scene of the play. Slowly, Chayo enters, opens the door and leaves her purse on the bed. She goes to the patio to look for Mother and finds her. Chayo does not know what to do and observes Mother for a long time. She turns around and wipes her tears. Chayo goes to the ice-chest, pulls a container and empties it on a frying pan on the stove. She stares again at Mother. The Father enters, walks to the door, and opens it. Chayo turns to look at Father and signals him to be quiet and get closer. The Father goes to the patio door and stares at his wife for a long time. He turns around and sits at the table, trying to control his emotions. Chayo goes to the stove, turns it off and empties the food onto a plate. She goes to the table and serves it to Father. He looks at her, but Chayo looks away and goes back to the door to stare at Mother. The Father stares at his plate. He gets up and exits in a hurry. Chayo turns to look at him, but can't decide between consoling Father or Mother. Fade out.)

SCENE 24

(Slowly, the lights fade in. The house is empty. The Mother still is sitting in the same place. Softly, she sings Maritza's song and wakes up from her stupor, goes inside and, from under the bed, she pulls a box with flyers and places it on the table. The father comes in. The Mother hides the diary under the box. The Father doubts, but finally enters the house. The Mother pretends to be busy with the flyers.)

FATHER: How are you, dear?
MOTHER: I made a flyer to post all over the place, to see if anyone has any information.
FATHER: You didn't go to work?
MOTHER: I called in and said I couldn't make it.
FATHER: *(The Father touches her shoulders. The Mother freezes.)* Why don't you stay home and rest? You didn't sleep all night and you've been on your feet all day.
MOTHER: How do you expect me to sleep wondering where my daughter is, if she's sick, if she's been kidnapped, not knowing what's happened to her? Why doesn't she at least call?
FATHER: *(Softly, the Father kisses her on the head. Pause.)* You haven't worked in two weeks and you're running yourself ragged. Why don't you let the police handle it, dear?
MOTHER: *(Violent.)* How can you even think I'm going to leave this up to the police!

(The Father moves away and stands next to the stove, looking through the door. Pause. The Mother gets up, takes her sweater and looks on the chest of drawers for coins. She picks up the box on the table and goes to the door. She stops and without turning...)

MOTHER: I told Chayo to stop at the market and get something. She'll be here soon.

(She exits. He turns around and looks at the diary on the table, takes it and opens it. Recognizing the writing, he's overcome with emotion. We hear steps. He leaves the diary on the table and returns to his position. The Mother walks in, goes to the table, takes the diary, looks at her husband and exits. He collapses, crying.)

SCENE 25

(Narrators read their lines seriously but it changes into mocking the recommendations. The Mother walks through the audience passing flyers and asking for help.)

NARRATOR 2:   Hundreds of women come here hoping to improve their lives and those of their loved ones. Once they arrive, they meet other women like themselves, all looking for a new identity - or any identity at all - that will keep them from becoming just another victim of poverty and unemployment. But everything works against them. Their worth as human beings is diminished by political and social indifference. They become disposable. If one disappears or dies, there are many more who will come and take their place.

NARRATOR 1:   In that way, murdering women is easy to explain, since here women are worth less than the garbage. Violence and impunity have turned us into point blank targets.

NARRATOR 2:   For example, the Chihuahua Penal Code says that a man that rapes women who has proof of provocation "shall receive a sentence of three to nine years in prison."

NARRATOR 1:   The same Penal Code, on the other hand, imposes a penalty of six to twelve years in prison for cattle thieves.

NARRATOR 2:   These recommendations are the property of the Prevention Campaign launched by the Commander-in-Chief of the police of the city of Juarez. If you go out at night, try to go with one or more than one person.

(The Mother reacts to the Narrators' mockery.)

NARRATOR 1:   If you do go out alone, avoid dark, desolate streets.

NARRATOR 2:   Don't talk to strangers.

NARRATOR 1:   Don't dress suggestively.

NARRATOR 2:   Carry a whistle.

NARRATOR 1:   Don't accept drinks from strangers.

NARRATOR 2:   If someone attacks you, shout "Fire!" so people will pay attention to your call for help.

NARRATOR 1:   Have your car keys and house keys out and ready.

NARRATOR 2:   If you are sexually assaulted, make yourself vomit, so your attacker will be disgusted and run away.

SCENE 26

MOTHER: *(Screaming, she falls to her knees center stage in a small circle of light. The Narrators exit.)* Enough! Enough! I have no strength left, dear God. I've lost it all. I don't want to live anymore. *(Like a mantra.)* How many deaths are too many? How many deaths are too many? How many deaths are too many? So many questions, so few answers. So many deaths, so few killers! How many deaths are too many? How many deaths are too many? How many deaths are too many? *(She cries desperately.)* Why did you leave me, *m'ija?* Don't you see that I can't live like this? Why did you leave?

(Blackout.)

SCENE 27

NARRATOR 2:   The media refers to "the dead women of Juarez" when speaking of these brutal murders. The name undermines the seriousness of these atrocious crimes, and that's wrong. One dies of natural causes, by accident, or as a result of an illness. But these women were brutally murdered just for being women and living in conditions that made them vulnerable. Every time we use this euphemism we downplay the atrocity of these murders. We abort the feeling of social urgency and injustice necessary in order to achieve public response. We have accepted the euphemism, without thinking of the repercussions, just because the media feels it is less offensive. But we can't accept that out of convenience, we grow complacent and allow the problem to reach a level of "normalcy." The public must feel all the horror a father or a mother feels when they see the daughter's body dumped in the desert like trash. If we refer to the women who were assassinated as "the dead women of Juarez," we will end up accepting that label such that it will no longer produce horror, or indignation, or even moral discomfort, and we will, in that way, assassinate these women over and over again.

SCENE 28

(The Narrators, the Mother and Chayo stand before the Policeman's desk. Narrator 1 has a file in her hands, which she throws on the desk during her first line.)

NARRATOR 1: How is it possible that the file is only one page, *señor?*

POLICEMAN: Well, what do you expect me to do? I'm not the investigator. You think we got nothing else to do. We're not obligated to look for them. If we do, we're doing you a favor and, if you don't like the work we do, then go find someone else to look for your daughter.

NARRATOR 2: It's your duty to look for them.

POLICEMAN: *Mire* [= "Look"]. Don't push it or we won't do nothing.

NARRATOR 2: But you've done nothing. How is such inefficiency possible? This shows complete incompetence, indifference, insensitivity and negligence. It's obvious there's been no full-scale investigation, that is, if there's been any investigation at all.

POLICEMAN: They asked for it. They were living a double life. Selling their bodies.

CHAYO: That's not true and you know it.

NARRATOR 2: Well, let's suppose it were true, what's so bad about that? The life of one of those women is worth just as much as anyone else's.

POLICEMAN: It's their own fault for hanging out at sleazy clubs. They're loose women. That's the problem. It's the result of a loss of values, drugs and alcohol. Those women just don't believe in the Virgin of Guadalupe any more.

NARRATOR 1: That's ridiculous and immoral. Nobody goes around asking to be penetrated with a PVC pipe, or have their breast bitten off or to bleed to death in the middle of the desert.

POLICEMAN: Look, I've had it. Either you shut up or we'll make you shut up. You'd better shut your trap! Here comes the City Attorney!

SCENE 29

(The City Attorney, 30-ish, comes in. He wears a suit and a tie and carries a briefcase. The Mother runs to him.)

MOTHER: Please, sir! Help us! Tell them to look for my daughter. They don't want to pay attention to us. But they will pay attention to you, won't they? I beg you, for your mother's sake.

(The City Attorney looks at the Policeman, who signals the Narrators with a gesture. Looking at the Narrators, the City Attorney understands the situation. They know each other well and the relationship is tense. During the scene, they try to be civil, but bit by bit they take the gloves off. The City Attorney adopts a public tone and repeats rehearsed explanations, trying to avoid direct confrontation with the Narrators.)

CITY ATTORNEY: We regret the laxity on the part of the previous government, of Francisco Barrios, part of the opposition party. They just left bags of bones and completely let the integrity of the previous investigations go to pot. Besides, he declared that the victims were at fault because they wore miniskirts, went out dancing, they were "easy," or prostitutes. Once the new government came into power, we found that there wasn't a single file on these cases, and that the City Attorney's Special Commission for the Investigation of Murders of Women was sorely lacking. We will do everything we can to resolve this matter.

NARRATOR 2: But you keep on ignoring clues.

CITY ATTORNEY: We are doing everything humanly possible to resolve these cases.

NARRATOR 2: In Chihuahua, kidnappings decreased, as well as car theft. Since the kidnappers' victims are rich, a special group was formed with personnel and material resources that have yielded results. Why has there been no attention paid, either in terms of manpower or resources, in order to investigate these serial murders?

CITY ATTORNEY: There are no funds available to create a special task force. Besides, a profiler from the FBI made an assessment and determined that there were no serial killings in Juarez.

NARRATOR 2: But the Canadian profiler sent by the U.N. Human Rights Commission stated that there were at least two serial killers.

CITY ATTORNEY: *(He begins to lose his patience and turns to the Mother.)* This situation is painful for us, and it's deeply embarrassing. These crimes are not only against women, but also against all of Mexico, humanity in general. But there's no budget.

NARRATOR 1:   The problem is indifference on the part of the government, impunity and machismo.

CITY
ATTORNEY: There are 93 people who've been detained and accused of homicide and abduction, including accomplices. You shouldn't think that impunity reigns, that would imply inaction on the part of the state.

NARRATOR 2:   The main thing is that there shouldn't be any more murdered women. These unpunished crimes against women are a matter of state. It demands intervention on all levels, both from the government and the private sector.

CITY
ATTORNEY: *(Screams.)* The women who've died are dead! *(He realizes his mistake and tries to save face.)* And it's painful for us, and we don't want this to remain unresolved, we want to know what goes on in Juarez, and for there to be not a single more murder.

NARRATOR 1:   This feminicide is a matter of global interest; it's a question of basic humanity, above all, when it's the product of organized international crime involving the authorities.

CITY
ATTORNEY: Careful, miss, that might be construed as defamation.

NARRATOR 1:   Well, call it what you like.

CITY
ATTORNEY: Excuse me, but I have a very important meeting.

MOTHER: *(Kneeling before the City Attorney.)* I beg you once more, sir! Find my little girl!

CHAYO: No, *mamá!* Don't beg! *(Grabs Mother by the arm and helps her up.)*

CITY
ATTORNEY: Yes, ma'am! Don't worry. We're going to find her.

NARRATOR 1:   How can this be possible! I'm tired. Tired of fighting every day for justice, where justice does not exist. How's it possible that so many women are being murdered and nothing happens? How is this possible? How can so much impunity, corruption, violence and ineptitude exist? We're all guilty. You're guilty. I'm guilty. Yes, we're guilty for the fact that, in Juarez, women can be hit and raped; guilty that all these women can do is work in the *maquiladoras* and that, in Juarez, there are five bars for every one school.

CITY
ATTORNEY: Relax, woman! *(Turns away to leave, but the women stand before him, cutting his exit.)*

NARRATOR 1:   The president should order the army to patrol the city of Juarez.

CITY
ATTORNEY: According to the constitution, those cases are under local jurisdiction. In other words, the case is in the hands of the state authorities.

NARRATOR 1:   What authorities? The ones who've spent ten years staging a spectacle of lies?

CITY
ATTORNEY: We're doing everything we can. *(Again, he tries to leave, but the women don't let him.)*

NARRATOR 1:   There are 340 factories in Juarez. These multinational corporations that earn millions of dollars in Juarez should provide financial assistance in order to guarantee public safety.

CITY
ATTORNEY: The *maquiladoras* work with us, providing jobs and a future for our people. *(He signals to the Policeman, who moves in between the City Attorney and the women.)*

NARRATOR 1:   They should collaborate with the Mexican government and the human rights organizations to put an end, once and for all, to the killing of these innocent young women.

CITY
ATTORNEY: And I've got to get going; I'm really late. *(Exits.)*

SCENE 30

NARRATOR 1:   *(Screaming.)* This feminicide, this massacre, where and when is it going to end!

(Narrator 1 tries to chase after the City Attorney, but the Policeman stops her. Narrator 2 gives a step forward. Coldly, the Policeman puts his hand on his gun. The Mother and Chayo embrace Narrator 1. She calms down.)

NARRATOR 2:   Don't worry. I'll take them home. You should rest.

(The Policeman exits. The Mother and Chayo say goodbye to Narrator 1 and exit behind Narrator 2. Narrator 1 stays alone on stage. She turns, looks at the audience directly, and controls her crying.)

SCENE 31

NARRATOR 1:   They found the lifeless body of my 12-year-old daughter, Rosita, in a cotton field. She had been strangled and raped, kidnapped the day before when she left school. Even if your father died, or your mother, or your husband, it's not the same as losing someone that belongs to you, who is a part of you. A child is a part of you…

(Exits. Blackout.)

SCENE 32

(The lights come up on the house. The radio plays an old bolero. The music shall play throughout the scene. Chayo sits on the ground, attaching, with a broken hammer, a piece of cardboard to a stick of wood. The cardboard reads: LOOK FOR MY SISTER MARITZA. The Mother moves up and down, organizing her box of flyers and instructing Chayo. The Father comes in and looks at his wife and daughter. Nobody moves. Pause.)

FATHER: What are you doing?

MOTHER: Posters. We're going to City Hall to protest.

FATHER: *(Goes to stove, to the table and back to the stove. Pause.)* Is there anything to eat?

MOTHER: *Ay, viejo,* I had to go to the hospitals and to the police again, and I was passing out flyers, I haven't had time to cook.

FATHER: *(Back to the table.)* You're never home. There's never anything to eat around here.

MOTHER: *Viejo,* this is much more important to me than cooking. Can you understand that?

FATHER: I understand. But it's been almost two months. There's never any food in the house or clean clothes for me to wear.

CHAYO: *Papá.*

MOTHER: *(With a harsh hand gesture, she tells Chayo to be quiet.)* Let him say it, Chayo!

FATHER: *(Screaming.)* It feels like I lost my whole family, not just my daughter!

MOTHER: *(The anger she has repressed for all these weeks erupts to her family's astonishment. The Father tries to say something, but she doesn't give him opportunity. Chayo begins hyperventilating.)* You want to eat! Do you! Well, go ahead, eat, eat, since you can! I can't eat! Whatever I eat gets stuck in my throat! I can't eat thinking about where my daughter might be! That's why I stay here, in this house, in this neighborhood, in the hopes that one day, if she comes back, she'll know where to find us! I won't lose hope! I can't lose hope and think that my daughter is dead! I'd rather believe what that policeman told me, that she ran off with some guy! I'd rather find out she turned into a drug addict, or a prostitute, whatever, but not that she's dead!

CHAYO: *(Screaming.)* Stop! It's all my fault! Before we left that morning, I told her to drop dead, that I didn't want to see her ever again! I cursed her! I killed her! It's no one's fault but my own! *(Chayo falls to the bed. Her parents run to her, embrace her and console her.)*

FATHER: No. No. It's no one's fault, not yours, or your sister's. *(The song is over and we hear the news jingle.)*

NEWSCASTER: Flash news from your favorite station, KILL in Juarez. Maritza Martinez Lopez's lifeless body, in an advanced state of decomposition, was found in the desert. The body was lying face down; the hands were tied behind her back using the straps of her purse. No prints or clues were found. She had two stab wounds to the chest and two to the back. The coroner said she had been dead for two months. Given the condition of the body, it was impossible to determine whether she had been raped.

(When they hear Maritza's name, the family freezes. They seem to be a photograph or a sculpture. Slowly, the Mother gets up and walks forward in a trance. At the end of the news flash, Chayo runs to the radio and turns it off, hitting it.)

MOTHER: Maritza!

(The Mother screams and falls. The Father runs, catches his wife and falls to his knees, with his wife's head on his lap. Chayo runs to them, hugs them and cries. Blackout.)

SCENE 33

NARRATOR 2:   In 1997, a seven-year-old girl disappeared. The police did nothing to help, and repeated with impunity that, according to the autopsy, she was neglected, had cavities and had a calcium deficiency. That little girl was my daughter, Irma. Her body showed signs of torture. Her eyes were ripped out. *(Pulls out a handful of pictures from his pocket.)* Look at these photos of Irma at her first communion, at her cousins' *quinceañera* [= "girls' 15th birthday celebration"], one in her school uniform that she liked so much. We buried her in it. Here's a photo of her body dumped in the desert. *(Swallowing his fury, tears and frustration.)* Who could do this to my baby girl? *(Screaming.)* Who! What monster is capable of doing such a thing to a child! *(A long pause to compose himself.)* Despite the years that have passed, I can't help getting choked up, I feel pain in my chest and anger in my heart when I think of my daughter. The impunity is so rampant that the only way to go on is to fight so that we don't become indifferent. *(Exit.)*

SCENE 34

(Chayo and the parents, dressed in black stand before a table. A white sheet covers what seems to be a body. The Policeman is standing next to the family.)

POLICEMAN: Here's your daughter. We identified her by the school ID she had with her.

MOTHER: But how could she be all bones in two months? A body takes longer to decompose.

POLICEMAN: If you don't want it, leave it.

MOTHER: Can't you do that DNA test to make sure that it's her?

POLICEMAN: Oh, *señora*. That costs a lot of money and it takes a long time.

You have to identify the body. *(He realizes the impact of his words and changes his attitude.)* You're lucky. There are more than 70 unidentified bodies.

MOTHER: I can't look at her. I just can't. *(Turns, burying her head on her husband's chest.)*

FATHER: We have to make a positive identification before they'll release the body to us.

CHAYO: We need to look at her, identify her. Be sure that it's her.

(The Father steps forward. The Mother stops him and gently pushes him back.)

MOTHER: I'll do it.

(She closes her eyes, breathes deeply and lifts the sheet, looking at the remains attentively.)

MOTHER: It's her clothing; her jeans, her blouse, but it's not her face, it's not her. *(Crying and laughing hysterically, she turns to her husband and hugs him.)*

CHAYO: *(Steps forward and looks at the body.)* Those are her teeth, her fingernails and her hair. It's her, *mamá*. Maritza is dead!

MOTHER: No! No! No!

(The Mother runs off crying, with the Father behind her. Chayo tries to follow them, but stops and cries and cries. She looks up and faces the audience. She calms herself.)

SCENE 35

CHAYO: That was four years ago. Ever since that day when she didn't come home, I knew she would never be back. I sensed it. She wasn't the kind of girl who would just take off. After the burial, we went out and painted crosses on a lamp post and wrote: "not one more." We wrote her name on every lamppost and telephone pole in sight. Other families joined in and a long list of names on crosses began to appear; Maritza...

SCENE 36

(The Mother walks into the house, wearing a black veil over her head. She hugs Maritza's teddy bear and packs it in a box. She does the same with the diary. She stops, retakes the diary and begins to write on it. At the same time the Mother walks on stage, the rest of the cast, except Maritza, come on stage too. They come in as actors not as the characters they play, and they are all in black and form a semicircle around Chayo. The men carry a lit candle and Narrator 1 wears a black veil over her head. After Chayo names her sister, they all, simultaneously, recite the names of the victims.)

FATHER: Adriana, Agustina, Aida, Alejandra, Alicia, Alma, Alondra, Amalia, Amelia, America, Amparo, Ana, Angeles, Angelica, Angelina, Araceli, Argelia, Berenice, Berta, Blanca.

JUAN CARLOS: Brenda, Brisia, Carmen, Carolina, Cecilia, Celia, Cinthia, Clara, Claudia, Cristina, Daniela, Deissy, Donna, Dora, Edith, Elaine, Elba, Elena, Elizabeth, Elodia, Elsa, Elva.

CHAYO: Elvira, Emilia, Epigmenia, Erendira, Erika, Esmeralda, Estela, Ester, Eugenia, Fabiola, Flor, Francisca, Gabriela, Georgia, Gladys, Gloria, Guadalupe, Guillermina, Helena.

POLICEMAN: Hilda, Idalia, Ignacia, Ines, Irene, Irma, Isabel, Isela, Ivette, Ivonne, Janneth, Jessica, Juana, Julia, Julieta, Julissa, Karina, Laura , Leticia, Lilia, Liliana, Linda, Lizeth.

CITY ATTORNEY: Lorenza, Lourdes, Lucero, Lucila, Luisa, Luz, Mabel, Manuela, Margarita, Maria, Maria de Jesús, Maria Salud, Maria Santos, Maribel, Martha, Merced, Mireya, Miriam, Nancy.

NARRATOR 1:   Natividad, Nelly, Norma, Olga, Otilia, Paloma, Patricia, Paulina, Perla, Petra, Raquel, Rebeca, Refugio, Reina, Rocio, Rosario, Rosaura, Sagrario, Sandra, Saturnina, Silvia,

NARRATOR 2:   Soledad, Sonia, Susana, Teresa, Tomasa, Vanessa, Veronica, Victoria, Violeta, Virginia, Wendy, Yareli, Yesenia, Yolanda, Zenaida, Zulema.

NARRATOR 1:   14 years, four hundred murders and no one responsible!

CHAYO: Not one more...

FATHER: *(Screaming.)* Alejandra!

NARRATOR 2:   14 years, four hundred murders, and a mountain of lies!

CHAYO: Not one more...

JUAN CARLOS: *(Screaming.)* Berenice!

NARRATOR 1:   14 years, four hundred murders, and a mountain of impunity!

CHAYO: Not one more...

CITY ATTORNEY: *(Screaming.)* Erica!

NARRATOR 1:   14 years.

FATHER: *(Screaming.)* Agustina!

CHAYO: ...four hundred murders.

JUAN CARLOS: Cecilia!

NARRATOR 2:   ...and walls of silence.

POLICEMAN: *(Screaming.)* Janneth!

ALL: *(Screaming.)* Not one more! *(They turn to the Mother.)*

SCENE 37

MOTHER: *(Steps forward and stops at the center of the semicircle. The Father moves behind her on her right and Chayo on her left.)* We don't ask for much: we just want justice; for the murders to be solved and the government to do something to stop it; to not live in fear thinking that one of us will probably not come home someday. We want to be able to live and work in peace, to walk without fear. We want someone to take a look at Juarez and say, ENOUGH! Is that too much to ask?

(The women cover their faces with the veils and the men blow out the candle. Blackout.)

Curtain

Acknowledgements

I wish to thank Ingrid Marquez for originating the role of The Mother and giving her a strength and stature I could only dream of; my translators and friends, Eve Muller and Liane Schirmer, for their great work; my brother Ariel for his love and undying support; and all my teachers and fellow actors for their patience and the lessons they have shared with me.

BOXCAR/EL VAGÓN

by Silvia Gonzalez S.

(El Vagon is a corollary to the original play BOXCAR,
and will be part of a trilogy)

Author's biography

Silvia is proud to be a Mexican-American. Her mother was born in Fresnillo, Zacatecas, and her father was born in Ciudad Mier, Tamaulipas, Mexico. Silvia started life in San Fernando, and lived in Pacoima, California, for her growing years. Silvia attended Loyola Marymount University in Southern California, and Loyola Rome Center in Italy, and graduated with a B.S. in Education from Loyola University of Chicago. Performance activity started with stand-up comedy and ventriloquism. Inspiration took over and Silvia began acting in community theater and improv groups in Columbus, Yuma, Phoenix and Chicago. Soon after, playwriting became a passion and Silvia has 30 plays to her credit. Sometimes writing several plays simultaneously with constant dabbling in teaching school and bird raising, most notably parrots, Silvia continues to see her work produced across the country, Canada and in New Zealand.

Writing accomplishments large and small can be found on www.SilviaGonzalesS.com Productions include: *El vagón* (derived from *Boxcar*), national winner of VOCES (2004) and production at Repertorio Español (New York City), Teatro Bravo, Teatro del Piel, Teatro Vision, Second Stage Theater's "Immigrant Project" (excerpt), Teatro de la Rosa The Original Theater Works; *The Migrant Farmworker's Son*, University of Texas-El Paso Chicano Theatre, The Empty Space, META at the University Theater, California State-Long Beach; *Alicia in Wonder Tierra (or I Can't Eat Goat Head)* Cara Mia Theatre Company with the Dallas Children's Theater, Utah State Theater, Teatro Humildad, Theater for Young Folk, Berkeley Repertory, The Côterie, Kennedy Center, New Voices/New Vision; *The Narcissistic Personality Disorder Radio Show*, Stockyard Theater; *Don't Promise (A Story of Women, Mormonism, and Survival)*, Stockyard Theater Project; *Border*, American Playwrights of Color Aquijon II Theater Company; *Los Matadores,* Paula Productions; *Waiting Women (Pearl Hart's Famous Stage Coach Robbery)*, Mutt Repertory Theater (New York City); *¡Fiesta!,* John F. Kennedy Center; *La Llorona Llora*, Whole Art Theater; *U Got the Look*, The Original Theater Works; *T for Torture*, Aquijon II Theater Company (bilingual production in repertory); *Samual and Daniela,* Wizard Oil Productions (New York City).

Introduction

In the spring of 2006, nationwide protests erupted across the United States, staged by immigrant advocates seeking to promote reform. One of the most clamorous rallies occurred right here in Phoenix, Arizona, at the same time that Teatro Bravo was staging Silvia Gonzalez's play, *Boxcar/El vagón*, translated into Spanish by Rubi Orozco. Many of our actors were involved in the protests, such as Luis Avila, a local actor and community activist who at the time was also a disc jockey at La Onda 1190 radio station. As the director of this particular production and a Chilean immigrant myself, I was personally invested in the issues involved in Silvia's play. The playwright honored us with her presence during the second week of the production and contributed to audience talkbacks at a time when many of us hoped that immigration reform would still be possible. But a Republican Congress chose to rebel against its own president and put off reform for another time and another administration.

These are the times we live in and no matter how portentous and frustrating, it's a pertinent time for the theater to mirror the struggles of its community. Unfortunately, in Phoenix, a typical day at the theater involves a revival of, say, *Annie* or an East Coast play approved by New York critics. Latinos who comprise thirty percent of the greater Phoenix population are often rendered invisible in local theater. The Phoenix critics avoided this production as they do all our Spanish-language presentations. There was a time when the *Tribune* employed a fearless critic, Max McQueen, who reviewed all our productions, regardless of language. His solution to the language barrier: he brought a friend with him to interpret. Those days were over by the time we opened this production. I'd like to believe that we at Teatro Bravo have remained relevant with regards to current issues affecting our community, but the leadership of our local theaters and the critics tend to ignore those efforts altogether. Not so members of the Latino community who attended the play and engaged in audience talkbacks about this production, just as the theater of the streets had erupted only blocks away, lending support and veracity to the play and the production itself. Our friend and Teatro Bravo founder, Daniel Enrique Perez, by then a professor at University of Nevada, Reno, invited the production to his campus where the Latino Research Center had us perform the play for their local audiences. On the same day we arrived, a rumor spread through the immigrant community that the border patrol would arrest and deport the undocumented on sight. When we talked to audiences after the show, they explained to us that several friends wanted to come see the play but were afraid that the border patrol would seek them out in a show about undocumented immigrants. Fortunately, there were no raids at our performance that night, but the fear in people's faces reminded us that the issues of the play had become frightfully real during the current anti-immigrant hysteria.

This play forces the audience to witness the painful process of dying through asphyxiation when immigrants become trapped in a boxcar in the middle of the desert. I projected the temperature that the migrants experienced inside the boxcar onto a wall at the John Paul Theatre, in Phoenix College, as it rose from about 50°F in the morning to the high deadly temperatures of 130°F and beyond. Those of us who live with heat in the Phoenix environment know precisely what this discomfort means, and the way intense heat robs one of the air one breathes. With an expert set created by designer Gary Imel, the boxcar felt like a trap and the lights by Merritt Smith got more intense and more infernal as the play progressed. By the end, the boxcar rotated in the John Paul Theater's mobile stage, looking like a hot furnace. The effect proved discomfiting and frightfully real.

Silvia had by then won first prize in the National Hispanic Playwriting contest, sponsored by Repertorio Español in New York City where the play had its premiere in 2007. As Silvia's play goes on to be produced elsewhere, as it should, it will continue to be relevant. Unfortunately, in this delicate situation politicians speak with ire and conviction, yet refuse to put their votes down on paper. The delay costs lives, as people continue to perish in the desert.

> Guillermo Reyes
> Phoenix, AZ
> December 2007

Production History

Boxcar/El vagón by Silvia Gonzalez S., was developed through Teatro Vision's new works program, CODICES, with the following cast and crew:

FRANCISCO	Andres Sinohui
PEPE	Mauricio Rivera
GÜERO	Gualo Aguayo
NOEL	Alex Perdomo
MANUEL	Jaime Avelar-Guzman
ROBERTO	Fred Silva
BILL	Ted D'Agostino

Artistic and Stage Director	Elisa Marina Alvarado
Dramaturg	Amy Gonzalez
Designers	Erin Kehr, David Ferlauto Andy Horenner, Gloria Grandy, and Caela Fujii
Stage Manager	Anna Licea
Translator	Rubi Orozco
Project Assistant	Josefina Cid

Project support was provided by Teatro Vision's staff:

Production Manager	Dianne Vega
Executive Director	Raul Lozano
Business Manager	Ben Soriano
Marketing Coordinator	Vanessa Rios

World premiere production by Teatro Vision, performed in Spanish and English at the Mexican Heritage Plaza, Theater, San Jose, California, March 11th – April 4th, 2004.

El vagón by Silvia Gonzalez S. was produced by Teatro Bravo in Spanish, as translated into Spanish by Rubi Orozco, in March 2006 at the John Paul Theater of Phoenix College, Phoenix, Arizona, directed by Guillermo Reyes with the following cast:

FRANCISCO .... Luis Avila
NOEL ....Daniel Chavez-Alcorta
GÜERO.. Pedro Osuna
PEPE ....Juan Gomez
MANUEL... Miguel Calvillo
BILL... Luis Melodelgado
ROBERTO .... Ismael Gaytan
GUARDS and DETECTIVES .... Angel Hernan and
....Obed Hurtado

For production rights in Spanish, contact teatro@teatrovision.org. Production rights in English go to website www.SilviaGonzalezS.com.

El vagón/Boxcar originated from the original play *The Empty Boxcar*, subsequently retitled to *Boxcar* by the author.

Boxcar
SCENE 1 - Desert

(Darkness before dawn. A slight,dry wind. In the distance, Mexican music from a radio station blends with the sound of the wind, then fades away. Country music from a radio station blends with the sound of the wind then fades away. What should be noticed is that the Mexican and American Country music are similar. In a faint dawn light we see Border Patrolmen, Roberto and Bill, scanning the horizon with binoculars. Roberto receives a call regarding the sighting of an undocumented nearby. Bill exits to check this out. Far upstage, an immigrant crossing the desert is sighted by Roberto. The immigrant is Manuel. Roberto points his gun toward Manuel's back.)

ROBERTO: Immigration! Put your hands up.

(Manuel drops his suitcase to raise his hands.)

ROBERTO: Now turn around slowly.

(Manuel turns around very slowly almost comically.)

MANUEL: *(Recognizing Roberto.) Roberto! Que me lleva la trampa* [= "I just got trapped"].

ROBERTO: *(Recognizing Manuel.)* Manuel.

MANUEL: *¿Si?*

ROBERTO: How many times do we have to go through this?

MANUEL: I don't know. One, two, three, four, *cinco?*

ROBERTO: This is the ninth time.

MANUEL: Nine? No, much less.

ROBERTO: Nine times.

MANUEL: *(Shrugs.)* Thank you for stopping to say hello. *(Manuel makes a meager attempt to keep on walking.)*

ROBERTO: *(Approaches.)* Don't you get tired of running in circles?

MANUEL: I don't get tired of eating? Do you? *(Waits for an answer.)* When a man stops providing for his family, he is nothing.

ROBERTO: You always find work here, don't you?

MANUEL: Yes, I do. And you must do your work. You mustn't lose your job. One of us should eat.

ROBERTO: I'm sending you home.

MANUEL: I am home. Number one, the employers want me. Number two, someone made a mistake with the history books. This all was Mexico.

ROBERTO: Like you said, I'm just doing my job. *(Roberto handcuffs Manuel.)*

MANUEL: And you're doing it so well. *(Beat.)* Is it a crime to improve your life?

ROBERTO: It's my job to return those who were born over there.

MANUEL: And where were you born?

ROBERTO: Here.

MANUEL: And your parents?

ROBERTO: *(No answer.)*
MANUEL: *(Eyes him.)* You are one of us.
ROBERTO: I...
MANUEL: *Se te ve en la cara. Traes nopal en la frente.* [= "It is written on your face. You have a nopal on your forehead"].
ROBERTO: What do you mean?
MANUEL: *Pocho.*
ROBERTO: *(Frowns.)*
MANUEL: Neither here nor there.
ROBERTO: Anything I should know about? *(Indicates Manuel's bag. Opens and searches it.)*
MANUEL: Did I ever tell you I have a gift?
ROBERTO: *(No answer.)*
MANUEL: I never told you? Let me look at your face more closely.
ROBERTO: What is it?
MANUEL: I can tell by the features of a face where someone is descended from.
ROBERTO: *(Waits.)*
MANUEL: Dark, penetrating eyes. I can barely see the pupils. I would say they are from the Southern province of Spain – ruled by the Moors for 700 years. Forehead – even with the nopal – Northern Spain or France. Lips, cheekbones are indigenous. Perhaps even the big head – heard of the *cabezones* [= "colossal heads"] of the Yucatan? If you had freckles, I would say a bit of Irish too.
ROBERTO: I have freckles on my back.
MANUEL: Well then, a trace of Irish from the maternal side.
ROBERTO: Irish?
MANUEL: Many Irish preferred Mexico to the United States where they faced much discrimination way back then.

(Roberto is silent.)

MANUEL: *(Continues.)* An anthropological lesson, for free. When I look at the features of a face, I can see the ancestors. You should realize, we are all related.
ROBERTO: Come on, Manuel, walk to the van. I'm sending you back.
MANUEL: Don't feel bad, Roberto. I'll cross again soon. I have to. Maybe next time it will go better for me. *(Manuel fades away.)*

SCENE 2 - Interrogation Room

(Noel is in a chair. Long uncomfortable moments. Roberto holds an identification card.)

ROBERTO: Is this you?
NOEL: ...Yes.
ROBERTO: A college ID card?
NOEL: ...University.

ROBERTO: Why did you cross then?
NOEL: I had to.
ROBERTO: El Salvador?
NOEL: Yes.
BILL: Not Mexico?
NOEL: *(No answer.)*
BILL: *(To Roberto.)* The rest were Mexicans, weren't they?
ROBERTO: *(Ignoring Bill's question.)*…What happened?
NOEL: I don't know.
BILL: You must know something.
NOEL: I just did what I was told.
BILL: By who?
NOEL: *(No answer.)*
ROBERTO: The *coyote* [= "smuggler"]?
NOEL: …Yes.
ROBERTO: Who is he?
NOEL: *(No answer.)*
BILL: Tell us.
NOEL: I don't know.
BILL: What do you know?
NOEL: I know if he says, run, you run. And if he says crawl, you crawl.
ROBERTO: And?
NOEL: If he says in the boxcar, it's in the boxcar.
ROBERTO: Don't play with me, kid. How did you get to the boxcar?
NOEL: I was taken there.
ROBERTO: By who?
NOEL: …I was driven there in a car. But not in the normal way.
ROBERTO: Go on.
NOEL: *(Slowly, resisting.)* With the seats taken out, we were stacked like sardines. One on top of the other in rows. We had to stay down. None of us daring to move. The *coyote* let some of us out at a truck stop. Me, he motioned towards the train tracks. He gave me the number of a boxcar, 17583, and told me to wait in there.
ROBERTO: Then what?
NOEL: I found the boxcar. Someone was already there.

(Crossfade to scene three.)

SCENE 3 - Boxcar

(Temperature: 76 degrees.)

(Boxcar brought/rolled onstage. Francisco enters the boxcar as it is moving. He hides inside, alert, wanting to make sure he wasn't seen. He then opens a cardboard box tied with rough rope, which contains his belongings. He pulls out a rosary and begins to pray. He hears sounds outside the boxcar. Moments later, the door of the

boxcar slides open. Noel quietly enters, and closes the sliding door to the exact position it was before. The two are silent, eyeing each other.)

NOEL: *Buenos días.*
FRANCISCO: *Buenos días…(Francisco places his bag against the wall of the boxcar.)*
FRANCISCO: How much?
NOEL: How much what?
FRANCISCO: How much did it cost you?
NOEL: He took all I had.
FRANCISCO: *Pinche coyote* [= "fucking smuggler"].
NOEL: He wants more.
FRANCISCO: And…
NOEL: My mother will pay him the rest later.
FRANCISCO: Your mother?
NOEL: *(Embarrassed.)* Yes. *(Pause.)*
FRANCISCO: Total?
NOEL: Five thousand.
FRANCISCO: *Pinche coyote.* You're from far away then.
NOEL: San Salvador.
FRANCISCO: Ah. That's why.
NOEL: Are you far away from home too?
FRANCISO: *Sí.* From the Sierra Tarasca to this desert is very far. Too far.
               I heard a long time ago it used to cost 200 dollars. I paid two thousand. Well, welcome to the ugly side of life.

(They sit quietly, sizing each other up a bit more as they rearrange themselves for the train ride. Outside, Güero approaches the boxcar. He has been walking hours in the dark desert. He is ecstatic at finally finding the boxcar his coyote *had told him of. He sings a favorite* Los Tigres del Norte *song, climbs the ladder on the boxcar and proclaims…)*

GÜERO: *¡Adiós México querido! ¡Ya me voy pa'l otro lado! ¡Ajúa!* [= "Goodbye my beloved Mexico! I am going to the other side! Yeah"]! *(He pretends he is saying goodbye to fans at the end of a concert. He climbs down, pounds out his song's rhythm on the boxcar, then throws open the door.)*
GÜERO: *¿Qué hubo querida Raza* [= "What's up my beloved people"]? This the ride to the stars?
FRANCISCO: *Este mero.* [= "This is the one"].
GÜERO: *Chido* [= "awesome"]. *(Güero tosses in a pillowcase. Francisco and Noel offer assistance. Francisco looks out of the boxcar then closes the boxcar door to the same spot it was before.)*
GÜERO: *¡Qué suave* [= "How cool"]! No walking for miles and no running from gun-crazy *migra.* Just take a cruise north. I have my Metallica T-shirt and my Lakers cap. *¡Puro Americano!*
FRANCISCO: And those jeans? Did you get them caught on barbed wire?

GÜERO: *¿Qué traes hombre* [= "What is your problem, man"]? You've
            seen Van Halen – these jeans are *estilo Norte Americano!*
            (Gives a yelp of delight.)
FRANCISCO: *Oye* [= "Hey"], we're not at a rock concert. Keep it down,
            güero.
GÜERO: *(Whispers at first, then gets increasingly louder.)* Oh, that's
            right. I can't get caught. I don't have money to cross for a long
            time. How did you guess my name was Güero?
FRANCISCO: It wasn't hard, *hijo.*
GÜERO: Everyone calls me Güero. The fair-skinned. I just blink my
            green eyes and say 'Okay,' 'all right,' 'no problem, my friend'
            and I pass. *(Rummaging through his possessions.)* I brought
            a bathing suit, sunglasses, and toilet paper – I'm going to
            California. But it isn't easy being so light – I get bad sunburn.
            Picked up some sunscreen to keep me from burning. *(He pulls it
            out.)* Watcha.
FRANCISCO: That's suntan lotion, not sunscreen. You'll fry in this grease.
GÜERO: What? Man, I won this in a dice game with the *coyote* - put in
            five *pinche dólares* for this! Well, guess I'll have to wear my
            long sleeve shirt when we get out into the sun.
FRANCISCO: You got dice?
GÜERO: *Simon que sí* [= "Of course"]. Never leave home without them.
            (Holds up dice. Then to Noel...) And you? What's in your little
            bag?
NOEL: Nothing much. Some water and a book.
GÜERO: A book? What you need is toilet paper.
NOEL: *(Looking around.)* Just us, then?
FRANCISCO: I don't think so. Not enough profit for the *coyote.*
GÜERO: Ah, the profit. Can't forget that. *(Güero finds a spot to put
            his belongings and prepares a location in the boxcar for his
            journey.)*
GÜERO: *(Hears something.)* Someone's coming.

(They all freeze and wait like quiet mice.)

GÜERO: *(Peeks outside.) Allá anda un viejillo* [= "There is an old man"].
PEPE: *Oye, no sean malos. ¡Ayúdenme* [= "Listen don't be mean. Help
            me"]!

(Francisco cautiously looks out of the boxcar.)

FRANCISCO: *Vamos* [= "Let's go"]. He's in bad shape.

*(The three go out and find Pepe, exhausted, on the track. Pepe is smeared with
black oil.)*

GÜERO: What's that smell?
PEPE: Your *pinche mamá, cabrón* [= "your mamma, asshole"].
FRANCISCO: What happened to you? *(Together they lift him up.)*
GÜERO: *¿Qué és?* [= "What is it"]? Oil?

PEPE: *Sí.* If the *coyote* tells you to get in a barrel, tell him to eat shit. *(Looks at himself.) Hijo de su chingada madre* [= "Son of a motherfucking bitch"].

FRANCISCO: We'll mix a little water with sand and clean you up. Do you have another shirt?

PEPE: In my bag.

(Francisco looks in Pepe's bag and pulls out a shirt and helps him with it. Güero gets his toilet paper and tries to help get some of the oil off Pepe. This is not much of a help. Noel also tries to help in any way he can. They then help Pepe towards the boxcar.)

FRANCISCO: *(Noticing the dirty shirt on the ground.)* Don't leave it there. They'll see it. Put it in his bag.

(Noel puts the shirt in Pepe's bag. They look around to see if they were seen, then help Pepe into the boxcar.)

PEPE: *¡Ora!* Watch the legs.

(Francisco closes the boxcar door to the same position as before.)

GÜERO: *(Smells his fingers, then to Pepe...)* What's the oil from?

PEPE: I had to hide in a barrel.

GÜERO: Did they use oil to squeeze you in? *(Chuckles a bit.)*

PEPE: *(Slightly insulted.)* No. I just let the others have the cleaner barrels. Mine had been used for old car oil.

FRANCISCO: *Pinche coyote.*

NOEL: Why barrels?

PEPE: *(To Francisco.)* He's new?

FRANCISCO: Very new.

PEPE: That is what he said to do. So we did it. We started out in a couple of cars. Stuffed in the trunk. I had people above me, under me, all around. Hours passed. An elbow dug deeper into my kidney. There were two babies – thank God they slept the whole time. I felt bad for the women who had strangers pressed against them. When we got to the desert, the *coyote* got us out of the cars and pushed us to a truck with barrels. Eight of us went into the barrels. A mother and her two children, me and four other men. The lids where hammered on tight.

NOEL: *La gran púchica* [= "the big hell"] – like being buried alive.

PEPE: My legs still ache.

(Fransisco offers to do an adjustment, estilo huesero *[= "bone-setter]. Pepe accepts help.)*

PEPE: *¿Eres sobador* [= "Are you a massage therapist"]?

FRANCISCO: *(Acknowledges his skill with a nod.)* Rest old man.

PEPE: Yes. Maybe I can forget that horrible ride.

(Silence. Noel goes to Pepe.)

NOEL: My name is Noel.

PEPE: I'm Pepe...Nice clothes.

NOEL: Thank you.

PEPE: Have luck with you?

NOEL: Sometimes.

PEPE: I consider myself one of the lucky ones. There were only eight barrels. The rest were left behind.

GÜERO: I once hid in a refrigerator. It smelled like rotten beef. I could barely stand the smell. The stench stayed on me for days. I tried to wash it off with gasoline.

NOEL: You're lucky you didn't fry like a *chicharrón*. [= "pork rind"].

GÜERO: *Mira, güey*, [= "look, dude"], I know how to get across this *pinche frontera* [= "fucking border"]. Do you?

NOEL: I...

PEPE: *(Cuts in to cut off conflict.)* Not exactly first class, *eh muchachos*?

FRANCISCO: *Mexicanos* never ride first class.

GÜERO: My sister crossed in a train two months ago with no problem. I know she misses home though. She was the closest to our mom. *Muy pegada.* [= "very close"]. But it takes both of us working up here to keep the family together.

PEPE: *¿Y tú Papá?*

GÜERO: My dad died in a tractor accident up in Oregon a couple years ago. My mom can't come up here – *tuvo mucho chamaco.* [= "she had lots of kids"]. She's got seven other kids at home. I'm her favorite though. *Soy el consentido* [= "I am the favorite"] because I'm the lightest.

PEPE: You miss your *mamá, verdad*?

GÜERO: *Ni hablar, hombre* [= "no kidding, man"]. I'm gonna work really hard this time. No partying. Going to save all my money so I can buy my mom a little house and get my sister back home too. They'll live good – my mom will get her nails done at least every six months. And my sisters will have pretty dresses. Then I'll buy myself a car.

NOEL: *¿Oh sí?* What kind?

GÜERO: *Pos,* one with a motor. *(Beat.)* My poor sister. She crossed all alone.

FRANCISCO: Every crossing is hard.

GÜERO: This is my fourth time.

FRANCISCO: A *veterano*.

GÜERO: First two times, I came on my own. Then I used a *coyote* – faster.

PEPE: My cousin crossed on his own his first time and almost got his throat cut by a robber.

GÜERO: *Ay, qué culero* [= "Man, what an asshole"] That's very bad luck.

PEPE: I crossed on my own once. I was robbed of everything. The *cabrón* even wanted my clothes.

NOEL: What happened?

PEPE: I pleaded with him. I said, "Please *señor*, you have all my money, my little radio, even my Dodgers cap. Don't take the clothes off my back. Are you going to leave a man as old as your father out in the cold in his *chones*" [= "underwear"]? He said, "I hate my father." And took off with my clothes.

GÜERO: *Que gacho* [= "that sucks"], that's very bad luck.

PEPE: Anyhow, let's have a good trip. I know this will be a good one.

GÜERO: It will be.

(More settling in.)

NOEL: *(To Pepe.)* Where were the others going?

PEPE: My barrel partners?

NOEL: Yes.

PEPE: Nebraska, I think.

GÜERO: I've been there. It's cold.

FRANCISCO: Yes, very cold up there, but there is a lot of work on the cattle ranches. Not like California these days. Used to be we could work in the canneries. Now you are lucky to get a job as a janitor or dishwasher. But in places like Nebraska, Oregon and Washington, they still wait for us with open arms.

GÜERO: Last time I was in California I worked in a car wash. The owner charged 18 dollars for a wash. We washed six or seven cars an hour. He made...

NOEL: One hundred twenty six...

GÜERO: Yeah, 126 dollars an hour and I made six dollars an hour. I heard my old boss is laying off guys, though.

FRANCISCO: I used to work on a flower farm in Watsonville...They shut down because florists are importing cheaper flowers from South America. The farmers had to sell their land to companies that build big houses for the *ricos*. So many farms are now covered by cement.

GÜERO: Not in Nebraska. *(Nods to Pepe.)*

PEPE: We're not the only ones having a hard time. I've seen *americanos* paying for food with these cards. Others wait in line at missions. Sleeping on the ground with cardboard. I think, if they are like that, then what's going to happen to us?

FRANCISCO: Nothing. Absolutely nothing.

PEPE: Besides all that, I want to believe the grass is greener on the other side. If I stop believing that, I lose all hope. Why live when there is no hope?

NOEL: *(To Pepe.)* So, where are you going for work?

PEPE: *Pos,* Houston. From there, maybe Idaho to work in the potatoes.

GÜERO: I'll go anywhere for work.

PEPE: Yes. Anywhere...*(Beat. Lowers his head.)*

NOEL: *¿Qué le pasa* [= "what's wrong"], *señor?*

PEPE: *(Long silence and then slowly surrendering his thoughts.) Sabes*
         [= "you know"], call me crazy, but I heard a strange sound when
         I was in the barrel.
GÜERO: What kind of sound?
PEPE: A sound like a man screaming inside a bottle. I don't want to
         think this, but I think a barrel fell out of the truck, with a man.
         I saw the woman when we were let out, but there was one less
         man.
NOEL: What did you do?
PEPE: *(Hurt.)*…What could I do?

(Silence. Pepe takes a blanket out of his bag and lies down to rest. He appears to be hiding from his thoughts. The men settle in a bit more. Pepe has an orange, which he peels and shares. A sudden pounding on the metal door.)

MANUEL: Open up! Immigration! *(Door slides open.)* Up against the wall
         now! *¡Manos pa' arriba, pantalones abajo* [= "Hands up, pants
         down"]! *(All men freeze, up against wall.)* Come on *cabrones,*
         give me a hand! *(Enjoying his joke.)*

(Noel helps Manuel. Train bells are heard.)

MANUEL: Just in time.
GÜERO: *¡Ya nos vamos!* [= "We're leaving"]!
FRANCISCO: *Todos callados.* [= "Quiet everyone"].

(Silence. All watch each other. Train bells continue. A big jolt. The men are thrown to the side. Francisco takes a look out of the boxcar.)

FRANCISCO: They're reconnecting the cars.

(Güero looks out.)

GÜERO: Someone's coming!

(The men hug the walls and stay very quiet. The sound of the door being latched from outside. All stare at the door for long moments.)

MANUEL: The door is latched for our safety. Less chance *la migra* will
         look inside.

(The train lurches forward, the men react to the movement. The sound of the train moving.)

MANUEL: *(Introducing himself to all.) Buenas. Me llamo Manuel* [=
         "Hello. My name is Manuel"]. This is the second time I've
         crossed since yesterday. *(The men look at him with skepticism.)*
         Es verdad [= "it's true"]. A few days ago I crossed, no problem.
         Then, just when I thought I had made it, *la migra* caught me
         and sent me back over the border. I knew the guy, too. Almost
         convinced him to look the other way. I spent the last of my
         money to cross again.
FRANCISCO: *(Acknowledging.)* Francisco.
MANUEL: *¿El chamaco* [= "the boy"]?

NOEL: Noel.
MANUEL: How about you, *güero?*
GÜERO: Güero.
MANUEL: Of course. *(Eyeing Pepe.)* Pepe?
PEPE: *El mismo que viste y calza.* [= "the same that you saw and got"]
MANUEL: I hardly recognized you.

(Pepe stands up.)

PEPE: How about now?
MANUEL: Now there's no question. I'd recognize that *panza* [= "belly"] anywhere.

(They hug Mexican style.)

MANUEL: *¡Te vez más viejo* [= "You look older"]! What has life done to you?
PEPE: Broken every bone in my body.
MANUEL: And mine, too. But with a little glue I pasted them back together.
PEPE: I should try that.
MANUEL: How long has it been?
PEPE: Years. Maybe since Chicago.
MANUEL: *(Sincerely.)* We had good times there.
PEPE: Maybe.
MANUEL: Come on. We danced with beautiful *rucas* [= "women"]. How could you forget Chicago? Remember when I was chased by the boyfriend of that skinny *rubia* [= "blond"].
PEPE: No?
MANUEL: And when the *güey* caught me, *zurco! Me partió la madre* [= "he beat the hell out of me"].
PEPE: *(Starts to smile.)* We were young and unmarried.
MANUEL: The Aragon Ballroom. On Fullerton Street. Northside Chicago. That fine palace was packed with beautiful girls ready to dance. They didn't care with who. I danced with every single one. Remember that, Pepe?
PEPE: No.
MANUEL: Remember *Suzy?* Come on, there's no way you could forget *La Suzy. ¡Estaba tan grandota* [= "she was a really big one"]!
NOEL: How big was she?
GÜERO: *¿Así – o así – de grandota? (Demonstrates hips, breasts.)*
MANUEL: More than you can handle. *Ojos grandotes. Labios grandotes* [= "really big eyes. Really big lips"].
GÜERO: *¿Nariz grandota* [= " really big nose"]?
NOEL: *¿Patotas grandotas* [= "really big feet"]?
GÜERO: *¿Orejotas grandototas* [= "really big ears"]?
MANUEL: *Y también un gran* [= "and also a big "]...
PEPE: Now I remember.
GÜERO: *(Really wants to know.)* A big what? What?

MANUEL: *(To Güero.) Vete a* [= "Go to"] Chicago – you can't miss her
and you won't want to! *(To Pepe.)* The most fun I ever had in
the United States was during those nights at the Aragon. The
women fought to dance with me.

PEPE: The women fought to get away from you, *cabrón.*

MANUEL: How they loved my profile.

PEPE: You mean the profile from behind, when you left.

(They all laugh.)

MANUEL: Pepe, you still have a sense of humor.

PEPE: *(To the others.)* No sense of humor. It was the truth. But all that
was before we were married. *Dime* [= "tell me"], is your wife as
beautiful as I remember?

MANUEL: Even more.

PEPE: Your *india.* Those girls in Chicago don't compare, *verdad?*

GÜERO: Is she *pura india?*

MANUEL: Yes. *Pura india. india pura.* From one of the few places the
Spaniards missed. She speaks the ancient language of her
ancestors. Even the best anthropologists have not deciphered the
language completely. *La quiero tanto* [= "I love her so much"].

PEPE: I've always wondered? How did you marry *una indígena?* I
know many *familias indígenas* who do all they can to stay away
from whites and mestizos.

MANUEL: *Es verdad.* Her father was so angry that we became *novios* [=
"sweethearts"], I thought he'd make *chicharrones* out of my
nalgas [= "butt cheeks"]. We had to run away to get married. I
was always afraid he'd come after us. *(Beat.)* I don't blame her
familia for trying to save what's left of their people. Several
weeks after we'd gone, her family told the others in their pueblo
that she'd fallen from a high cliff. They even built a shrine at
the ledge where they said she fell. We watched from across the
valley. There was a procession, then a funeral. Her *mamá* threw
flowers over the cliff. We imagined it was our wedding. I think
of her every day. She is who gets me through hard times.

PEPE: *Sí, compadre* [= "buddy"]. The memory of a *mujer* [=
"woman"] can carry you across any desert. *(Beat.)* I think of my
wife every day. Sometimes every hour. I know that right this
minute she is worrying about me and our Sarita.

MANUEL: *¿Que tiene la niña?* [= "what's wrong with the girl"]?

PEPE: The doctors say they don't know yet. She is very sick. There is
a good doctor in the village who let us pay with what we had
– chickens, *frutas – lo que había* [= "fruits – whatever we had"].
Then the doctor said he could not help her. He said our daughter
needed special tests in the *capital.* Ones that cost a lot of money.

*(Güero has been examining the ceiling. Then he holds out his arm as if he is holding
a torch.)*

NOEL: If you find a way to let some air in, let me know.
GÜERO: Haven't found any openings…Hey, gues who I am?…The Statue of Liberty.

(Sounds of train bells.)

MANUEL: *Señores,* here we go!
FRANCISCO: Soon we'll pass the check point.
MANUEL: Then we better be quiet. *Que Díos nos bendiga* [= "may God bless us"].

(Train sounds. They all sit there for long moments listening to the sounds of the train. Crossfade to scene four.)

SCENE 4 - Interrogation Room

ROBERTO: And that accounts for everybody.
NOEL: Yes.
ROBERTO: Everyone have the same *coyote?*
NOEL: *(No answer.)*
ROBERTO: The name of the *coyote* that brought you?
NOEL: I don't know.
BILL: Did the smuggler tell you not to tell us?
NOEL: Those guys never give a real name.
BILL: So what fake name did he give you?
NOEL: *(Pause.)* I heard someone call him *El Chapulín.* That's all I know.
BILL: *El Chapulín?*
ROBERTO: Means "the grasshopper."
BILL: *(Under his breath.)* Figures.
ROBERTO: *(To Noel.)* Can you tell us what he looked like?
NOEL: I couldn't say.
ROBERTO: How did you find this *coyote?*
NOEL: I heard from a friend of a friend that he could help me.
ROBERTO: And?
NOEL: We met briefly. Made arrangements.
ROBERTO: What kind of arrangements?
NOEL: How to travel. What to wear, what to bring, what to say and not to say. He told me he would be in charge of everything.
ROBERTO: And?
NOEL: I did what he told me to do, that's all.
BILL: You put your life in the hands of a stranger? Not very smart for a college kid.
NOEL: I had to.
ROBERTO: What else do you remember about him?
NOEL: May I have another drink of water?
ROBERTO: Sure. *(Roberto gives him water. Noel takes a long time to drink.)*
NOEL: Thank you.

BILL: Can you tell us anything else about him?

NOEL: You've seen more *coyotes* than I ever have and ever will. He was a *mexicano*. Black hair, brown eyes. I don't know anything else.

BILL: *(Aside to Roberto.)* It's the usual.

ROBERTO: Yeah, usual.

BILL: What's eating you?

ROBERTO: *(To himself.)* It's a crisis.

BILL: Our health insurance covers that.

ROBERTO: Not me! This! This here. They are dying!

BILL: They are also breaking the law. *(To Noel.)* We spoke with your mommy.

NOEL: How did she find me?

ROBERTO: The news wire here, and then the story was picked up over in Central America.

NOEL: May I talk to her?

BILL: When you tell us more.

NOEL: More of the horror story?

ROBERTO: You don't have to.

BILL: Yeah. We'll find out with the forensics. But if you tell us, we can get your side of the story.

NOEL: What will happen to me afterwards?

BILL: That's not for us to decide.

ROBERTO: We'll do something for you. I promise.

NOEL: Thank you.

(Bill takes Roberto aside.)

BILL: Why did you say that?

ROBERTO: I want to help him.

BILL: You can't go saying you'll help. You're a border guard.

ROBERTO: He's just a kid.

BILL: They sneak across!

ROBERTO: Why isn't something done about the enticers?

BILL: And who are they?

ROBERTO: …Us. *(Beat.)* Noel. You have anything else to tell us? Anything you can give me so I can help you?

NOEL: I want to talk to my mother.

BILL: You will if you tell us everything.

NOEL: Can I talk to her today?

BILL: After you tell us what we need to know.

NOEL: Why do you have to know all this?

BILL: For our report.

ROBERTO: You'll call your mother today. On my phone.

NOEL: Thank you. *(Misty.)*…May I take a moment?

ROBERTO: Take your time.

(Noel puts his hands over his face.)

BILL: *(Aside to Roberto.)* You're crazy. Just damn crazy. It's another day at the office. You can't go making promises.

ROBERTO: It's just a phone call.

BILL: You don't do that with them.

ROBERTO: ...It's no big deal.

BILL: Well, it is a big deal. You'll be accused of harboring a criminal.

ROBERTO: I told you he's a kid.

BILL: He's a criminal.

ROBERTO: Says who?

BILL: Says everybody.

ROBERTO: ...Not everybody.

BILL: Even so, we don't want them.

ROBERTO: Them?

BILL: Look at your uniform, *señor* Robert. What're you goddamn wearing, and what is your goddamn job? There's just too many of THEM.

ROBERTO: Too many of me-types?

BILL: Too many of them-types. Don't give me that look. I'm concerned with them.

ROBERTO: You are?

BILL: They're exploited, and that's not the American way.

ROBERTO: You exploited them before. Every time you hire one to work on your ranch.

BILL: I pay a fair wage.

ROBERTO: I know what you pay.

BILL: What're you trying to say?

ROBERTO: Willing workers are an attraction. We're all guilty of it in one way or another. Even if you sit in a restaurant and watch one clear the tables, you have in your consciousness, that if he sounds like he's from another country, he's probably working for less. Living in sub-housing, maybe with 5 or 8 other men because we pay them less. So we see the exploitation and we say nothing...I just want to help one guy.

BILL: Think of it like high school. When you don't have a pass, you can't walk around the school. You get sent to the principal's office.

ROBERTO: You've been sent to the principal's office.

BILL: Yeah, I have. But, I'm telling you the goddamn truth. And no one is saying it because it is so damn politically incorrect.

ROBERTO: Surprise me.

BILL: You want to hear it?

ROBERTO: I've been hearing it.

BILL: Too many, Robert.

ROBERTO: You said that.

BILL: Then I'll say it again.

ROBERTO: How many is too many?

BILL: We're just sick of it. They should go back so they don't get
            exploited. They take our jobs, our taxes, our health services, our
            welfare. They got to stop sneaking around and disappearing into
            our system. Taking advantage of us.
ROBERTO: You said they get exploited.
BILL: Well, then it's both.
ROBERTO: We give them the low-paying jobs, we tell them to use the
            health services and welfare. We encourage it! I know, before
            I worked here I was an interpreter. I remember how we told
            them about every service they can apply for if they were making
            a very small income! For godsake, we told them about it and
            forced them to go to the appointments for breast screenings. We
            gave them birth control patches! We even gave them a ride to
            the health department.
BILL: Must have been democrats in office.
ROBERTO: Bill, how many is too many?
BILL: I know what you think. Let everyone in at anytime!
ROBERTO: I just want to see people being treated like humans. But if
            you are asking me my opinion, I'd say this: I'd like to see
            a registration, with a health check, a respect for the human,
            appreciation for their desire to work, and like you said, a pass
            to come and go as they wish. Able to go home and see families
            without fear. I'd like to see fair treatment when they work, and
            not blame all societal problems on these hard workers. I'd like
            to see justice for those who want to improve their lives and be a
            part of the fabric of this country.
BILL: I'm not saying they can't come.
ROBERTO: What are you saying?
BILL: They gotta wait in line and do the proper paper work.
ROBERTO: That's where they tell me the problem is. The paperwork is a
            joke and not an avenue to opportunity. A stone wall. But you
            say you're sick of seeing people like them. Are you sick of me?
BILL: You're okay.
ROBERTO: I'm okay?
BILL: I don't want to see you go.
ROBERTO: I'm an American. My heritage is Mexican, *baboso*.
BILL: I know what that means.
ROBERTO: *(Frustrated.)*I don't know what law tells you to let your family
            starve. When I see their hands…their hands…their hard working
            hands, the hands leathery from work, I know that's all they
            want. Not a free ride. Just a little time over here to make money
            to send back to their families. To know in their minds that
            they are helping their loved ones to the last possible recourse.
            There's pride in giving your family members something to eat.
            Some nicer clothes to wear. Some hope.
BILL: Some hope?
ROBERTO: Hope.

BILL: Hope. I hope that drugs stop trickling into this country, that terrorists don't use the wet-back trail to get across.

ROBERTO: I hope for those things too.

BILL: Still, with your Spanish, you even do a better job.

ROBERTO: A better job?

BILL: You tell them they are being detained.

ROBERTO: ...Before I started working here, I used to read the paper where a man was found dehydrated in the desert. I thought, what a way to die, but worse if the vultures get to it. Soon after I took this job...Now, I'm tired of scraping dozens of dehydrated bodies off the ground.

BILL: Then they shouldn't cross.

ROBERTO: I'm imagining that some time ago, someone in my family must have had to do this. No one speaks of it. And the way people are talking about it now, why would anyone admit it. Why become a victim to people like you?

BILL: So what do you want to do about it?

(Silence. Crossfade to scene five.)

SCENE 5 - Boxcar

(Pepe is softly whistling "Dos arbolitos.")

GÜERO: *¿Oye, don Pepe, qué no es "Dos Arbolitos"* [= "Hey, don Pepe, isn't that "*Dos arbolitos*"]? *Mi 'amá* liked that song. *(Güero listens a while.) ¿Me la canta* [= "will you sing it to me"]?

(Pepe sings. Francisco joins. Manuel begins singing as if in a cantina.)

MANUEL: *Cerveza.* Beer. I need a beer, Pepe. Is Corona still your favorite?

PEPE: I don't drink anymore.

MANUEL: Wife's got you well trained!

PEPE: Ulcers. The doctor said that one more beer will kill me.

MANUEL: That's not true. Beer is good for you and it's the national drink of *la mexicanidad.* I favor Negra Modelo.

GÜERO: *Hui,* too dark! Budweiser's my beer now. Might as well get used to it if you're going to live *en el norte.* All the *raza* drink it up here.

MANUEL: It tastes like piss.

PEPE: Coors tastes like piss.

GÜERO: *Neta.* [= "seriously"]. Gotta agree with you there.

MANUEL: Getting back to Mexico, you want to talk about piss, Moderna is piss.

PEPE: All beer is piss when it burns your ulcers.

MANUEL: You and your ulcers. See a doctor.

PEPE: I did. He said no more drinking beer.

MANUEL: Get another doctor. One who drinks.

PEPE: *(To Noel.)* What do you drink?

NOEL: I drink red wine.

(They stare at him. Dead silence.)

FRANCISCO: You remind me of someone.

PEPE: He reminds me of my son.

MANUEL: Number five or number eight?

PEPE: Number twelve.

MANUEL: He reminds me of my oldest son. Same age.

PEPE: What's his name?

MANUEL: Jose Alberto, but we call him Pepe.

PEPE: Get out of here.

MANUEL: We do. And when he's not looking we call him Pepito for the little *pepito* he has.

PEPE: He got that from you.

MANUEL: Maybe he did. If I had one as big as yours, I would have 15 kids.

FRANCISCO: You want to hear a story?

MANUEL: Are you going to tell us about your *pepito*? I'm not interested.

FRANCISCO: I'm going to tell you about my friend Sanchez. *Se inspiraba mucho* [= "he was very inspired"] with the stories of fortune in the United States.

PEPE: Fortune…

MANUEL: *Anda,* [= "go on"], tell your story.

FRANCISCO: So he gathered his courage and climbed through a hole in the fence.

GÜERO: What fence?

FRANCISCO: The fence that runs along the border. The *tortilla* curtain. He got through and ran as fast as he could to the river.

GÜERO: *A lo mojado* [= "like a wet-back"].

FRANCISCO: He took off his shoes and pants and held them above his head. He crossed in the dead of night, through a strong current of deep, cold water. On the other side he would hide till he knew he wasn't followed by *la migra* or by the vicious *cholos* [= "Mexican gangbangers"] who rob and sometimes murder *los que cruzan* [= "those that cross"]. He would make his way through the desert to a farm to work. He crossed this way for years.

GÜERO: I can relate to that story, but I always wear pants.

FRANCISCO: *Escuchen* [= "listen"]. One day he was caught. Here's where the story is different. *La migra* looked up his record, and right there in the computer, right there on the screen, they found out he was an American citizen!

GÜERO: Ah, come on! Why didn't his mother tell him?

FRANCISCO: She was dead.

GÜERO: His father, then?

FRANCISCO: He had a stepfather who didn't know.

GÜERO: *No mames* [= "no shit"]! Unbelievable story. I know that I'm a
           mexicano. I don't need to check no computer.

(Güero takes off his shirt and pulls out the label.)

GÜERO: It's right here: *Hecho en México* [= "Made in Mexico"].

(All laugh. When they quiet down ...)

FRANCISCO: I ran into this man several years later. We worked side by side
           picking tomatoes in Texas. He was being paid the same as I was.
           Up here he was just another Mexican.

MANUEL: A man I knew, a desperate man – not like us, we never were
           that desperate – He didn't have enough money for a *coyote*, so
           he had this idea. He found a dead cow. There were buzzards
           circling all over it. Some of them were jumping on it, excited
           over the rotten meat. When the buzzards were almost finished,
           he took a knife and cut the hoofs off. You know what he did
           with the hoofs? He tied them to his feet! He knew the border
           patrol looked for human footprints. Then he started to walk
           across the desert – all the way to the border. *Pobre güey* got
           caught. The border patrol noticed a cow that didn't stop at
           patches of grass. They followed the prints till they found my
           friend exhausted on a rock, like beef jerky drying in the sun.

NOEL: *(Looks around and then tweaks his crotch.)* What do we do if
           we need to go to the restroom?

MANUEL: *Amigo mío,* it's very simple. *(Manuel takes an empty soda
           bottle).* And remember, one size fits all. In your case, *te va a
           quedar güango* [= "it will be too loose"].

NOEL: It will not.

GÜERO: I'll need a bigger bottle.

MANUEL: I'll need a barrel.

PEPE: No barrels.

*(Noel takes the Coke bottle and walks toward the corner. Before he gets there,
Manuel swipes the bottle from him and tosses it to Güero. Both play 'keep away'
with it.)*

NOEL: Will you stop that. I have to go.

MANUEL: How bad?

NOEL: Do you want me to pee right here?

MANUEL: Better in the corner.

NOEL: No!

MANUEL: How badly do you want this bottle?

NOEL: Give it to me.

MANUEL: How badly?

NOEL: You mean money?

MANUEL: I mean, your pride. How badly do you want it. Bad enough to
           sound like a rooster? Let me hear you crow like a rooster.

NOEL: *(Hesitates.)*

GÜERO: *(Chiming in.)* You know how a rooster sounds.
NOEL: That's not the point. I'm not going to do that.
MANUEL: Then where are you going to pee?
NOEL: *(Reluctantly crows like a rooster.)*
MANUEL: Not good enough.
NOEL: That was good.
MANUEL: No, that was terrible. Try again.
NOEL: *(Crows like a rooster.)*
MANUEL: *(Contemplating.)* I don't know.
NOEL: Come on!
MANUEL: One more time.
NOEL: *(Crows like a rooster.)*
MANUEL: *Bueno*, that deserves an applause. Everyone.
NOEL: Can I have the bottle now?
MANUEL: Sure.
NOEL: *(Outraged.)* You're all making fun of me.

(Güero 'pecks' at him like a rooster.)

MANUEL: Of course. If we didn't make fun of someone, it would be boring in here, *chamaco*. The trick is to enjoy it.

(Güero then pecks at Manuel who pecks back. Pepe and Francisco join in on a pelea de gallos [="cockfight"].)

NOEL: I don't enjoy ridicule and abuse.
MANUEL: Abuse? We better stop then. This can be classified as harassment and we don't want to be a part of that.
NOEL: Absolutely, you are harassing me!
MANUEL: *Bueno. Ya con eso* [= "fine, enough of that"].
GÜERO: I don't want to stop.
MANUEL: *Ya estuvo* [= "enough"].
NOEL: Thank you.

(Noel cautiously walks away from them.)

GÜERO: Hey, you have a fancy bag.

(Güero kicks it or picks it up and drops it.)

GÜERO: Oh, what's in there? A brick?
NOEL: It's a book, I told you. Don't go in there.
GÜERO: What?
NOEL: *(Feeling challenged.)* Don't go in there.
GÜERO: What kind of book do you have?

(Güero sticks his hand in and takes out a book and frowns.)

GÜERO: It would be better if you had a *Playboy* magazine.
MANUEL: Wait a minute. Let me see this book. Anthropology? Are you a student of anthropology?
NOEL: Yes.
MANUEL: Give him back his book.

GÜERO: But I can use it as toilet paper.
MANUEL: No more jokes on him.
GÜERO: But...All right.
NOEL: *(To Manuel.)*...Thank you.
MANUEL: Any student of anthropology is a friend of mine.
GÜERO: What about me?
MANUEL: You're a pest.
GÜERO: *(Smiles.)* So they say.
MANUEL: The university?
NOEL: Yes.
MANUEL: Which one?
NOEL: *La UTEC* – uh, *La Universidad Tecnológica de El Salvador.* I am studying pre-Columbian cultural interchange between North and South America.
MANUEL: In my youth, I had a dream of becoming an anthropologist. Maybe even a professor. But I couldn't afford the university. I had to work. But, I read many books in my spare time. What made you choose that field?
NOEL: I'm interested in people.
MANUEL: So am I, Noel. So am I. You know what impresses me the most, after traveling like I have? As different as people are on the outside, on the inside we're really all the same. *Todos somos parientes* [= "we are all related"]. Remember that. Deep down we're all related.

(Crossface to scene six.)

SCENE 6 - Interrogation Room and Boxcar

ROBERTO: Go on, *muchacho* [= "boy"]. What happened in the boxcar?
NOEL: I was told by the *coyote* that it would be a long ride. So at first we just tried to pass the time.

(Manuel is pretending to drink a beer. He savors it.)

NOEL: *Disculpe* – [= "pardon me –"]
MANUEL: *¿Sí?*
NOEL: May I ask you something?
MANUEL: Of course.
NOEL: What are you doing?
MANUEL: *¿Qué no vez?* I am drinking a beer.
NOEL: There is no beer in your hand.
MANUEL: *Chinos en el frente* [= "right in front of me"]! Who took my beer? Well, that's life, isn't it? Pepe, buy me a beer later, okay?
PEPE: I will buy you a whole *cantina* if we get out of here soon.

(Noel is becoming uncomfortably hot.)

GÜERO: What's the matter with you?
NOEL: The heat. Why did the train slow down? My hair is dripping
           with sweat.
GÜERO: You got the "wet look." When I was up here last year my hair
           was purple and spiked. I thought I looked just like an American
           rockero – muy Steven Tyler.
MANUEL: Who the hell is Steven Tyler?
GÜERO: You know, the *vato* [= "dude"] who sings, "Crazy." *(Imitates
           Steven Tyler.)* Anyway, nobody would give me a job. My
           mother called asking when I'd be able to send some money. She
           had lots of bills. I got that color out of my hair fast. Now I am a
           man who will do what he has to do get a job. My *jefita* told me
           that when I get married I should stop supporting her. I'll have
           my own wife and kids to take care of.
NOEL: When are you planning to get married?
GÜERO: I'll give you an answer when I find myself a woman.
MANUEL: *Las chichis grandes son las mejores, Güerinche* [= "big boobs
           are the best, whitey"].
GÜERO: Any breasts, for that matter.
MANUEL: You're such a *joto* [= "gay"] and you don't even know it.
GÜERO: I'm not a *joto*. But if I were, you'll be the first to know.
MANUEL: Pepe…Pepe. *(Pepe is dozing. He doesn't answer.)* Pepe!
PEPE: *¿Qué pues, hombre* [= "what, man"]? What?
MANUEL: Go to sleep.
PEPE: *Ya*, leave me in peace!
MANUEL: You keep falling for it, *sonso* [= "dummy"].

(SOUND: Train bells, brakes. The train stops.)

GÜERO: *¿Y ahora qué* [= "and now what"]? The train has been inching
           along for hours. Now we stop.
MANUEL: It's usually because they are hooking on new cars, waiting for
           another train to pass or changing tracks.
NOEL: This boxcar is no place for humans. Not even for animals.
           (Takes a measured drink from his bottle of water.)
MANUEL: *(Seeing Noel drink, also takes a sip from his water.) Oye*, Noel,
           turn on the air conditioning.
NOEL: *(Becoming even more uncomfortable due to heat.) ¿Dónde* [=
           "where"]?
MANUEL: If you can't find it, just open the window.
PEPE: *Ay, por favor.* [= "Oh, please."] I could use a little breeze.
GÜERO: A little sea breeze.
FRANCSCO   A soft wind.
NOEL: *¿No tienen calor* [= "aren't you hot"]? How can you ignore this
           heat? I need air!

*(Noel goes to boxcar door, tries to open it. It continues to be locked from outside.
He frantically attempts to pull and pound it loose till breathless.)*

PEPE: You've never crossed before. You haven't known the suffering. You'll learn how to cross. Look at me – I've made this journey over and over.

MANUEL: *(Goes to him, tries to get him to sit.) Joven, paciencia* [= "young man, patience"]. Patience. I have ridden these trains before. Trust me, the trick is to stay calm. *Tranquilo* [= "calm down"]. *(Beat.)* Now is the time to find your *aguante* – your strength. It is obvious you have a good heart. Your father must be a good man. He taught you kindness, but maybe you are having to find your *aguante* with us.

GÜERO: My father taught me *el aguante – a lo bruto* [= "toughness – the hard way"].

NOEL: *(To all the others.)* You have no right to speak of my father.

FRANCISCO: Yes, you are right. But you have the right to speak of him. Perhaps he can teach you, even here. *Anda.*

NOEL: *(Struggling.)* My father was a newspaper man. He hated the corruption in our government. He knew who was making a lot of money.

MANUEL: Sounds like Mexico.

NOEL: Seems my father had been getting death threats for almost two years. He never told my mother or me. He had only told his best friend, one of the few honest judges left in the country. My father would have publicly denounced the threats but he did not want to alarm my mother. She knew his work was becoming more dangerous though and begged him to leave the country. One day, he got to his office and found it trashed. The walls filled with bullets. Graffiti on the walls called him a communist.

FRANCISCO: *Ah, sí.* Called a communist for wanting the truth known.

NOEL: Two weeks later, as he left home one morning for a meeting with the judge, *(Beat.)* he was killed. I went to his office to see if I could find evidence. My mother panicked. She insisted I leave the country immediately and made arrangements to get me to the Mexican border.

FRANCISCO: Must be very hard for your mother to be without her husband and son.

NOEL: I can't stop thinking about his car exploding. I see him open the door, get in, turn the key…the fire. *(Anguished.)* We must find air!

MANUEL: *Óiganme, todos* [= "listen to me, everyone"]. If we save our air, if we sit quietly and not move too much, we can survive this.

GÜERO: Listen to me. We have two choices. We stay quiet, like you said, and hope the train continues on it's way before we die of heat and no air. Or, make noise until someone hears us. If we get sent back, we can cross again, no?

(First Güero and then Noel bash their fists on the walls of the boxcar. Francisco, then Manuel start banging the walls with their shoes, their bags, screaming for help

for a long time. There is hysterical yelling and groaning and banging on the walls in frustration. The heat becomes even more intense. Noel searches for an opening, a loose plank. Güero joins him, climbing all over the boxcar.)

FRANCISCO: *Sí, mis hijos* [= "yes, my sons"]. Look for a way out. *Mira* [= "look"]. *(Points to seam in floor.)* Maybe you can pry that piece of floor up. Do you have a key or anything metal?

GÜERO: I have a knife – here. It's pretty small but maybe it will work.

MANUEL: Pepe, *¿qué te pasa* [= "what's wrong with you"]?

PEPE: I've been thinking about it over and over. I am sure of it now. One barrel fell off the truck.

MANUEL: *Párale* [= "stop"].

PEPE: What do you think it feels like to die in a can?

MANUEL: Pepe. *Ya.*

PEPE: I keep imagining what it is like. *Pues, tú sabes tanto* [= "since you know so much"], tell me what it is like.

MANUEL: I don't know and I don't want to find out. *Mira*, think about that job that's waiting for you. Think about how you are going to be able to help your daughter.

PEPE: *Sí. Sí. Tienes razón* [= "you are correct"].

(Noel has been starting to bore a hole. Pepe goes to help. Pepe, with great effort, takes up the task till exhausted. Manuel works. He is able to pry up the metal and finds wood planking below. He begins to carve a hole. He works, then becomes exhausted. Noel resumes working, carving at the hole till he must rest. The temperature has been rising steadily, and the oxygen available for the men lessens. The task of making a hole becomes increasingly difficult. The breathing of all the men is labored. During this time, each man periodically takes sips of water from his bottle. Francisco, then Manuel, finish their water. Güero takes up the task. He begins carving methodically when a panic creeps up and overtakes him. He stabs at the wood below the metal frantically. He cries out –)

GÜERO: *¡Ay 'ama!* I made you a promise! *(He cries, is unable to continue carving.)*

(Francisco gently takes the knife from Güero and continues to work at making a breathing hole. Crossface to scene seven.)

SCENE 7 - Interrogation Room

(Noel sobs. Roberto and Bill step back to give Noel some space.)

BILL: *(Beat.)* You know, there's a lot going on. I mean…it's not as easy as it used to be. It was easier before 911. After that, we got all sorts of instructions.

ROBERTO: Why do you do this?

BILL: I think it's okay.

ROBERTO: Is it really okay?

BILL: When I don't think about it, it's okay.

ROBERTO: And when you think about it?

BILL: …It's got to be done by someone.

ROBERTO: When I think about the origins of this country, labor was absolutely necessary. People were encouraged to come. They worked as laborers to lay down the train tracks, roads, buildings, make parks, put up dams. My father worked on a dam. Without them, this country wouldn't be that strong. It was made great on the backs of people from other countries. And when they were done, they were rejected.

BILL: I don't know much about history.

ROBERTO: Chinese worked on the tracks, too. They worked from the east, the Mexicans were working on the tracks from the west, until both groups met in the middle.

BILL: The gold spike.

ROBERTO: Pictures were taken of men in top hats shaking hands as west met east. In the background, the Chinese and Mexicans were shaking hands, but there's no pictures of them. Then they were sent home. And they are still being sent home. *(They watch each other.)*

BILL: We have to uphold the law.

ROBERTO: When I see the face of a man with calluses on his hands, I know he's here to work. Risking everything to feed a family. People dreaming, who despite all that is done to them, still have to dream that there is a better life.

BILL: …It's because of that kid, right?

(Long beat. Noel seems to awaken from his fog.)

NOEL: *(Takes a breath, then –)*…We continued to sweat. Most of us were delirious. We worked hard on a small hole to help us breathe.

(Crossfade to scene eight.)

SCENE 8 - Boxcar

(Temperature: 162 degrees.)

(A few hours later. The men are sweating profusely. Shirts and pants spread about the boxcar. Manuel, who has been working on the hole, finally bores through the thick planks in boxcar floor.)

MANUEL: You can draw a full breath now.

(Manuel slowly moves away from the hole. Both Güero and Noel dive for the hole at the same time. A frantic fight ensues. Güero slams Noel's face on the floor.)

GÜERO: Breathe your *pinche* air, *cabrón!* I know how to survive without you!

(With much effort Manuel and Francisco intervene. Güero grabs his water and

finishes it, throws bottle, hard, at boxcar door. He lays down. Noel breathes air in deeply from hole. All are quiet as if listening, breathing with him. Noel looks around at all the men, notices Pepe, who is very still.)

NOEL: *Don Pepe. Venga, respire* [= "come, breath"]! *(No response.)*
            Don Pepe!

MANUEL: *(To Noel.)* Let him rest. Noel, it's Güero's turn. Then you,
            Francisco.

(Güero crawls to the hole, breathes awhile. He's worried about Pepe, goes to him, nudges him. He thinks Pepe is only unconscious. With great effort, as he is feeling weak, ill, he sings "Dos arbolitos" to revive Pepe.)

GÜERO: "Han nacido en mi rancho dos arbolitos
            Dos arbolitos que parecen gemelos
            Y desde mi casita los veo solitos
            Bajo el amparo santos y la luz del cielo…

(Franciso and Manuel softly join Güero in singing.)

            Arbolito arbolito bajo tu sombra…

(Güero's voice fades, Manuel and Francisco continue. Güero lies down near Pepe, semi-conscious. As the scene continues, Güero dies.)

            Voy a esperar que el día cansado muera
            Y cuando estoy mirando al cielo
            Pido pa' que me mande una compañera…"

(Beat.)

FRANCISCO: I saw them in the desert. They kept going and going till lost.
            They were Salvadorians. Your people.

NOEL: *¿Qué dices* [= "what are you saying"]?

FRANCISCO: The *coyote* had taken all their money. Told them to walk a few
            miles west and another *coyote* would meet them to guide them.
            No one ever appeared. They had no water. Nothing. Only one
            survived. The one who failed at slitting his own throat.

MANUEL: Francisco, *cálmate.*

FRANCISCO: *(Becoming delirious.)* Every year the monarch butterflies came
            home to my mountains. How did they travel so far with those
            fragile whisper wings?

MANUEL: This *coyote* has never failed me. Each time I cross with him I
            get a job, make a little money and return home to my wife and
            children.

FRANCISCO: *Mi rancho del cielo* [= "my heavenly ranch"]. It was to be my
            son and daughter's inheritance. Their home forever. A place
            they would never have to leave. Confess me.

MANUEL: *¿Qué? No, hombre. Espera* – just wait.

FRANCISCO: There is no movement. The soul is still. Thorns prickle my feet.
            I've never noticed my feet until now. The toes separate as they
            touch the ground, then they press together for one more step.
            (Beat.) We should confess our sins.

MANUEL: Don't knock on the door of death.

(Silence.)

FRANCISCO: I want peace. Sins to be lifted. They lay heavy here in my heart.
They are a huge weight. *Pesan* [= "they weigh]...*pesan*...I can't
breathe...

MANUEL: Stop it! You scare...me.

NOEL: What is he talking about?

MANUEL: He is hallucinating. Francisco, look at me.

FRANCISCO: I like picking oranges the best. They smell so pretty, so round.
Hermano, vamos a piscar naranjas [= "brother, let's go pick
oranges"].

MANUEL: *Tranquilo*, Francisco, *tranquilo*.

*(Francisco lies down. Though Manuel weakens, he encourages Noel to breathe
at the air hole. Noel breathes while Manuel speaks. As Manuel speaks, he carves
words into the boxcar floor.)*

MANUEL: Did your teachers tell you about the great migrations of our
people? The long walk to find our nation is a story of my wife's
abuelos [= "grandparents"]. *Dicen que* [= "they say that"], way
back, many of us *mexicanos* were from up here, the desert of the
North. These Pueblos up here are our relatives. *Dicen que* we
were told to leave and keep walking South till we saw a sign,
an eagle on a nopal devouring a serpent. They say we had to
walk to learn who we really were. We would not be able to see
the *aguila* [= "eagle"] and nopal till we learned how to do our
journey.

MANUEL: *(Looking at the message he has carved.)* Todos somos parientes.

(The boxcar slowly is turned door side out to audience. Crossfade to scene nine.)

SCENE 9 - Interrogation room

(Several long beats. Bill and Roberto pace.)

BILL: Thinking?

ROBERTO: Remembering.

BILL: What?

ROBERTO: When my dad became a citizen, he had land in Mexico by
inheriting it from his father. If he became a citizen, he would
lose it.

BILL: Yeah?

ROBERTO: He decided to lose his inheritance because he saw how he was
able to work and feed a family. His kids got a good education.
He worked hard in a terrible job, but it helped him feed his
family. He decided to turn in his green card. I remember him
jumping with joy with a paper saying he was now a U.S. citizen.
This gray-haired man was skipping down the sidewalk like

a child, waving it in his hand. I thanked him for giving me the honor to witness this great event. I looked at hundreds of people from every nationality possible staring at the American flag, being sworn in as citizens. They had tears in their eyes holding that citizenship paper against their heart...People know this is a great country. People like me and you forget. People from other places can see the difference. Because why would Europeans overstay their visas? People in boats or flimsy rafts risk all to come here. A 13-year-old kid walked for a year from the southern tip of Mexico to get to the United States. He heard it was a great place. Of course when he got here, he had to get deported.

BILL: Did he?

ROBERTO: I don't know. Last I heard, a church group wanted to help him stay. Such a brave child fending for himself is special...Other children are appearing in the desert now. Their parents paying *coyotes* anything to get them in.

BILL: That's wrong.

ROBERTO: *(To no one.)* But when you get here, you'll see me. You'll see Bill. And we have to say: This is a great country, we want you to be like us, but don't come here. We want you to adopt our values, but don't come here. We will let you fight in our war and then we'll give you citizenship – sometimes after you get killed on the battleground. We'll thank you at your grave site for giving us your life. Here's the paper saying you are a citizen. Bless you. *(Getting misty.)*

BILL: Robert!?

ROBERTO: *(Hesitates, then –)* I knew one of the men who was in that boxcar. Manuel. I caught him a few days ago and I sent him back. He is a good man. A man who never did any harm to any one. A smart man.

BILL: Not that smart. He got into that boxcar.

ROBERTO: To feed his family. *(Beat.)*

BILL: You're worked up about knowing someone in there.

ROBERTO: ...I knew them all.

BILL: We're almost done with this case. Look, I'll arrange for the transport van. You take Noel back to his cell. Then we all go home. Okay? Okay. *(Bill exits.)*

(Roberto goes to the interrogation room. Crossfade to scene ten.)

SCENE 10 - from Interrogation Room to Boxcar

(Roberto is alone with Noel. Roberto puts on his hat, readies to leave interrogation room.)

ROBERTO: Come on.
   NOEL: Where are you taking me?
ROBERTO: To that boxcar.
   NOEL: No, please, I don't want to go back there. Please, please, no!
ROBERTO: I can't leave you here by yourself. Come. Don't be afraid.

(Roberto and Noel exit the interrogation room. They go to the boxcar. They both stand in front of it, back to audience. Roberto goes to the boxcar, slides open the door, enters. Inside, he finds Manuel's carved message. Roberto removes his badge, gun and the other equipment he has used to hunt the undocumented. He places them near the air hole or carved message, as if on an altar. He takes a moment to reflect then returns to Noel. Roberto motions for Noel to run.)

ROBERTO: *Ni uno más* [= "not one more"].

(As lights slowly fade to deep dusk, Roberto takes off the handcuffs.)

ROBERTO: *Todos somos parientes.* We are all related.

Curtain

14

by josé casas

Author's biography

José Casas is a playwright and director hailing from Baldwin Park, California. He holds a B.A. in Dramatic Arts from the University of California, Santa Barbara, M.A. in Theatre Arts from California State University, Los Angeles, and an M.F.A. in Creative Writing (Playwriting) from Arizona State University, Tempe. His plays have been produced across the country. Works written include *Mindprobe/Freddie's Dead*, *the vine*, *la rosa still grows beyond the wall*, *somebody's children*, *14* and *la ofrenda*. His play, *Mindprobe/Freddie's Dead*, was awarded a Sherrill C. Corwin-Metropolitan Theatre Award for Best One-Act (1992). His play, *la ofrenda*, was the winner of the 2005 Bonderman National Playwriting for Youth Competition and the 2007 American Alliance for Theatre and Education Award for Distinguished Play. His play, *la rosa still grows beyond the wall*, was awarded a 2005 AriZoni Theatre for Excellence Award for Best Production – Original Play. His play, *14*, was awarded a 2003 AriZoni for Excellence Award for Best Production – Original Play. It was also a finalist for the 2004 Nuestras Voces National Playwriting Competition. *La ofrenda* is published by Dramatic Publishing and *14* is published in the book *Ethnodrama: An Anthology of Reality Theatre* (AltaMira Press). He has been commissioned by a number of theaters including Cornerstone Theater Company, Found Spaces Theater Company, and Artists Repertory Theatre. He is currently the Literary Manager of CASA0101 in Los Angeles, California, as well as a Company Member of Breath of Fire Latina Theatre Ensemble in Santa Ana, California.

introduction

José Casas wrote *14* as a graduate student in the playwriting program at Arizona State University (ASU). In May 2001, fourteen immigrant workers died attempting to cross the U.S.-Mexico border in an incident near Yuma, Arizona. They became known as the Yuma 14. This event was also chronicled in the book, *The Devil's Highway,* by Luis Alberto Urrea. José (or C.C.) chose to document the reactions of local residents to this incident and later to dramatize them. He interviewed residents in the Phoenix, Tucson and outlying areas, out of which emerged this series of monologues. The play was first included in the ASU New Plays Festival in 2003, at which time I, as the supervisor of the program and the reading series, decided to take the play to the next level, to a production with Teatro Bravo. Christina Marin, a Ph.D. student at Arizona State University at the time, agreed to direct the play for the Triple Fest of New Plays produced by Teatro Bravo in the Fall of 2003.

The play incorporates elements of what my colleague Professor Johnny Saldaña calls "Ethnodrama," also the title of his authoritative book on the subject, which anthologizes various plays in this genre. This form of theater develops out of ethnographic studies, interviews, or documented reality in general. Professor Saldaña chose to publish selected portions of the text. We publish it in its entirety for the first time. *14* fascinates by chronicling various voices in the debate around illegal immigration. Arizona sits at the crossroads of *la ola migratoria,* the wave of immigration, both documented and otherwise, which promises (and some might say "threatens") to transform the cultural, racial and sociopolitical destiny of the Southwest, indeed alarming social commentators, such as Patrick Buchanan, who warns us we are living in a "state of emergency," which will destroy Anglo America as we know it. These voices are best exemplified in the play by people such as the rancher who has appointed himself to guard the border. As a counterbalance, C.C. gives us the voice of the undocumented immigrant himself, this vulnerable, modest man trying to earn a living, not exactly the Genghis Khan invader Mr. Buchanan seems to invoke in his writings. A greater complexity of divided loyalties is exemplified in the Latina widow of the border patrolman killed by *coyotes* or human smugglers, showing a family of Mexican-Americans divided by the issue.

Again, strife and passion, ethnographic verities of our times and region get transformed into performance. If it's happening in our community, it surely belongs on the stage, does it not? It's a no-brainer for us at Teatro Bravo, but the overall theatrical community in Arizona shies away from controversy, fearing that someone somewhere will be made to feel uncomfortable. According to this aesthetic, theater's supposed to be soothing. In the Fall of 2003, after our initial run at Playhouse on the Park, the production was invited to stage a special performance for the students of Phoenix College. An outraged Anglo student wrote to the president of the college to complain that taxpayers' money was being used to fund a play that the student deemed "one-sided," that "white people were shown in a negative light as racists," that "minorities are viewed as victims, not in charge of their destiny." This student's complaint brings up the dilemma of how to discuss urgent political issues of social justice without appearing didactic or biased. The play does show sympathy for the plight of undocumented workers and, as such, it is "biased." Yet, the people interviewed speak for themselves and offer a diversity of opinions. The Anglo citizens range from the outraged rancher to the compassionate preacher who distributes water in the desert. This is a social document, and it's up to us as viewers to take sides, to identify with one character over another, to become "biased," if we choose to do so. I consider it progress that this one student was moved enough to write such a strong letter of protest. If theater leaves us indifferent, then it has failed. Still, this fear of controversy permeates our local stages. Somewhere in Arizona the hand of self-censorship constantly seems to conspire to silence the playwright and limit him to safety. This play defies that norm, and that's one good reason for producing it and publishing it.

Guillermo Reyes
Phoenix, AZ
December 2007

production history

14, by José Casas, was produced by Teatro Bravo in September 2003 at Playhouse on the Park in Phoenix, directed by Christina Marin, with the following ensemble in the various roles:

Barbara Acker
Christina Marin
Christopher Miller
Adrian Villalpando

For production rights, contact José Casas at chicano_power_14@yahoo.com.

table of contents
prologue

characters

roger tate: hardware store owner, 48 – yuma, az

marta ramirez: secretary & member of the YUMA PARENT/ TEACHER ASSOCIATION, 46 – yuma, az

omar castillo: state senator, 34 – flagstaff, az

alexis franco: artist, 57 – sedona, az

luz ortiz: maid, 60 – guadalupe, az

denise hudson: cashier, 42 – chandler, az

matthew (mateo) logan: actor, 32 – phoenix, az

michelle rodriguez: editor of MODERN LATINA magazine, 39 – phoenix, az

antonio loera: ASU law student, 27 – tempe, az

charlie clarkston: rancher & head of VOICES FOR A FREE ARIZONA, 71 – douglas, az

dr. snezena kuftinic: emergency room physician, 40 – tucson, az

jose reynoso: soldier, 19 – goodyear, az

monica flores: kindergarden teacher, 25 – chandler, az

lacey williams: boutique owner, 34 – scottsdale, az

oscar garcia: day laborer, 30 – mesa, az

reverend clay nash: pastor & head of WATER FOR LIFE, 50 – tucson, az

set

the setting consists of a variety of different locales located in different areas of the state. a video screen located upstage center (or a barren back wall) is the only set piece location that is specific. the other set pieces are to be placed at the discretion of the director. some of these set pieces may be used for more than one monologue if needed (or desired). the set pieces/locales are:

-a desert water station. the water station consists of a large plastic barrel painted light blue which is placed atop a makeshift stand. a water valve is located at the end of the barrel and above it are stickers spelling out the word "agua." next to the water barrel/station is a tall pole that stands anywhere from ten to twenty feet. atop the pole sits a blue flag – an indicator to immigrants that a water station is present.

-a makeshift altar adorned with pictures, flowers and an assortment of candles and personal objects.

-chairs and a desk to indicate an office, restaurant, etc.

-an artist's space filled w/discarded materials used to make sculptures, one sculpture should be in the process of being built.

casting

-four actors are required for this play in order to emphasize the two main cultural groups (whites & latina/os) associated with the issue of immigration in the areas along the border. the play calls for:

one white actress	one white actor
one latina	one latino

-any production that seeks to cast these roles differently, <u>must</u> get permission before doing so.

production notes

(1) a slide/video projection should be shown at the beginning of each monologue (interview) giving the name of the name of the piece, the name of the character, their occupation and their hometown (as is shown in the script). there are also specific slide requests within the text of the script. also, slides can be used to suggest setting if setting requirements for specifics pieces are too cumbersome. the section headings are meant only to create a tone for the director to explore.

(2) throughout the play, there is extensive use of the (extended beat). these are meant to give the characters unspoken dialogue. they can range from an extended

pause to a character action depending on the context in which they are inserted. actors are encouraged to experiment with the extended beats...to explore their "true" meaning.

(3) the play was written with no intermission, but an intermission is strongly encouraged. if a director chooses to include an intermission, it must be between "color" and "a man's home."

(4) translations of the pieces "*virgencita linda*" and "*muñequita*" are included with the script as a courtesy, but those pieces <u>must</u> be performed in spanish.

> **"a man's dying
> is more
> the survivor's affair
> than his own."**
>
> **- thomas mann**

prologue

(in the darkness a spotlight shines on the back wall/video screen. the slide reads:

may 19, 2001
a smuggling guide abandons more
than 30 mexicans crossing
east of yuma.
dehydration kills 14.
their deaths trigger renewed
binational debate over immigration.
the dead are:

the next series of projections are individual slides showing the names of each victim. there should be a beat between each slide. the names of the victims are:

lorenzo hernandez ortiz
raymundo barreda landa,
reynaldo bartolo
mario castillo fernandez,
enriquez landero
raymundo barreda maruri,
julian mabros malaga,
claudio marin alejandro,
arnulfo flores badilla,
edgar adrian martinez colorado,
efrain gonzalez manzano
heriberto tapia baldillo.

final slide of prologue:

two others have yet
to be identified

(extended beat)

*as the projection on the screen slowly fades into darkness, guns-n-roses'
"welcome to the jungle" begins blaring.)*

"welcome to the jungle"

roger tate & marta ramirez
business owner & secretary
yuma, az

(with "welcome to the jungle" still playing, two spotlights go up – one downstage right and one downstage left. located downstage right is a chicana in her mid-forties. her name is marta ramirez. she is sitting on a chair behind a desk. a picture of her family sits prominently on the corner of the desk. standing downstage left is roger tate. a white man in his late-forties.

it is apparent that he has not had much sleep. he is standing in front of his family-owned hardware store. the store has been vandalized and roger is sweeping up broken glass. these interviews are taking place in different locales so neither of these characters knows of each other's presence on stage. marta ramirez begins to talk as the song slowly fades away.)

marta: the theme of this year's prom was "welcome to the jungle."

roger: i had never ever heard of guns-n-roses.

marta: i had never even heard of guns-n-roses.

roger: they's being singled out.

marta: nice enough looking kids. the girls' dresses were beautiful and those boys looked so handsome in their tuxedos.

roger: their pictures on the front page of the newspaper.

marta: smiling for the camera.

roger: they had their entire lives ahead of them.

marta: *(annoyed)* there they were. chests puffed out...beaming with pride.

roger: each story has two sides to it.

marta: *(incredulous)* giving a white power salute...in the middle of their prom photos!

roger: they're teenagers.

marta: their parents should be ashamed of...

(extended beat) (roger starts pacing around a bit and then rubs his tired eyes.)

roger: you'll have to forgive me. i haven't had much sleep lately. reporters have been calling me and my family all hours of the night. we changed our phone number to an unlisted one, but that still hasn't stopped them, though...it isn't right, i tell you. all this attention is insane. (beat) this hasn't been easy for my family. my little girls have had to stay at home because of all this commotion...some other kids threatened them at school. my wife went grocery shopping the other day and was harassed by a mob of people. she had to have the police escort her home. fortunately for us, we have some good neighbors. they've offered to take turns buying our groceries until this whole thing's blown over. i can't even go a single day without somebody wanting to talk to me...a man can only – (beat; angrily) a man deserves the right to some privacy!

marta: i don't sit here and tell you that there's no racism in this town. border cities aren't built that way. instead of black versus white, it's mexican versus white. different colors, but it's the same fight. after a while, you actually get used to it. that's not to say, you accept it. all i'm saying is that most of the time around here people's barks are worse than their bites. as long as it's just a bunch of people yelling at each other or shooting a dirty look now and again, things remain somewhat tolerable. (beat) then, those boys had to ruin what little peace there was.

roger: no one knows exactly what happened.

marta: francisco and javier did nothing wrong.

roger: people want to make it out to be a race war or something. nonsense. they're painting a false picture...that's not the truth. my son and his friends were only doing what they felt they needed to do. are you telling me those kids should have let those boys walk all over them? the one mexican kid grabbed that girl inappropriately. no one seems to mention that...and, what about the girl? what about concerns for her safety? who knows what could've happened! everybody knows that section of town isn't very safe...my son and his buddies were protecting her.

marta: all the jocks and their friends go to the peak to drink and smoke pot...and, whatever else it is that high schools do up there.

roger: they weren't out to hurt anybody.

marta: all because they smiled at a girl...imagine that.

roger: that mexican boy and his friends –

marta: (angrily) friend!

(extended beat)

there were only two of them. two skinny little mexican boys against half a football team.

roger: they were defending themselves like anyone would in that situation.

marta: six football players...three of them close to three hundred pounds.

roger: hell, i got into plenty of scrapes when i was younger...that's part of becoming a man.

marta: francisco and javier were held to the ground and kicked in the head while the others kids watched and yelled, "kill the beaners!"

(extended beat)

not one person lifted a finger to help them!

(extended beat)

but, as long as the stands were full of people cheering for touch-downs...

roger: i'm a respected man in this city.

marta: people would look the other way.

roger: i'm a businessman and i'm on the city council. my great grand-father. gerald xavier tate was considered one of the founding fathers of this area. there's no better place in this world to raise a family...people trust me.

(extended beat)
(roger looks at the sign.)

take a peek at that sign...tate hardware store. been in my family for generations. it's more than a hardware store. this is a place where townsfolk can come to unwind. *(looking at the broken glass)* they come here to relax and shoot the breeze. this building is a living piece of history. *(beat; unconvincingly)* i'm a respected man.

(extended beat)
(a look of pain crosses roger's face. he looks off into the distance for a beat, then turns back towards the interviewer.)

my son's also respected. honor society. captain of the football team. girlfriends left and right...he would always help a friend in need. he wasn't a follower. he was a leader. he was the most popular kid in yuma. he wouldn't do anything to damage that.

marta: especially, the tate boy. he always had this air of arrogance about him...like he was entitled. thought he could get away with murder. (beat) who knows? maybe, he will. the trial doesn't start for another few weeks.

(extended beat)
(nonchalantly)

i wouldn't be surprised.

roger: i'm getting him the best lawyer money can buy. i'll do whatever it takes to clear my boy's name. he has a bright future ahead of him. *(defiantly)* he has a scholarship to play football at the university of utah. strong safety...that's his scholarship. he earned it!

marta: *(sadly)* i think about those boys. both groups and i think to myself, every single one of these boys were once little babies...with little fingers and little toes and flashed the kind of smiles that only babies can.

roger: jason is my son...he isn't guilty of any crime.

marta: i've met the tate boy's father on a couple of occasions...he was cordial. seemed like a nice enough man...but –

(marta picks up the photo of her family; stares at it.)

sometimes i wonder how i got so lucky with my kids.

(beat; marta puts the picture frame back on the desk.)

my kids are grown up and in college now, but i won't sit here trying to convince you that they were perfect angels. believe me, they were a handful. i'm sure there are things they did that i don't ever want to know about. but, uhm...but, i don't know. *(beat; contemplative)* they seem to have turned out alright from what i see.

roger: i am not a racist. my son is not a racist! *(beat)* some of my friends are mexican.

marta: those boys ruined two lives. two families. they need to be punished. they need to know that what they did was wrong...everyone in this city needs to know!

roger: *(pleading)* my son is a good boy! why can't some people see that!?

marta: *(defeated)* how did they manage to learn so much hate?

(the spotlight focused on marta fades to black.)

roger: people from all over town have been writing letters to the judge on his behalf. the principal and some of his teachers. all of his friends and family, too. coach taylor even wrote to the univerisity to reassure them that this whole incident was just one big misunderstanding.

(extended beat)

(unconvincingly) in the end, i believe my son will be exonerated. then, everyone will know that it wasn't his fault...and, that things just got out of hand.

(extended beat)

(sadly) that kids will be kids.

(the spotlight on roger fades to black.)

"all in the family"

omar castillo
state senator-arizona
flagstaff, az

no! i don't feel that bilingualism is a necessary component of the educational system. it's not the responsibility of our school systems to carry that load. it's an unfair burden to place on staffs and faculties...tests scores are at an all-time low...do you understand what i'm saying!? the more time and resources we dedicate to bilingual education the longer it will take to get our scores up...if at all. *(responding to a question; sarcastic)* yes...i'm sure that your numbers say what you want them to say. you're not the first person to throw out statistics at me and you won't be the last, but i can throw out numbers as well as the next guy. however, the reality of the situation is that bilingual education hasn't proven to be of any benefit to the general popula-

(extended beat)

(angrily) and...where does it stop!? spanish, vietnamese, chinese, french? what next? maybe gaelic? or latin? just look at the problems in california. if we have to adjust for one group of the people then we must adjust for any and all groups of people. (beat) that is not a possibility...parents need to be responsible for the welfare of their children...that includes their ability to learn the langauge.

(responding to a question.)

these students are not studying in mexico. they are studying in the united states. they need to know the official langauge of this country. in the end, it will benefit everybody. *(beat)* other countries have official languages. mexico...has an official langauge. *(sarcastically)* yet you're here...in my office claiming racism against this government.

(extended beat)

the hispanic community needs to rely less on the kindness of others.

(extended beat)

anti-latino!?

(extended beat)

i'm anything, but that...what you need to understand is that bilingualism in our schools has to be dealt with pragmatically...yes, i understand that it's a volatile subject to discuss but, ultimately, what we are talking about is economics; a fact you seem to ignore. *(beat)* the point that i am trying to make is that cutting bilingual education from the current curriculum is of the most vital

importance. we need to divert money into better school facilities, computers and better wages for our teachers...are you telling me our teachers are overpaid? you stand there scribbling in your little notebook about how unfair this situation is, but what are the alternatives? i doubt you have any to offer. *(responding to a question; beat)* cutting bilingual education is not about ignoring

our students' cultural roots...once again, and i'm sorry if i'm sounding like a broken record, but that is not the responsibility of our school systems. eliminating this program won't affect that.

parents need to understand that immersion is the best way of approaching the subject. *(beat)* it is the only way.

(extended beat)

(he begins tapping his fingers on the table) my mother understood this...she would take me with her on her cleaning jobs. while she was working i would be watching television...she'd have me sitting in front of that thing for hours at a time. always telling me to pay attention...sesame street. soap operas. the price is right. you name it. *(beat; fondly)* by far, though, my favorite show was all in the family. they would play the reruns at two o'clock

every afternoon on c.b.s... i know it sounds simple and, believe me, more went into my upbringing than that, obviously, but what it represents, in a very small way, is the spirit of my mother's determination...of her desire to make a better life for our family. the point is – *(beat)* my mother knew what was needed of me to survive here...and, that is exactly what i've done. my eyes glued to a t.v. set...well, that was just the beginning.

(extended beat)

my mother didn't know english. *(proudly)* but...i taught her. *(beat)* and...she taught me spanish. *(beat)* look at me now...i am one of the youngest senators in the history of arizona and one day i will be the governor of this state. i firmly believe that. *(beat)* you see, i've succeeded! there is no reason others shouldn't be able to do likewise...it's all a matter of priorities.

(extended beat)

i turned out just fine.

"selective amnesia"

alexis franco
artist
sedona, az

(alexis franco is an artist who is working on a sculpture made up of found objects. she works while she talks. she is in her early fifties and is a native new yorker with the heavy east cost accent; animated and lively. the sculpture she is making appears to be that of a disjoined american flag, made up of glass, tiles and other assorted materials; a plunger is being used for the flag's handle and the letters "NY" replace the stars.)

(animated) it literally broke my heart. do you hear what i'm saying!? it wasn't like mr. october had come up to the plate and knocked one out of the ballpark. luis gonzalez hit a freakin' bloop

single! that's no way to win a world series!

(extended beat)

i'm still a little bitter.

(alexis finds a piece of material and begins to use it on the sculpture. (beat) she reacts to a questions.)

> well...uhm...no, i mean, you see, i – *(beat)* the move out west was for my husband. i love the big lug, you know...and the doctors made it all too clear that his arthritis wasn't getting any better so we had to go someplace where the weather was...what did he say, uhm, to slow down some sort of degenerative process in his joints...so...we're...uhm, here. (beat) when we made the decision to move we narrowed it down between taos, new mexico and
>
> sedona, arizona. people back home figured we'd go to california or someplace like that but, let's get one thing straight, there is no way in hell a self-respecting yankee fan would ever live within driving distance of the dodgers...hu-uh, no way! *(beat)* i do miss the city moments. i mean, we try to visit as much as we can, but it's not nearly the same thing. to me, new york is like no place
>
> else. different type of people and flavors...that east coast attitude. *(beat; picking up a piece of glass)* i know phoenix is supposed to be like the seventh or eighth biggest city in the country, but it doesn't feel like a big city. to tell the truth, i don't much think it's that interesting. the only times i drive down to phoenix is to see the occasioinal ballgame or to go to an art gallery. *(beat)*
>
> you see, i had been to sedona before for an art exhibit about ten years ago...i mean, i'm not too hip on the new age hippy vibe, but i like the fact that it's quiet. a different kind of quiet than phoenix...peaceful, not boring.

(extended beat)
(alexis responds to a question.)

> no...that's the one thing i don't get about this place. all the fuss about people coming over here; crossing the border. i don't know if they've noticed, but mexicans aren't the only ones coming into town. hell, it took me ten months of living in arizona before i met someone who had actually lived here their entire life. *(cleaning her hands with a rag.)* they're only doing what any one of us would be doing if we were in their shoes...those who deny that
>
> don't want to admit the truth...and, that my friend, is bullshit! when a person goes to the market they like the fact that they can buy a head of lettuce for about a buck, though, most people

don't really think past that. people don't do that because then they would have to deal with their own insecurities and biases. the ones that tell them that they don't want those people in their communities but, at the same time, they don't want to have to pay more for veggies and fruits than they already have to. they want to believe that that head of lettuce magically found its way into safeways. they want to believe that those hotel beds never get messy. they want to believe that toilets automatically clean themselves overnight. *(beat)* they want to believe that if they don't think about it...it doesn't really exist.

(extended beat)

just look at 9/11...and, i know this might piss off some people, but i don't care. *(beat)* there were some good things that came out of that...a lot of bad did as well. the kinda bad that shows how people truly feel. *(beat)* when the families of the victims were being compensated financially for what happened at the twin towers i was livid. that's not to say that i had no sympathy for the families. of course, i did, but people die tragically every freaking day in

this country and i don't see them getting a cent. a single mother in the *barrio* loses her son to gang violence. i don't see her getting a check. a wife with four kids and no job skills loses her husband to a deranged ex-coworker who's gone postal...no check being given to her and, believe it or not, you'd be surprised by how often that happens. i'm not talking out of my ass. my husband

used to work for the government, tabulating those type of things. *(beat)* but, the twin towers...that, uhm...anyone who wasn't a citizen received nothing! they were working...like everyone else in those two buildings. *(solemnly)* but, no one seems to be mentioning that fact.

(extended beat)

yes! i like creating art from old pieces of junk...things that have been tossed off to the side...giving them life; back from the dead, so to speak.

(alexis responds to a question, looks at the sculpture, then back to the interviewer; impressed.)

thanks...i'm glad you got the reference. i call this piece... uhm...selective amnesia *(beat; annoyed)* people so willing to sing giuliani's praises and how he dealt with the tragedy of september...and, how crime has decreased during his tenure...but, what about abner louima!? *(beat)* where was giuliani when those policemen were shoving that plunger up his ass!?

(extended beat)

(angrily) terrorists fly planes into office buildings and every arab on the face of the earth has now become a suspect, but a timothy mcveigh blows up half of oklahoma city and there's no state department advisory warning people to be wary of any white male roaming the streets sporting a crew cut...selective amnesia.

(extended beat)

(alexis begins to walk around, looking for a piece of tile to add to the sculpture.)

you and me, both. *(beat)* i look around arizona and i feel sick to my stomach. american flags on every minivan from tucson to the grand canyon after 9/11. elections roll around a year later and only, what? twenty something percent voted!? *(beat)* that's eighty percent of these talking heads complaining about so-called illegals...complaining that this isn't their home, but what about us, huh? this is our home and we don't even appreciate that. this city. this state. this country, for that matter...we act like home owners, but if you think about it, we're all only renters...that's all.

(extended beat)

look at the yankees...renting randy freaking johnson. can you believe that?

(extended beat)

sorry...like i said...i'm still a little bitter about that whole world series thing.

"virgencita linda"

luz ortiz
criada
guadalupe, az

(la entrevista se está llevando acabo en la yarda de luz ortiz, una mexicana de sesenta años. está sentada en una silla. está rodeada de estatuas de la virgen de guadalupe. es temprano en la tardecita. luz ha llegado del trabajo de criada.)

perdón que estoy tarde, m'ija tenía que ponerle gas al carro. normalmente camino al trabajo ahí a una cuadra en el *holiday inn* hotel. el *express*, ahí en frente del mercado. *(responde al comentario de su hija; entretenida)* oh, perdón quise decir el mall. a m'ija le encanta caminar por horas ahí, pero como yo no tengo mucho dinero yo no voy. *(pausa)* pero es nomás quince minutos al trabajo. una caminada corta. mi viejo o uno de mis hijos vienen por mí y me caminan a la casa. les digo que no tiene que, pero se preocupan por mí...no quise llegar tarde y cuando mi hija me dijo del gas...aagh. gracias por ser paciente y me vas a tener que perdonar porque no tuve tiempo de cambiarme después del trabajo. *(pausa)* estoy muy emocionada de tenerte aquí. habla mucho de ti m'ija y dice que eres muy buen escritor. *(responde)* ah, muchas gracias, estoy muy orgullosa de ella. es mi niña más chica y la tuve ya casi a los cuarenta. dice que quiere ser maestra.

le pregunto si no quiere ser doctora o abogada como su hermano. eso paga mejor, pero dice que quiere ser profesora, que quiere ayudar a los niños. siempre piensa de los otros antes de pensar en sí misma. *(pausa)* ¿tú naciste en arizona? ¿eres de los angeles? hmm...yo fui una vez. se me hizo bonito. me gustó la playa, pero no me gustaría vivir ahí. se me hace muy grande y con mucha gente. estoy muy feliz aquí en arizona. *(pausa; entretenida)* no

te preocupes por su español. no eres pocho. te entiendo bien. no te debes de avergonzar. yo entiendo que tan difícil es ser bilingüe. ¡mi hijo mayor siempre me contesta en inglés! siempre le tengo que decir, "en español, m'ijo" pero a él no le importa, nomás se ríe. pero es buen hijo. ¿y tus papás? ¿en dónde nacieron? ah, ¿zacatecas...y tu mamá? monterrey. ¡ah ya lo sabía! yo también soy de monterrey. casi toda mi familia está ahí. colonia metalúrgica,

colonia nueva sonora, colonia torreón jardín. ¿no sabes de dónde es tu familia? ¿colonia vencedora? ah, sí...tengo dos tíos que son de ahí. pregúntale a tu mamá que si no conoce a la familia gallegos. juan carlos gallegos y eduardo gallegos. *(pausa)* trato de ir a méxico, pero se me hace más difícil ahora que estoy vieja. ¿todavía tienes familia en monterrey? ¿cuánto que no los ves? ¡oye, m'ijo, hace mucho tiempo! tienes que ir a verlos. es tu familia. *(responde)* sí es difícil, pero ahórrate unos *pennies* para

ir porque nos hacemos viejos y tienes que recordar que méxico es tu país como es de tus padres...sí extraño méxico mucho, pero me gusta la ciudad de guadalupe. es muy similiar a méxico. no es muy bonito y a los gringos no les importa mucho de lo que pasa aquí. es lo que yo pienso, pero yo no tengo que decírtelo. mira nomás a la calle baseline. es como cruzar tijuana a san diego. el *mall* y todo. todo nuevo y bonito, hasta tienen un parque bonito y a ellos no les importa si guadalupe es bonito. no les importa si las escuelas están mal. *(pausa; fastidiada)* a los niños les hicieron un parque para que jueguen al béisbol. es bonito y me alegro por los niños, pero es muy poco. al lado de la iglesia donde juegan

los hombres es pura tierra y basura. así es aquí. es como si se estuvieran riendo en nuestras caras, es casi decir, "si quieres jugar en lugar bonito tienes que cruzar la calle que tiene, vas a tener que volver a cruzar." *(pausa; disculpa)* ah, perdón pero me hace enojar. no quiero ser maldita. soy una mujer muy católica. yo creo en dios, jesús cristo y en la virgencita linda, pero no soy ciega...pero con eso dicho, estoy muy agradecida. agradecida que tengo mi casa y comida que comer, una tele para ver mis novelas.

mi viejo me quiere mucho y tengo buenos hijos. guadalupe se ha portado muy bien con nosotros. la mayoría de la gente aquí no tienen mucho dinero, pero ahí seguimos dándole duro siempre encontramos tiempo para convivir y tomarnos un cafecito. en guadalupe familia es familia. créeme, lo poco que tenemos aquí es mucho más de lo que una gente tiene en méxico. nosotros estamos

contentos con cosas como el papel del baño y el jabón. esas son las cosas que les llevo a mi familia en méxico, cosas que mucha gente no les pone importancia. *(pausa)* es porque la virgencita nos protege. somos muy afortunados de tener a la virgencita en nuestras vidas. por eso casi todas las casas en guadalupe tienen a la virgen de protección. tenemos que recordar que ella fue la que

nos ciudó, cuando cruzamos la frontera. *(pausa)* yo tenía 26 años cuando me vine, yo sola con gente que no conocía. *(responde)* no...mi mamá no quería que me viniera, pero en méxico no le puedes decir a nadie que no se venga, nomás que vas a rezar por ellos. *(cerrando sus ojos; pausa)* la primera noche me dormí con mucho miedo porque podía oir a los coyotes y el calor estaba

muy pesado. esa noche me dormí con mi virgencita bien cerca. fue la noche más larga de mi vida. *(pausa; emocionada)* unos días después cuando cruzamos, el coyote nos estaba empujando en una troca como si fuéramos animales. cuando me metí a la troca se me cayó mi virgen. le pedí al coyote que me la diera y me gritó bien feo que me callara. cinco horas después estaba en

una cochera en tucson. dos días después estaba en una siembra de sandías en el oeste de phoenix. cuando tenía unos minutos para tomar agua, pensaba en mi virgencita que quedó pisoteada y abandonada en el desierto como muchos que rezan por ella. *(pausa)* todavía rezo por ella...nunca me ha dejado, hasta cuando miro al otro lado de la calle y veo a ese *mall* y a los carros nuevos y a las casas bonitas, todavía. *(pausa)* ella está conmigo.

"...just"

denise hudson
cashier
chandler, az

(denise hudson is a white woman in her early forties. she has been crying. she wipes her eyes with a handkerchief.)

> thank you...i'm sorry. i didn't mean to...uhm, it's been almost three years.

(denise finishes wiping her eyes. she composes herself.)
(extended beat)

> you never think you're going to get that knock on the door or the late night phone call...it's such a surreal experience. no matter how many times you see other people talk about their stories...you don't know.

(extended beat)

> *(responding to a question)* that's right...michael wanted to have some pizza with some friends. it was a school night, but he had been doing so well in shcool. we were so proud of him.

(extended beat)

> in a few months, he would have left for college. i wanted him to go to arizona state. i would tell him that it was a really good school and that he'd save money being at home, but he was leaning towards one of those california schools...kept saying he wanted to learn how to surf. *(beat)* it was a school night...if i had...just.

(extended beat)

> it took place at the corner of ray avenue and mcclintock...waiting for the light to turn green. *(beat)* i can picture him singing alongside his music...listening to the rolling stones. that's all he ever listened to. i blame that on his father. they were so close. *(responding to a question; beat)* uhm...you can try to talk to him but – *(beat)* our divorce became final a couple of months ago. *(reassuring)* no, no, no...that's alright. how were you supposed to know? no need to apologize.

(extended beat)

> michael never had a chance. alone in that interesection driving a dinged-up '92 hyundai...a sports utility vehicle speeding at about ninety miles an hour. *(beat; angrily)* those machines should be illegal! they're nothing but glorified tanks...they weren't meant for streets. they were meant for the wilderness. the outdoors...but,

(extended beat)

i guess that's the mode nowadays. the bigger the better.

a police officer at the scene had claimed it was a miracle that my son could've made it to the hospital alive, much less in one piece...he was on life support for almost two weeks. *(beat)* i thank god we were there with him at the end.

(extended beat)

a second after he was pulled off life support i felt his hand gently squeeze my hand. that doctor said that was normal...only an involuntary spasm. *(beat)* no. no...he was wrong.

(extended beat)

(quietly) that was michael saying, "goodbye."

(extended beat)

the other boy was only a couple of months older than my son.

(extended beat)

he was running from the police. the car he was driving was stolen. they had been chasing him all the way from scottsdale. the impact of the crash tore my son's car in half and scattered pieces of it as far as two hundred yards away. the young man suffered two broken legs and a ruptured spleen, but nothing life-threatening. at the time of the accident i was working part-time as a cashier at walgreens. my husband had just begun working at circuit city, but he hadn't worked there long enough to earn any benefits. (beat; desperation in her voice) we're still getting hospital bills. my husband and i – *(stopping herself)* i mean...my ex and i were living from paycheck to paycheck as it was...we didn't have any health insurance at the time of the accident. we had three thousand dollars in a checking account and not much more. *(angrily)* but they told us we made too much to qualify for public assistance! my credit history has been destroyed! i had to move back in with my mother!

(extended beat)

(defeated) i lost my only child.

(extended beat)

that other boy never paid a cent. he can walk again. the doctors fixed his legs...he's not paying for what he did. *(beat; incredulously)* and, he even had the audacity to sue the police because he claims that he'll be walking with a limp the rest of his life. can you believe that!? he sued the police department. the chandler police department paid out millions in lawsuit damages!

(beat) that police chase, they say, killed my son...that's all i hear. "they" say. they say i should be suing for some money as well...no! never! those police officers didn't kill my son...he did!

(extended beat)

(angrily) it's like he won the lottery!

(extended beat)

(coldly) i hate him. *(beat)* as a christian, i know that i shouldn't, but i'm sorry...i do...i can't help myself.

(extended beat)

he was an illegal alien...my son wasn't.

(extended beat)

where's the justice in that?

(lights go dark.)

"type"

matthew (mateo) logan
actor
Phoenix, az

(matthew "mateo" logan is a latino in his early-thirties. he is an actor who lives in los angeles, california, but is visiting family and friends in phoenix, his hometown.)

...phoenix is what it is. my family and some of my friends are still here, but i had to leave. seriously...being an actor in phoenix. i think not. *(sarcastic)* a life of bashas markets commercials? no thank you...any actor worth his salt would want to be almost anywhere else...anyway, l.a. suits me better. it's home for me now, but i did not grow up there so, sure, i have somewhat of an attachment to the place.

(extended beat)

(amused) you might as well ask. i know it's killing you.

(matthew pulls out a cigarette and a lighter from his pocket.)

you mind?

(matthew lights the cigarette and puts away the lighter. he takes a puff. beat)

my cousin warned me about you. *(beat)* she told me you were one of those chicano power militant types. *(responding to a question)* naw, it's cool...we're each entitled to our own opinions.

(extended beat)

no...i don't see any reason to feel guilty. why should i? i didn't grow up with visions of becoming a revolutionary. all i ever wanted to do was act. it's that simple. the way i go about accomplishing this...is my business. *(responding to a question)* matthew, mateo. same difference? it's only a name; not who i am. *(annoyed)* of course, i respect my parents. do you respect yours!?

(beat) he's my father. i love the man, but the sanchez name does't sell very well in hollywood, but i'm not telling you anything you don't already know. *(beat)* are you going to sit there and deny that? to tell you the truth, i don't even know why we're having this discussion...you jump through the same hoops that i do so give me a break...and, if you're anything like me, which

i'm assuming you are, then, i know you have to be sick of this nonsense. every damn year you read the same articles i do. the ones in the l.a. times or the washington post; the ones saying minorities are making strides in the film industry. you know how utterly bullshit those numbers are? how those numbers are manipulated? the kind of roles they're talking about? preaching and preaching how this is the year of the latino.

(extended beat)

check it, mr. writer...i'm still waiting.

(extended beat)

my father is brown and my mother is white, but she's just as much part of me as my father...or, should i forget that? i'm proud of both sides of my family tree. if you have a problem with that, then, that's on your conscience...not mine. *(beat; annoyed)* i look at the expression on your face and it looks like you've just heard an endorsement for the aryan nation...but, you don't know the first thing about me.

(extended beat)

(responding to a question) no...i don't know much spanish. *(beat)* and, yeah, that was me on that commercial...hey, what can i say? people have accents. it was a character. that's all.

(extended beat)
(matthew takes a long drag from his cigarette. he throws the butt to the floor. beat)

the righteous brown man fighting against the system...good for you, but i need to pay the rent. i need to get credits. i need to hustle. *(beat)* we need to hustle.

(extended beat)

see...that's the difference between you and me. you want people to acknowledge you. brown this. brown that. i'm not like that. all i want is for directors to look at me and see a good actor. i'm sick and tired of people ignoring that. i do shakespeare because it challenges me. chekov. ibsen. i love them and i don't want anyone to tell me i can't do those plays because of my ethnicity. *(beat; responding to a question)* luis valdez? *(sarcastically)* ooh, how did i not see that one coming? *(matter of factly)* no...i've never done any of his work...sorry to disappoint you, but i can't say it bothers me very much either.

(extended beat)

(responding to a question; annoyed) dude, i'm tired of the gardener and gangbanger roles! i'm trying to fight those stereotypes. that's a good thing...i want to open this shit up for the rest of us. i'm tired of being a type so if i have to use my mother's maiden name and fake my smile a little more often than so fucking be it! life goes on.

(extended beat)

this is the only thing i know how to do.

(extended beat)
(matthew pulls out his card and extends it to the interviewer.)

here's my card...give me a call when you get back into town.

(extended beat)

we both know we'll be running into each other.

"a thin line"

michelle rodriguez
magazine editor
phoenix, az

(it is four o'clock in the afternoon, michelle rodriguez, an energetic and attractive chicana in her late-thirties. she is multitasking as she does the interview on her cell phone; using the headset.)

thank god for computers. you cannot believe the impact they've had on my life. i don't know where i'd be without them. yes, i'm grateful that they allow me the chance to spend some of my time in phoenix. *(beat)* sure...believe me, i wanted to run my magazine from arizona, but it made more sense to start up in los angeles. *(beat)* oh, i don't know, *sabes*? l.a. is alright, i guess, i'm not its biggest fan. obviously, there are parts of the city where i feel more comfortable, but, overall, there's this pervasive attitude of, *como se dice*, uhm...it's a very "me" kind of place. at times, i feel very insecure...just imagine multiplying scottsdale by fifty and then you got l.a. *(beat)* plus, i don't much like earthquakes...yeah, i know it's a generalization and an unfair one at that but, when all is said and done, i prefer the calmness of phoenix...having my *familia* around.

(extended beat)

sometimes i feel conflicted about running the magazine from here, but i feel fortunate that i have a magazine to run at all. *(responding to comment) gracias*...i appreciate that. yes...there was a time when i didn't think modern latina magazine would see the light of day. being a woman is hard enough in today's society but, to be a woman of color trying to make it in a male-dominated business...you can only imagine the difficulties i've had to endure.

(extended beat)

(proudly) modern latina celebrated its three-year anniversary a couple of weeks ago. something i'm very proud of. i hope it stands as a role model for chicanas to go after what they desire...that, through hard work and dedication, they can accomplish anything...*pura chicanisma*! *(beat)* i apologize for being self-indulgent, but this is like my child. i've –

(the caller keeps cutting off. michelle pushes the redial button to call back the interviewer.)

hello? hello? can you hear me? *(beat)* oh, i have you now. i'm sorry, i suppose technology isn't always as convenient as we would like it to be...you and me, both. *(beat)* yes, i heard that you were writing a play or something of that nature. i'm still a little confused. my assistant wasn't very clear about why you called –

(michelle nods a few times; beat)

the story...so...you've read it?

(extended beat)

i wish it weren't true.

(michelle beings to pace.)

that's right. el tepeyac. the one off of evergreen and wabash. *(amused)* me, too...i love the food and the different mix of people always amazes me. think about it. where in the world can you get yuppies, working class *gente*, cops and *cholos* in one place getting along? *de veras*! it's east l.a.'s own version of the united nations.

(extended beat)

> *(responding to a question)* yes..i was waiting for a friend of mine and i was getting a little worried because you know how it gets at that place during lunch time. it's a madhouse and with my friend on chicano time, i was getting a little frustrated...manny was already out on the sidewalk handing out shots of the tequila...well, to make a long story short, my cell phone rang and i know that it

> was going to be my friend bailing out on our lunch date and, at this point, i dashed all hopes of a decent lunch because the line in front of that place was like waiting in line for a ride at disneyland. *(beat)* oh, well...another day going through the drive-thru at mickie d's, i thought...so i begin walking back to my car when i see a little group of *cholitas* just hanging out across the street from the

> *restaurante.* you know, putting on their make-up and talking chisme. *(beat)* for some reason, i had the urge to strike up a conversation with them. maybe, even promote my magazine a little.

(extended beat)

> not one girl had ever heard of my magazine. not even glanced at it while they were in the grocery story. nothing...a little humbling, but i understood. i didn't need an explanation...i guess that's why i wanted to talk to them. you see, one of my main goals for the magazine is to reach as much of a cross-section of the latina community as possible and, apparently, i wasn't doing as good a job as i had

> imagined. *(beat)* but, i was truly enjoying my conversation with these girls – veronica, rosy, gladys y la ginger. *(beat; excited)* i just loved those names...loved the way they weren't afraid to express any feelings whatsoever. we talked about education, the lack of jobs, *vatos* with no game...you name it. it was refreshing, but it's not like i didn't understand what they were going through. i grew up in the same type of *barrio* in south phoenix. trust me, i can spray aquanet with the best of them but, for the most part, i was your typical catholic school kid, but some of the stories these girls were telling me. *(beat)*

> reminds me that i've been spending way too much time with the suits and not enough time with...well...*tú sabes*. *(beat)* suffice it to say, i appreciate everything my parents have ever done for me.

(extended beat)

i promised the girls i would send each of them a free subscription to the magazine. i didn't think it was that big of a deal, but they were totally psyched that i would do that. it meant so much to me that they would be so appreciative. like i said, i didn't think it was that big a deal...yes! of course, i wanted to continue talking with them...i wish we could have had more of a gabfest, but i had a

business meeting to go to and they had to get back to the class they were already fifteen minutes late for. *(beat)* i wrote down their addresses and we said our good-byes and as they began walking away i told myself that this conversation would make for a great article for the magazine and, that's when –

(extended beat)
(michelle pulls the phone away from her ear. it is apparent that she is upset.)

(disbelief) i couldn't believe my ears.

(extended beat)

as the girls were entering the gate back to school, a little *viejita* with the cutest smile was walking by them. you know, the kind i'm talking about...the kind of woman who reminds you of your own *abuelita. (beat)* well...uhm. this poor little woman accidently bumped into gladys...and gladys looks at her and says, "watch where you're going, wetback." a second later, as the woman crossed the street, the girls disappeared into the schoolyard.

(extended beat)

at that moment, my article suddenly changed. it was no longer about a group of girlfriends.

(extended beat)

(angrily) when are we going to learn that there's a thin line between love and hate? a line that becomes even thinner when that hate is directed at ourselves. is that where our young *gente* are heading? i wonder sometimes. *(beat)* with each new generation our *raza* becomes more assimilated. more separated from their past. they're not only forgetting their *cultura*, they are now beginning to resent it.

(extended beat)

that's why i started this magazine...because i love *la mujer*. la chicana. i love my *gente. (beat)* i want them to love themselves.

(extended beat)

funny how a seemingly insignificant little bump can –

(the cell phone gets disconnected. beat; as lights fade to black.)

hello? hello?

"color"

antonio loera
law school student-arizona state university
tempe, az

(the interview is taking place in a coffee shop outside the business administration building on the campus of arizona state university. the sounds of people talking and cell phones ringing can be heard lightly in the background throughout the interview. antonio loera is a chicano in his mid-twenties and a law student.)

...like i was saying. there's no way around it. it's about color. those who choose not to believe that should stay in their utopian little world and shut the blinds.

(beat; antonio blows into his coffee and then slowly takes a sip.)

believe me, i'd rather not deal with the issue of color altogether. it's too time consuming, but – *(beat)* that's not living in reality.

(extended beat)

i'm labeled by the way i look. *(beat)* in arizona...well, in arizona brown, uhm, let's just say arizona would benefit from catching up with the times. as my friend likes to say, "arizona is the south without the humidity."

(extended beat)
(antonio looks around at the other students; responds to a question.)

this issue of color...you see, that's the problem with most discussions on the topic of race. it all begins with the physical. how could it not? it's the first thing people see...they look at you and automatically want to define you as something. even at an institution of higher education where students of color are continually being forced to justify their positions within the system...having to defend their academic backgrounds in the name of affirmative action...the political turmoil happening at the university of michigan and other universities will become commonplace.

(extended beat)

do you honestly believe the majority is going to let it go!? all of a sudden, they're complaining that they're being denied equal opportunities, yet, i didn't hear those same people speaking up when we weren't being admitted and we weren't being offered the same opportunities.

(extended beat)

call a spade a spade.

(extended beat)

we have no choice in this matter. our world is a world of distinctions...from the moment we're born until the moment we die...a continual barrage of applications and surveys where our existence is contingent on what box we check. black, white, latino. asian. *(sarcastically)* and, of course, the ever popular...other.

(extended beat)

me being in law school at a.s.u., i, uhm, consider myself somewhat fortunate. if you look at statistics, the law program here is actually one of the better schools when it comes to diversity. *(beat; defiantly)* but...let's get one thing straight! that's not enough of a reason to view the world with rose-colored glasses...i'm more than sure there are a few people walking around this campus who believe i'm at a.s.u. solely

because of the color of my skin. forget the fact that i was at the top of my program at Berkeley. doesn't matter. in their minds they don't ask the questions because they've already come up with their own answers. what is fascinating to me is how people deal with race. to tell you the truth, i have a small sense of admiration for blatant racists. i mean, when i see news footage of the klan it's not like i jump up for joy or anything like that

but, at least, they're honest about the way they feel. it's the other type of bigots i have more of a problem with. *(animated)* the type of people who deal with race like cowards. people who whisper their bigotry behind your back; never face-to-face...i have no tolerance for that type of person. *(beat)* the other type of people, i don't, uhm, the other type of people who drive me nuts are those

people who want to go beyond the call of duty, so to speak. the polite ones who think they're helping the plight of the brown man. people who think they're doing the right thing when all they're really doing is perpetuating some sort of fucked-up cultural melodrama as a way of coming to terms with this whole notion of white guilt. here at arizona state, that's what it's all

about. color isn't dealt with on a personal level, but as different compartmentalized boxes filled with words like ideology and pedagogy as they go off into the distance to publish some journal article full of pretentious musings; saying in fifty pages what they could have easily said in two. i mean, really, do you think the average everyday homeboy gives a fuck about perspectives in

critical theory? i say, "talk to me in a language i can understand."
(beat; amused) then again…you are talking to a future lawyer.

(extended beat)

but, for once, i would just like one of these academic types to actually relate to me as they would anyone else. i'm tired of professors automatically turning to me when questions of ethnicity pop up in class discussion. they should be buying me a beer and talking about the next oscar de la hoya fight, instead of poking and prodding me like some sociological guinea pig…if

you think i'm kidding, just look around. i wouldn't know the exact number, but i would say that, easily, seventy-five percent of all theses and dissertations at this university deal either with the native-american and or the latina-latino community and since i know these two cultures don't make up seventy-five percent of the student population…well…i think you can do the math. *(annoyed)* it's like don't do us any favors.

(extended beat)

sometimes, i get so annoyed that i want to go up to a person, shake them, and say, "hey! aren't there any poor coal miners in west virginia that you can make a case study of?" *(beat)* they just don't get it.

(extended beat)

once…while i was talking to one of my white law professors during her office hours, she says to me, with this enlightened look on her face, "antonio, is it possible for me to be a chicana?" *(beat; angrily)* what the fuck is up with that!?

(extended beat)
(antonio finishes his coffee with one long final sip.)

man, i don't know how i could survive without my coffee. *(beat; tired)* i tell you, though, i can't remember the last time i had more than five hours of sleep. my professors weren't lying when they said law school would be tough. (beat) you do know that the first year of law school is intended to weed out as many students as they can, right? it's about the numbers. i mean, between you and me, really, we both know this world has way too many lawyers. law schools know that, too.

(extended beat)

(solemnly) like i said…it's about color.

(extended beat)
(checks his watch; to reporter.)

shit! *(apologetic)* uhm, i'm sorry, but i have to cut this interview short. i lost track of time. i have class in about five minutes. hope you don't mind. (beat) you, too…good luck with these interviews…hope something positive comes out of them.

"a man's home"

charlie clarkson
rancher
douglas, az

(this interview is taking place in the early morning hours (dawn), outdoors on the ranch of a mr. charlie clarkson, a white man in his early seventies. he is the leader of "VOICES FOR A FREE ARIZONA," a group of ranchers united together to combat immigration on the border. he holds a remote control and in the distance (offstage), on the desert floor, is a drone. a large model airplane. atop of it lies a tiny camera.)

this is the next wave of technology. *(responding to a question)* the fancy name for them is drones. it's plain to see that they're model airplanes…but, these are amazing little things. they got these little cameras on top of them. complicated, though. they work off these sensors that have been placed in strategic areas and – *(beat; annoyed)* i know this isn't a toy!

(extended beat)

we need all the help we can get. times are changing. america is under siege. the world isn't a safe place anymore…or haven't you liberals been watching the news lately?

(extended beat)

i started voices for a free Arizona about five years ago. a couple of friends and i got to the point where we were sick and tired of seeing our land destroyed. empty water jugs. food and candy wrappers. dirty clothes. human waste. you name it. there was trash as far as the eye could see. i spent half my time picking up after them…one day i said, "enough is enough!" this is my land and

i'm going to see that it stays that way. *(beat)* we're just a bunch of old ranchers sticking together to maintain our way of life. i don't see what all the commotion is about? this is my home. i paid for it. *(beat)* let me ask you something. if someone was breaking into your house, what would you do? exactly…no one would give you any gruff over it. you got to understand something. the need to protect ourselves is even greater now. *(beat)* my wife and i aren't getting any younger.

(extended beat)

if we don't protect ourselves, no one else will.

(a noise in the bush can be heard. charlie and the interviewer notice an animal running across the way from them. (beat) charlie takes a bag of chewing tobacco out of his pocket and places some in his mouth. he offers some to the reporter, but is rebuked. charlie shrugs it off. he places the bag back into his pocket. (beat) looks out again. he begins chewing his tobacco, which he spits out throughout the rest of the interview.)

just a jackrabbit…you hunt? shoot, next time you come for a talk give me more of a warning. i'll take you hunting. there's some good hunting in these parts. *(beat)* it's a shame what happened to those people. but, those are the chances you take, you know? you have to be brave to challenge mother nature. *(beat)* the desert sun can do some vicious things to man. destroys both his body and his

mind. poor saps didn't know what hit them. that's for sure. ain't much i can do about it. i don't make the laws. if someone wants to test fate, let them. who am i to say otherwise? as long as they take it someplace else…you enter my land, you're trespassing. you trespass, you get shot. no ifs, ands or buts…i won't like it, but i'll shoot you down without thinking twice about it…nothing personal.

(charlie reacts to a comments. beat)

(annoyed) of course, i know why they come! i know they got families like me…that they want to make a living. feed their children, but who's to say that one of the people crossing isn't one of those drug dealers or terrorist fellas. how am i supposed to know, huh? i can't assume they aren't. one of them shot at an

agent a couple of weeks ago. logic tells me i got to protect what's mine. *(beat)* people crossing the border got to know these things. it's only common sense. you walk into a man's home you don't- *(beat)* you don't litter. you don't treat another man's home like it's your own personal toilet. you respect a man's home as if it were your own!

(extended beat)

(defensive) my friends and i are not vigilantes!

(extended beat)

listen, i won't shoot at anyone during the day. if i catch them on my property i call border patrol and they come and pick them up. shoot, other ranchers aren't as generous as me. but, like, i was saying…during the day, i'm cool as a cucumber…at night…that's a totally different story.

(extended beat)
(charlie turns on the remote control and turns on the drone. the sounds of its flying can be heard. charlie looks up at the sky.)

watching these things soaring through the air brings me a sense of calmness.

(extended beat)

i'd probably do the same thing. a man has to be strong for his family...needs to be able to provide for them. if a man can't do that then he ain't a man. *(beat)* can't say that i blame them. *(defiantly)* just not on my property.

"very very"

snezena kuftinic
emergency room doctor
tucson, az

(snezena kuftinic is a white woman who is forty years old. she is a native of bosnia who has been living in the united states for a couple of years. her accent is very much evident. the interview is taking place somewhere in the confines of a hospital. she manages to keep her same expression and tone throughout the entire interview as if she is used to this type of conversation.)

...first detroit. eh, st. louis. then, i come here to arizona. a colleague from back home also works here. i came to visit and decided to stay. *(beat)* i prefer the sun to the snow.

(extended beat)

yes, many horrible stories. many injustices during the war. torture. rapes. i don't think my people will ever recover from what happened...difficult to ask of anyone.

(extended beat)

i am the only one left in my family. my mother died when i was young. my father died of stroke during the war. my brother was a soldier. the last time i saw him was thirteen years ago...some people in my village tell me, "be strong. he may still be – *(beat)* i know the truth. i will never see him again.

(extended beat)

after my father passed away i joined a group of doctors traveling from city to city...no reason to stay home. our war was very very bad...people hurt and ill...too many villages destroyed...many landmines. *(beat)* still many landmines at home. government has yet to take them away.

(extended beat)

i almost stay, but…uhm, went back to visit my borovica…five years after i had left for my medical training. hoping to find my brother. hear some news. most neighbors were gone. the few who were there had heard rumors. nothing more. *(beat)* people from

other neighborhoods…used to be nice…the muslims convinced them to destroy our village. many of the older people refused to leave. they were tortured and shot. their houses destroyed. my father's house was also destroyed. nothing, but ashes…i look around where it used to stand. i picked up my catechism book from when i was little girl. my home was like ghost town. *(beat)* that was december, ten years ago.

(extended beat)
(responding to a question)

differences? yes, i suppose, but many similarities, especially, working near the border. so many people come into the hospital. very sick…near death. remind me of the war. many i cannot help. i try, but by the time i see some of them, it's too late…these poor people have same look as people from my country. their eyes. very very sad. searching for a little peace, but knowing none. most unfortunate…too much like home.

(extended beat)

many times i hear people in this country speak of war in a casual tone. i do not understand how that is possible. i see children on the news…in iraq. crying in pain. *(beat)* the cry of a child who wants something very very different from the cry of a child in pain. i don't understand…many people live in a constant war.

palestine. africa. colombia…many places. life is different. more precious. americans say the real war is in front of us…in america. similarities. yes. i say that, but still not the same. my family. my home. bosnia. no longer exists…that is war. this is not war. america is more peaceful. yes, a lot of pain and problems that need to be dealt. with…but, not the same. america is very very, how do i say it? *(beat)* americans do not know the true meaning of war…only what they see on cnn.

(extended beat)

people don't want to leave their homes. war changes everything. the people in this hospital who come in…those found in the desert…all alone in the world. lying here thinking of their families…of their country.

(extended beat)

their eyes…very very similar.

"right here"

jose reynosa
private, first class-u.s.m.c.
goodyear, az

(marine corps private first class josé reynosa is a chicano. he is nineteen years old. he has a muscular build and close-shaven head. he is wearing camouflage pants, a t-shirt and boots.)

…they do that for every soldier in combat. it's just that, in this case, they had to go to zacatecas to do it. it took them a couple of weeks to locate his sister and her husband. they knocked on her door at 3 o'clock in the fucking morning. i don't want to imagine what she was thinking because who's to say my sister or my *amá* aren't going to be hearing the same thing real soon. i don't know.

(extended beat)

luis and his sister were real tight. *vato* got more mail than anybody in his unit. his sister was always so worried and shit. homeboy would send as much money as he could spare and he would always try to send her a picture of himself to make sure she knew he was alright and he would even send pictures of all of us hanging out…he dreamed of becoming an architect one day. he wanted to make something of himself…help his sister and her husband get into the states anyway he could. *(beat; solemnly)* he can't do anything about it now.

(extended beat)

him and his sister were orphaned when they were little kids. *vato* used to tell me stories about him and his sister working at a steel factory at the *pinche* age of ten. that's some fucked-up shit, *ese*. he decided that when he was eighteen he was going to go to *el norte* and find some work. they hid his ass in this truck carrying chickens. there was a fake bottom underneath the chicken pen. he

paid a thousand dollars to nearly suffocate to death in that truck. over a hundred degrees and the smell of that chicken shit driving him crazy; some of it dropping into where he was hiding. he had to lie there for hours…after a couple of weeks, though, the border patrol caught his ass and were about to send him back, but he told them that he was a minor with no family. shit...*vato* was a true babyface so

they treated him really good. *(beat)* even though he was close to being twenty-three, he made it through high school. he learned english, played soccer and drew a lot...*vato* did alright...after graduation, he joined the marines to pay back a little of what he'd gotten for the u.s.

(extended beat)

the more and more we watched the news, the more we know that the shit was gonna hit the fan, but he was proud to be in the service so he was ready. you see, i ain't like that. i'm too pissed off to feel that way. but, this *vato*...this *vato* wanted to prove himself. he wanted to throw down some chingasos.

(extended beat)

he died a week after he was shipped off. a sniper shot him in the side of the neck as he was helping his united rescue these Iraqis from a burning building...he never knew what hit him. the bullet shredded his vocal chords and hit pretty much every artery you could find...he didn't event have a chance to fight. *(beat; angrily)* i don't understand why he loved this shit so much! he

gave up his life for a country that didn't give a fuck about him! *(defeated)* fighting for something that wasn't his...say what you want, but that's what i believe. *(beat)* over here, there's a couple of paragraphs about his death in the local rinky-dink paper, but in mexico...shit, in mexico he's received a *chingón* of attention... those were his *gente*. they cared what happened to him.

(extended beat)

do you think people in this country truly appreciate what he had to do to get here? honestly, *vato*...what do you think?

(josé listens to his response. beat. nods his head.)

simón...that's what i'm talking about.

(extended beat)

(angrily) now, they're calling him a hero! for what!? because he managed to stand in the way of a fucking bullet!? because fools holding up posters telling everyone to "support our troops" say so.?*(facetiously)* hell, *vato*...it's great now. his death has ensured democracy for these *pendejos*, but when he was up crossing the border, he was nothing but a fucking wetback to them!

(extended beat)
(jose looks down at the floor. it seems like he doesn't wish to continue. he

continues looking down at the floor, shaking his head. he responds to a question, not bothering to look up.)

> fuck, homes…it was a stupid thing for me to do, but i didn't know what else – *(beat)* you see, my girl was pregnant and her parents kicked her out of her house. *(embarrassed)* my parents have been real cool about it. she's living with them, but she isn't their problem. she's my problem.

(josé realizes his last comment may have come off as insensitive. he raises his head and looks at the interviewer.)

> hey, *vato*… i didn't mean it like that. i love my girl. i love her with all my heart. what i meant to say was that she's my responsibility, not my parent's…that's all. *(beat; responding to a question)* what other choice did i have? i went to a shitty school, man. all they cared about was getting me out and it's not like they taught me

> anything. i ain't got no skills…you see, *ese*. that's the thing. they look at me as just another *cholo* with nowhere to go…the army, navy and *pinche* calvary depend on that shit. ain't no coincidence that there's always recruitment centers near unemployment offices…man, that's like sticking candy in front of a baby. these young *vatos*…uhm…i didn't know any better.

(extended beat)

> they said the war ended months ago and that our duties have changed…we're like supposed to be peace keepers or some shit like that…*pero*, every fucking day, our soldiers are dying. ain't nothing peaceful about it, *ese*.

(extended beat)

> we're still getting sent to the front lines. still casualties of war… but, what burns me is that we have a fucking war right here in our own house and we don't deal with the shit. fuck sadaam! i hate him as much as the next motherfucker, but this country shouldn't be playing daddy to a kid that doesn't belong to him!

(extended beat)

> george w. bush calling out a country on the nightly news because they have weapons of mass destruction…the last time i checked so did we so who is the evil empire here!? motherfucker almost loses the election because of the fact that one dumb-ass state didn't know how to punch a hole in a card…and, that state is governed by his brother. if that's not some political incest, i don't know what is…but, i guarantee you one thing, *ese*. if that mess had happened someplace else, you know we'd be the first ones to raise our hands and say, "that shit ain't right!"

(extended beat)

>the life of a brown man in america is predestined, *vato*...my homeboys been killed off left and right...here or across the ocean. dead is dead. dead brown kids belonging to us and dead brown kids belonging to someone else. does it really matter anymore? i mean, war is a business nowadays. i mean, just the other day, one of the president's buddies just asked congress for billions of

>*pinche* dollars to fight this war. dude! why not build some schools with that cash? create some jobs. make sure people have health insurance. shit like that. fuck, *vato*...my ass is gonna be in the desert soon enough. i'm preparing for it. i'll go fighting if i have to, but it's a shame. i'll be protecting and serving this country yet. my girl isn't sure how we're gonna afford to raise our baby. hell, *vato*...pampers and formula cost money.

(extended beat)

>i saw the news the other night and the pro-war *vatos* were arguing with the peace *vatos*. the pro-war *vatos* were yelling "you're against our troops." i yelled at the tv screen, "fuck you, *cabrón*. you're the ones who don't support us." those *vatos* don't want to see us dead. i don't want to see us dead. shit...anytime one of us dies, all they do is shed a tear and write a country song

>to commemorate it. naw, naw..those other people want us home with our *familias*. they don't want us killing innocent children. they want the government to start thinking with their heads and not their dicks. you want to support the troops? go get a gun, sign up and be one yourself, *cabrón*!

(extened beat)

>*(quietly)* i'm scared, *vato*...i don't want to go, but i know it's only a matter of days. i can feel it.

(extended beat)

>i gotta kid to think about, but when i really think about it, i realized that i didn't think about it at all. *(beat)* i regret the day i signed my name on the fucking dotted line...if i don't come back, my kid ain't gonna have a daddy. that's another *familia* without a father. that's another *familia* that the *pinche* republicans are gonna bitch about when reelections come back around.

(extened beat)

>like i said, we need to deal with the war right here at home because the fact is, *ese*...this country is losing that war, too.

"our song"

monica flores
kindergarden teacher
chandler, az

(the heatwave's "always and forever" is playing. we see monica flores. she is a chicana in her mid-twenties. located onstage is an altar. it contains candles and pictures of monica's deceased husband, pedro. she is lighting a candle. monica crosses back to her chair. (beat) the song plays for a while and as it slowly starts to fade away, monica begins to talk.)

>he dedicated that song to me during our senior prom…always and forever by the heatwaves. *(beat)* i knew right then, that he would be the man i would marry.

(extended beat)

>he was the nicest guy you would ever want to meet. he was smart…funny…polite. *(beat; fondly)* and, he had this smile that, i don't know, there was something about his smile that was just so perfect.

(extended beat)
(monica responds to a question.)

>he wanted to make sure he did something positive with his life. you see, for him, it was more than just about getting a job. to him, anyone could do that. that's not what he wanted. *(beat)* he had gone to community college for a couple of years to sort things out in his mind, you know, try to find himself. but, all along, i

>knew he'd do something i didn't want him to do…i figured he'd be a fireman or a policeman, something of that nature. i think he just went to school to make me feel better. to show me that he was making an effort to explore his options…but, it wasn't in his nature to sit behind a desk shuffling papers and crunching numbers.

(extended beat)

>from the first moment they met, pedro and my father had a great relationship. since my two sisters and i were the only children my parents had, my father took to him as if pedro was his own son. *(beat)* things would never be the same, though.

(extended beat)

my father couldn't even look at pedro in the eyes. it was as if my father had his heart ripped out...to make matters worse, it felt like the rest of my family was following his lead and i was caught in the middle. *(beat)*. i didn't agree with pedro's decision and he knew i wouldn't, but it didn't stop him from going through with it and that caused problems between us because i knew there was no way i was going to be able to change his mind.

(extended beat)

(near tears) and...and, uhm...the thing is...a few years ago during the i.n.s. raids in chandler...uhm, my father had been one of those taken into custody. when they stopped him, he had been on his morning run and didn't have his i.d. on him...he was kept in a cell for three days *(beat)* for pedro to stand there in front of my father and tell him he had applied to work for the department of immigrat-

(extended beat)

(quietly) i had to stand behind pedro...he was my husband.

(extended beat)

i remember when he began his training and how it would affect him. i can't tell you how many times we would have conversations where he was on the verge of quitting. i could hear it in his voice and every time it killed me but, at the same time, it gave me hope that he would go on to something else. *(beat)* i remember

this one night, he told me about this thing called tonking...he was instructed that tonking was the sound one of those heavy metal flashlights makes when it's smacking someone's head, but it wasn't necessarily seen as a bad thing...only part of the job. this was the type of thing my husband was learning!

(extended beat)

growing up, my father used to say that the only good border patrol agent was a dead one. *(beat)* so, i asked him if he still felt that way knowing that pedro was working for them...without the slightest hesitation, he said, "yes." that was my husband he was talking about! the future father of my children...of his future grandchildren.

(extended beat)

i haven't spoken to my father since.

(extended beat)

i'd yell at pedro. "why is this job so damn important to you!? don't you see what you're doing to this family!? don't you care about your people!?" he'd yell back, "don't you ever tell me what i'm thinking! i've told you the stories of my father crossing the border. the shit he had to go through to get here. what? you think this is just one big fucking game i'm playing!?" *(beat)* and, he stopped for a moment…because he had realized he had been yelling at me, then, he pulled me towards him. he kissed me on my cheek and held me for what seemed forever. like he didn't

want to let go…and…he, uh, whispered to me, "would you rather have some racist white dude dealing with our people…*(beat)* or…me…someone who's going to make sure they're treated like human beings?"

(extended beat)

you hear stories all the time about latino border patrol agents who are worse than the white officers…they're so afraid of appearing weak that they go to the extremes to build a reputation…in the process, not only do they lose their souls, but they lose their dignity. *(beat)* pedro wasn't like that. he treated every single person he stopped with respect. didn't matter what color they were…because of that, he was respected by most, resented by others.

(extended beat)

it almost never failed. pedro would catch someone and a few days later he would catch them again. the funny thing is, believe it or not, some of them didn't mind being caught…as long as it was pedro, that is. they would even greet him friendly, "hello." it wasn't like they didn't know the routine. they get caught, processed…and given a happy meal from mcdonalds…then, tomorrow would roll around.

(extended beat)

after a few years, i came to understand that pedro wasn't there to hunt down people crossing the border. he was there making sure they would have another chance to try again. *(beat)* i once remember him joking around one day…he said, "if they get past me, the more power to them." i didn't think much of it at the time, but now that i look back at those words, i realize that he

meant them. he knew people living in this neighborhood who were here illegally. didn't matter. he'd strike up a conversation with them. maybe, share a story or two. but, he didn't turn them in…you see, the borderline was his workplace. anyplace other than that…wasn't.

(extended beat)

he was having some drinks with some of his football buddies at his bar. nothing unusual about that…he was just relaxing.

after his friends had left, he struck up a conversation with some other guys at the bar and, from what i was told, they seemed to be nice guys. apparently, during their conversation, pedro had mentioned to them that he was an agent for the border patrol. *(beat)* they found his body a few feet away from the border. he was murdered execution-style. authorities told us that they think those guys might've been drug dealers or *coyotes*, and, that, uhm, when they found out my husband was an agent, *(beat)* they didn't take anything from him. he had all his money and his keys.

(extended beat)

(near tears) they found his badge laying on top of his chest…for everyone to see.

(extended beat)

(angrily) i don't care what any goddamn person has to say…even my father!

(extended beat)

my husband was a good man.

"skewed"

lacey williams
business owner
scottsdale, az

(lacey williams is a white female in her mid-thirties; stereotype of a sorority sister grown-up. she runs a jewelry boutique in the heart of downtown scottsdale. this is where the interview is taking place. she is sitting in a chair.)

…a play! that sounds so exciting! *(proudly)* i go to the herberger to see shows as often as i can. have you been to the herberger? how silly of me to ask. of course you have…you know, if you're not too busy, you should head straight down there…i saw the producers a few days ago.

(extended beat)

and…what was your play about again? *(responding)* border issues? race? why would you want to write about that? you have to understand one thing…it isn't a question of race. it's a question of economics. arizona is already in a budget crunch as it is. add them. yes, that's right. them! the immigrants you were talking about. *(beat)* add them to the equation and you'll see that the solution to this problem is nowhere in sight. we have our families to think about. if we want a future, we need to plan for it right now and i don't see how that's possible if we keep allowing those people to enter this country illegally. it's not like there aren't legal ways of getting in. other people have gotten in legally. i don't see why they can't. we can't take care of everybody, especially if we're having trouble taking care of ourselves.

(extended beat)

i read stories all the time about the cities in southern arizona. all the difficulties they're dealing with…and, i know firsthand. my brother did his medical residency in tucson a few years ago and he – *(beat)* first hand…second hand…same difference. like i was saying, the problems at my brother's hospital were never ending. the hospital was in debt beyond belief. they needed extra medical

supplies. nobody had insurance…they even needed to hire a staff of translators. not translator, but…translators to accommodate so many people. the money used for those positions could've been used better in other areas. *(beat)* is it wrong to believe our citizens should have first right to the amenities entitled to us as taxpayers? education, social services, etc. is it fair that some foreigner has access to our resources? my husband and i have worked hard for what we have. this jewelry shop has made a

name for itself in scottsdale and my husband's accounting firm is very well respected in this community…and, you see, this is what scottsdale is…it's a community. a community of like-minded people. *(feigning apology)* no, no…what i mean is that scottsdale is a very refined place to live. we have an image to

uphold. we want our property values to remain high, we want our children to attend the best schools. exactly! you're starting to get the picture…we don't want what's happening to places like tucson and yuma to happen here. that wouldn't be acceptable. *(responding)* no! you're still not understanding what i mean. just listen to what i am saying. this isn't about me disliking mexicans or anything like that. i love the mexican culure. i practically live

at baja fresh. and…my nanny, rosa, is like a member of the family…when i was a student at arizona state, my sorority sisters and i spent every spring break in mexico…my husband and went there for our honeymoon so, you see, it's not about disliking another group of people. it's about the fact that there is not enough money to go around.

(extended beat)

i know that scottsdale has a reputation of being exclusive, but that's just not true. no one is being excluded from living here, albeit living here does require a certain level of success, but that's not a question of exclusivity, but of hard work. if you reach those levels no one is going to stop you from coming here, regardless of what race or religion you belong to...we want people to feel

welcome. *(proudly)* north scottsdale, to be precise. and, i am a proud member of the scottsdale chamber of commerce so i know what i'm talking about. people want to come to scottsdale. that's why we try so hard to pamper them. all the high-end shops are intended to attract high-end clientele, but also to give other people an idea of what might be possible if they work hard

enough. we have only the finest restaurants and hotels. plus, there's a reason why scottsdale has more spas than anywhere in the world...it's because we want people to feel comfortable. in a world full of problems it's a blessing to be able to lose one's self in a body treatment or a round of golf. and, at night, this town is electric. *(beat)* seeing that i have a family now, i don't go out as

often as i would like but, on those rare occasions, there's nothing better than dancing the night away with friends. the clubs here are so inviting. they're so the place-to-be. *(beat)* this isn't mesa, that's for sure.

(extended beat)

(embarrassed) you live in mesa? uhm, well...i'm sure it suits you just fine. *(beat)* did i mention the weather?

(extended beat)

you can't beat the weather. eight months out of the year i dare you to find another more beautiful and charming locale. it's picture-perfect. i can't say that i have an answer for the heat, but that's what air conditioners and pools were made for and, really...a little heat never hurt anybody. *(confused)* no...i don't think so. what do you mean? *(beat; responding, unsympathetic)* yes, yes, the fourteen immigrants. *(beat; responding)* simple. they should've brought along some more water.

(lacey responds to the interviewer furiously writing away in his notebook.)

is everything alright? what's the problem then? *(shocked)* what do you mean by that!? *(angrily)* no...i don't agree! i don't believe i'm ignorant at all. honestly, i think you should be ashamed of yourself for saying something like that. i agreed to do this interview for your little play and i wasn't expecting to be chastised for my opinions. *(beat)* you're just like the rest of them with your skewed sense of who we are. you talk about how we stereotype people when you're no better. i don't know you anymore than you know me, but i agreed to have this conversation anyway. unlike you, i try to look at people as people...and, not race. *(beat)* nothing i've told you today has anything remotely to do with that. it's about maintaining standards. there's no sin in that.

(extended beat)

(standing up) this discussion is over. furthermore, i'm going to have to ask you not to use any of this interview in your project. i don't feel you've portrayed me in a positive light and the thought that you would put this up onstage disturbs me. i am very serious. i will take legal action if you decide to go through with using this interview.

(extended beat)

(pointing towards the door) please leave!

"muñeca"

oscar garcía
obrero
mesa, az

(es mediodía. la entrevista está llevándose acabo en una calle en la ciudad de mesa con mucho tráfico dónde obreros buscan trabajo. oscar garcía, de treinta años, es mexicano. es flaco y por los afectos del sol tiene más oscura la piel que lo normal. su ropa está acabada por lo viejo y lleva un cinto de herramienta. su lonchera está en el piso a su lado. al fondo está el letrero HOME DEPOT con letras borrosas. se pueden escuchar los ruidos de hombres hablando en español.)

así es, yo conocía a enrique. era muy bueno...muy amable. es que él era camarada de mi primo y siempre que iba a visitar a mi primo ahí estaba pisteando y sacando curas. como dije, era muy payaso.

(pausa larga)

no, no supe...ni cuando vi las noticias. era la misma historia cada día. así es, todos lo sabemos, siempre hay chansa que no lo logremos. eso está muy gacho pero no hay de otra. méxico es un país muy pobre como su gente...me salí de la escuela, hmm...a los siete años. mi familia necesitaba mi ayuda para chambear. así es allá unos pocos pesos ni al caso. *(mirando al piso)* seremos pobres, pero no

pendejos. sabemos que la muerte nos persigue...ni modo. pero me siento mal por ellos. la cosa es ver tanta gente muerta en un solo lugar, nunca me había tocado ver eso. y sí, ese día me sentí retefeo porque ellos también venían de sinaloa, chin…sinaloa es mi tierra. ellos eran mis camaradas. *(pausa)* yo no supe de enrique hasta unas semanas después. yo sabía que se iba a venir, ya habíamos platicado de eso, pero me había dicho que se iba a

esperar un rato porque su vieja estaba embarazada y él quería conocer a su bebé. tampoco quería que su vieja estuviera sola. el era ese tipo de muchacho. *(pausa; triste)* cuando recibí la carta de mi primo me dijo que enrique era uno de los catorce…creo que no aguantó esperar y su mujer acababa de tener su bebé la semana pasada…lo nombró enrique. *(cambiando el tema)* ¡pinche calor! ¿verdad? ¿quieres un refresco? tengo extra por si quieres.

(oscar se agacha y agarra una soda para él mismo y le ofrece una soda al entrevistador.)

¿seguro? bueno, pero aquí en confianza, lo que es mío es tuyo.

(oscar se pone de pie. abre la soda y prácticamente toma toda la soda. un poquito se le cae en la barba y se limpia.)

¿yo? varios meses. desde agosto. *(le contesta)* agosto es el mejor mes nomás porque es el mes más difícil. el clima es mejor en el invierno pero es cuando hay más migra. ellos saben que es el tiempo en que nosotros más tratamos de cruzar. pero yo no. yo traté de hacerlo más difícil para que me cacharan así como fue difícil para llegar aquí. a lo mejor suena raro pero así soy. *(hablando con los otros obreros)* ¿qué no compas?

(se escucha el ruido de los hombres que están de acuerdo. oscar empieza a hablar en voz alta para comunicar sus pensamientos al grupo y al entrevistador.)

pues la migra también odia el calor igual que nosotros…nomás hay una diferencia. para nosotros es pensar en vida o muerte y para ellos es solamente pinche inconveniencia. ellos nomás se queman y dicen que es la culpa de los mojados. se pican con un cactus y es la culpa de los mojados. *(carcajeándose)* no encuentran vieja para casarse y es culpa de los pinches mojados.

(se escucha la risa de los obreros. cuando se baja la risa, oscar se queda pensativo.)

¿oyes eso? los chistes…es lo único que tenemos. cuando batallas tanto para sobrevivir…en una manera ya estás muerto. por eso es bueno reír y es una risa buena…pues ya sabes.

(oscar termina su soda y aplasta la lata.)

extraño la risa de mi niña. mi niñita preciosa…estrella. ella es niña de navidad. está bendecida. ¿gustas ver una foto de ella?

(oscar saca una foto de su hija y la enseña al entrevistador.)

esta foto es de ella recién nacida. lo recuerdo como si fuera ayer…es tanto como su madre. ¿no es la bebé más bonita que has visto? sí, ya sé que todos los papás hablan así de sus bebés pero en este caso es en serio.

(oscar pone la foto en su cartera.)

empezó la escuela la semana pasada y tiene ya seis años y es más inteligente que su papá…quiero que ella sí vaya a la escuela. no quiero que ella…

(se escucha la bocina de una camioneta. también se escucha el ruido de los obreros buscando trabajo. oscar brinca para agarrar la atención del chofer. después de unos momentos, oscar se para y mira como se va la troca; pausa.)

(avergonzado) perdón, no quise ser gacho. ¿seguro que no quieres nada de tomar?

(pausa larga)

guardé un poco de dinero…varios bolas. esta navidad podría mandarle algo chiquito a mi familia. tengo suficiente para un colchón para mi vieja y niña para que lo compartan. lana para comida y otras cosas, a lo mejor me sobrará hasta para un radio chico. nuestro radio viejo ya no sirve pa' nada. a ellas les gusta oír la radio juntas.

(pausa larga)

el año que viene…aunque me mate…voy a darle un regalo de navidad a estrella pero va a ser de los buenos y también un regalo de cumpleaños muy bueno también. *(pausa)* es que mi niña siempre tiene su muñeca fea. es de plástico chafa. está casi bichi y no tiene un brazo. mi niña se merece mejor. le voy a comprar una barbie americana, pero no es todo. le voy a completar toda la

barbie. un novio de barbie. la casa grande. el carro. todo el *set*. ya saqué la cuenta de cuánto me va a salir todo…15 bolas cada barbie. la barbie y el novio. 20 bolas para el carro y la casa 80 bolas. ¿lo puedes creer? ¡tanta lana para una barbie! *(haciendo cuentas en su cabeza)* otros…creo…puede…pienso que debe de salir a…no sé, a lo mejor 50 bolas para enviarlo…casi 200 bolas. *(preocupado)* ¡200 bolas! *(pausa)* no me gusta la muñeca que tiene. está sucia. está quebrada. las muñecas deberían ser bonitas.

(pausa larga)
(oscar mira alrededor por unos momentos con la esperanza de un trabajo. pausa. orgullosamente.)

yo chambeo duro. estas son mis herramientas que uso para hacer y arreglar cosas. yo no soy ratero ni nada así. yo soy un hombre honesto. no es justo lo que piensan de mis camaradas. ¡nos tratan como animales! y eso no es cierto. ellos no saben cómo nos sentimos…cuánto extrañamos nuestras familias. yo amo a méxico pero no hay chamba en méxico. yo sólo hago lo que debo hacer. no estoy lastimando a nadie. asegúrate de decirle eso a la gente. ¡no somos criminales!

(pausa larga)

(seriamente) los criminales no compran barbies americanas.

"agua/water"

reverend clay nash
pastor
tucson, az

(in the darkness, america's "horse with no name" is playing. after a few moments, the lights go up. the interview is being held in the desert outside of tucson. reverend clay nash is a white man in his early fifties and has a texas drawl. a cross hangs from his neck. he is putting up a water station. it is the middle of the afternoon and the temperature is easily over 110 degrees. reverend nash wipes his brow with a handkerchief. the song slowly fades away as reverend nash beings to talk.)

oohee…i'd say it's about one-twelve maybe. but the day is still young.

(extended beat)

the day those fourteen people died, the temperature was well over a fucking 117 degrees.

(clay places his handkerchief back in his pocket.)

this area is classified as a "high risk zone" by authorities…no surprise there. right at this second, there's some agent wandering around "the devil's road" looking for some poor souls. *(beat)* immigration is changing their policies; rerouting immigrants so that they have to travel the most treacherous geography you can imagine…now these poor folk are being forced to travel to god knows

where…only to die…not to be apprehended. the powers that be know that all too well. *(looking at the water spigot.)* you don't mind if i check this right quickly, do you?

(clay checks a water spigot.)

(angrily) damn *coyote* stole their money and left them out there to

die.

(extended beat)

there were over thirty people in that group. did you know that? the youngest survivor was sixteen. *(beat)* think about that for a second. a sixteen-year-old.

(extended beat)

think about this even more…two weeks earlier, agents found the body of a ten-year-old girl…a ten-year-old…still just a baby.

(extended beat)

when the survivors reached the hospital they were burned black and were covered in cactus spines from the cacti they were trying to eat for food…one doctor at the hospital described the survivors as looking like mummies…you spend enough time under these conditions and your kidneys are liable to explode…and, i definitely mean that in the literal sense.

(clay walks around, looking for immigrants.)

(to himself) pretty quiet on the warfront.

(extended beat)

these people really have no idea what it's like. no one can really. you hope for the best and you hope god is carrying you, but unless god is carrying jugs of water you're shit out of luck…there's no habitation, no ranches, no roads, no water. *(beat)* they start off their journey, if they're lucky, with one maybe two gallons of water. they think it's going to be all they need, but it gets real clear real soon that the shit isn't going to last.

(extended beat)

(pointing) over there…about thirty miles southeast from here we found the body of a woman, a mrs. juanita ramos, near a creek bed. her body had been picked clean by animals and her bones were spread over an area of about fifty feet. the woman had tried to cross with two of her children. she was a heavyset woman which, in and of itself, was a horrible idea…but she wanted to be with her husband in texas. *(beat)* the things people will do when they're in love, y'know?

(extended beat)

you married, son?

(extended beat)

(solemnly) one day…maybe.

(extended beat)

well…this poor woman fell ill and couldn't continue. the *coyote* took her young daughter who made it safely across. her teenage son stayed with her as long as he could before getting help, but he was caught and sent back home. a few weeks later, her father got permission to find his baby girl. he asked us for help and we helped...we spent twenty-one days looking for her. during that time we found the remains of another seven people.

(extended beat)

señor dominguez identified his daughter by the necklace lying near her remains. it was the necklace he had given her for her quinceañera. *(beat)* at least, juanita is at peace now...now many of these poor souls can say the same...if they're lucky, they'll be sent home in a wooden box. for the ones that are never found, well...a person should die amongst the living...not the dead.

(clay picks up a rock and throws it out into the distance.)

most people don't think about water...even when there's a drought going on, they don't think about it. how many times have you left the sink on when you're brushing your teeth? and...what about when you shower? ten...fifteen minutes. do you realize how much water that is? that's more water than some families in this world have in a week...probably, even longer in most cases. water is life. without it...you ain't nothing but a heap of fucking ashes...that's why i decided to put up these water stations. too many brown faces dying.

(extended beat)

(responding to a question) yep...i can go on and on about the policies and, trust me, there isn't one politician in arizona who doesn't know me. i'm a texas preacher with a big mouth and i know how to use it.

(extended beat)

not like i have much of a choice. hear what i'm saying? i don't do this for publicity. i'd prefer y'all just leave me the hell alone...i only live to serve the lord.

(extended beat)

(responding to a question) hmm...let me see. the first two that we built were in the organ pipe cactus national monument. the others were placed on some private land south of tucson and just north of rio rico, but that was just the first of many to come...there are going to be plenty more. believe you me. *(beat)* there's no way of knowing exactly how many people are being saved, but it's helping. that i know for sure...proving this water is nothing more than an act of faith and conviction.

(extended beat)

what irritates me are those people who criticize what we're doing…saying that we are not only contributing, but encouraging illegal immigration…and, i use the word, illegal, loosely. that word should be reserved for those who are truly breaking the law…rapists…murderers…that isn't the case here. the only thing these people are about is survival.

(extended beat)

it boggles my mind to see how desensitized civilization has become…the sight of fourteen deceased bodies on a dried up riverbed and the only thoughts that pass through their hollow minds is "we got to do something about illegal immigration. it's getting out of hand."

(extended beat)

(angrily) regardless of which arguments you side with, when you see a person dead in front of your eyes, your thoughts should be on him or her. honoring that person while, at the same time, being grateful that you get the chance to see another day!

(extended beat)

i doubt that people are risking their lives for a sip of hot water in the middle of the desert! nothing you or i –

(extended beat)

(composing himself) we can't forget that these people are our brothers and sisters…children of god…they're human beings, people with dignity, dreams and desires who have enriched this country with their work and talent. for every penny they've taken out of this country, i believe they've put two pennies back in…and, there are some realities that, as a people, we are going to have to face.

we can no longer look at ourselves as two nations divided by a river or some fence. we have to look at ourselves as a region that's going to live together, that's going to work together, that's going to make some damn progress together.

(extended beat)
(clay sees a person in the distance and waves him down.)

(yelling) aquí, señor…agua, aquí!!!

(clay looks off into the opposite direction.)

john…over there! see him? bring him on over to the station!

(extended beat)

(clay stands silent for a moment, then begins to quietly say a prayer; ends it with a sign of the cross.)

(extended beat)
(clay looks back towards the interviewer.)

        (solemnly) looks like today's your lucky day…care for a cup of water?

(lights go dark as a spotlight hits a screen that is either located upstage center or on a back wall. the final slide appears. it is a quote that reads:)

**"a man's dying
is more
the survivor's affair
than his own."**

- thomas mann

(extended beat)
(lights fade to black.)
(end of the play)

translations for:

"virgencita linda" & "muñeca"

"virgencita linda"

luz ortiz
maid
guadalupe, az

(the interview is taking place in the backyard of luz ortiz, a mexicana who is sixty years of age. she sits near a makeshift altar that her family has created; the virgin of guadalupe being prominently displayed. the time is early evening. she has just returned from the hotel where she works as a maid.)

forgive me for being late. *m'ija* needed to put gas in the car. i usually walk to work. it's just down the street. the holiday inn hotel. el express...right down the street, across from the big market. *(luz responds to a comment made by her daughter; amused)* oh, forgive me. i meant to say "el mall". my daughter loves to spend hours walking around that thing. me? i don't

have much money so i don't bother. i don't see the point in it. *(beat)* but, it's only fifteen minutes to walk to work. short walk. at night, my *viejo* or one of my kids will come and walk home with me. i tell them it's not necessary, but they worry for me...i didn't want to be late tonight. when *m'ija* told me about the gas...aagh. i just want to thank you for being patient and to

apologize about my appearance. i didn't get a chance to change out of my work clothes. you sure it's alright? *(beat)* i'm so excited to have you in my home. my daughter goes on and on about you. she says you're a very good writer. *(responding)* thank you so much. yes, i am proud of her. she was my youngest; i was almost forty

when i had her. she says she wants to be a teacher. i ask her if she would rather be a doctor or a lawyer like her brother. something that pays better, but she just wants to help kids. she's always thinking of others before herself. *(beat)* were you born here in arizona? are you from los angeles? hmm...i've been there once. i thought it was nice. i very much liked the beach, but i wouldn't want to live there. no offense. i just think

it's so big and there are so many people there. i'm happy where i'm at. *(beat; amused)* don't worry about your spanish. you aren't a *pocho*…i understand you just fine. it's nothing to be embarrassed about. i know how difficult it is to juggle two languages. i'm always running around in circles with my oldest son. i'll talk to him in spanish, but he usually answers me in english. i constantly

have to remind him, "in spanish, *m'ijo*" but he jokes it off like it doesn't matter. i know it does, but he's getting better at it. he's a good boy, though…and, your parents? were they born here? ah, zacatecas…and, your mother? monterrey. i knew it. there was something familiar about you. i couldn't pin it down, but now i can. i grew up in monterrey. most of my family still lives thereabouts, colonia metalúrgica, colonia nueva aurora, colonia torreón jardín. do you know which one your family lives in? colonia vencedora? ay, yes…two of my uncles are from there. next time you talk to your mother ask her if they

know anyone from the gallegos family…ask her if that name sounds familiar. juan carlos and eduardo gallegos..ask her. *(beat)* i try to visit mexico every few years, but it gets more difficult as i get older. do you still have family there? how long has it been since

you've seen them? *ay, m'ijo*, that's much too long. you need to go and see them. they are your blood. *(responding)* yes, things cost money. it's an expensive world, but if you get the chance, start saving your pennies because your family won't be around forever. none of us will. plus, you shouldn't forget that mexico is as much your home as it is your parents'. please don't ever

forget that…i know that i miss mexico so much sometimes, but i love guadalupe. it's the closest thing to mexico that you can find around here. it's not as nice as the other places, but it's home. the white people, they don't much care about what happens here. at least, that's what i think. i don't have to tell you. i know you know that. you can see it yourself. look at baseline street. look at

the other side and look at the guadalupe side. it's like crossing from san diego to tijuana. the mall and everything. all nice and new. lots of places to spend. down the street there is this beautiful park that is so green. but they don't care if guadalupe isn't green. they don't care if the schools are bad. *(beat; annoyed)* around the corner they just made a place for the little ones to play baseball. it's pretty. i am happy for the kids. it's green like the big park, but one little piece of land still isn't enough...guadalupe is still nothing but dirt and rocks. next to the church where the older men play sports, that's all it is. dirt and rocks. sometimes broken pieces of glass and trash. there are many open areas like that. it's almost like they are laughing in our faces...as if to say to us, you want to play somewhere nice, then cross the street to do so. we don't care...you eventually have to cross back anyway. *(beat; apologetic)* forgive me. i am angry, yes, but i don't want to come off hateful. i am a good catholic. i believe in god and jesus and the lovely virgin mary, but i am not blind...but, with that said, i am thankful. thankful that i have my small little house and food on the table. a

television to watch my soaps. my old man treats me good and my children are good people...guadalupe has been good to us. to most people here. i mean, there isn't a lot of money, but we go on because we must. even with all the bad around us, we still find the time to share our stories and coffees. in guadalupe family is family. believe me, what little we have is a world's more than what most people in mexico have. we appreciate the little

things like soap and toilet paper. those are the things i bring to mexico to give to my family...the little things other people don't think twice about. *(beat)* it's because the virgin mary protects us. she looks over us. we are lucky to have her in our lives. that is why almost every house in this neighborhood has a virgin mary standing guard over them. we must always remember that she

was the one that watched over us as we crossed the border. she protected us. she held us when nobody else would. *(beat)* i was only sixteen when i crossed...alone with people i didn't know. *(responding)* no...my mother didn't want me to go, but in mexico you can't tell anyone not to cross, you can only tell them that

you will say a prayer for them. that is all. *(closing her eyes)* that first night with the coyotes howling and the heat unbearable i can still remember how tightly i was holding onto my tiny statue of the virgin of guadalupe; nearly crushing her. it was the longest night of my life. *(beat; emotional)* a few days later when i snuck across, a *coyote* was herding us into the back of this big truck like cattle

and i slipped as i got on...i dropped my little virgin onto the ground by accident, but i didn't see her until i was all the way inside. i sat down with the others when i noticed. i yelled for the *coyote* to please pick it up. "please give her to me," i said... but, he just yelled at me to shut up and with those words he slammed the door in our faces...five hours later i found myself in the back of a garage in tucson. two days later i found myself in a watermelon field west of phoenix…when i had a minute to get a drink of water, i thought of my little virgin of guadalupe…being stepped on…forgotten in the desert…like so many of the poor souls who prayed to her during their journeys.

(extended beat)

i still pray to her because she has never left me…even when i look out across the street to el mall and the new cars and nice houses…even now. *(beat)* she is with me.

"muñeca"

**oscar garcia
day laborer
mesa, az**

(it is the middle of the day. the interview is taking place on a busy mesa intersection where day laborers gather, searching for employment. oscar garcia, thirty, is a mexican. he is slight of build and the effects of the arizona heat has his skin looking darker than it usually would be. his clothes are worn and he carries a weathered tool belt (with a few basic tools). his mini-ice box/lunch pail lays next to him. in the background an out-of-focus but, definitely recognizable, HOME DEPOT sign can be seen and the sounds of men talking in spanish can also be heard.)

that's right. i knew enrique. he was a good guy…very friendly. you see, he was my cousin's friend, so whenever i'd visit my cousin he was usually there talking shit, making jokes, sharing his beers. like i said, he was a funny guy.

(extended beat)

no. i didn't know…not even when i saw the news on t.v.; same story every day. that's the way it is. we all know that. there's always a chance we won't make it. that shit is fucked-up, but there is no other way. mexico is a poor country, like its people…i quit school when i was like, uhm, seven. my family needed me to help. a few

pesos isn't enough. not even close. *(looking down at the floor)* we may be poor, but we're not stupid. we know that death is following us…that's the way it is. i can still feel bad for them. the thing is to see to see so many dead people in one place…all the same time. i had never seen that before. and yes, that day i felt really bad because they also came from sinaloa, damn, man! sinaloa is my land. those were my brothers. *(beat)* i didn't know about enrique until a few weeks later. sure, i knew he was going to make the crossing. we all had talked about it. i knew that, but he said he had told that he was going to wait a while. his wife was pregnant and he wanted to see his child be born. he didn't want his wife to be alone. he was that kind of guy. *(beat; sadly)* when i finally got my primo's letter, he told me that enrique was one of the fourteen...i guess he couldn't wait long enough. *(beat)* his wife had her baby last week. a son...she named him enrique. *(changing the subject)* it's fucking hot! you know? want a soda? i have an extra one if you'd like.

(oscar bends down and grabs a soda for himself; and he offers a soda to the interviewer –)

you sure? alright, then, but don't be afraid to ask. what's mine is yours.

(oscar stands back up. he opens the soda can and practically drinks the whole can in one motion. a little bit of the soda runs down his chin. he wipes it off.)

me? a few months...ever since august. *(responding to a question)* august is the best month because it's the most difficult month, my friend. the weather is better in the winter. more *migra* patrol then. they know more of us will try when the weather is cooler. not me, though. i wanted to make it as hard for them to catch me as it was for me to get here. i know that sounds crazy, but that's just me. *(talking to the other workers)* isn't that right, fellas!?

(the sound of men agreeing can be heard. oscar begins talking in a louder voice to communicate his thoughts to the whole group as well as the interviewer.)

shit. la migra hates the heat as much as we do...only difference is that for us it's a matter of life and death. for them, it's a damn inconvenience. if they get a sunburn, it's the immigrants'fault. if they prick themselves on a cactus, it's the immigrants' fault. *(chuckling)* if they can't find a woman to marry them. it's the immigrant's damn fault.

(laughter erupts from the group of day laborers. as the laughter dies down, oscar becomes a bit pensive. beat; to interviewer –)

hear that? the laugther. that's the only thing we own out here. when you struggle so much to try and survive you're already dead...in a way, that is, but a good laugh...well, a good laugh... well, you know.

(oscar finishes his soda. he stands the can on the floor and crushes it.)

i miss my daughter's laugh. my little baby girl... estrella. she was a christmas baby. she's blessed. would you like to see a picture of her?

(the interviewer agrees to see the picture. oscar pulls out the picture and shows it to the interviewer; pointing.)

this was her when she was born. i remember it like it was
yesterday…she's so much like her mother. look at her. isn't she
the most beautiful baby you've ever seen? yeah, i know. every
father talks like that but, in this case, it's true.

(oscar puts the picture back in his wallet.)

she just started school last week. six years old and already she's
smarter than her dad. i want her to go to school. i don't want her
to…

*(a truck horn can be heard. the sound of men responding can be heard. oscar
begins jumping up and down, hand waving in the air, trying to get the truck
driver's attention. after a few moments, oscar stops his actions. he watches as the
truck drives away. beat.)*

(embarrassed) sorry, i didn't mean to be rude. sure you don't
want anything to drink?

(extended beat)

(to the interviewer) i've saved a little bit…a few dollars. this
christmas i'll be able to send a little something to my family.
i have enough to get a simple mattress for my wife and child
to share. money for food and other things. there might even be
a little cash left over for a small radio. our old one is no good
anymore. *(beat)* they like to listen to the radio together.

(extended beat)

next year, though…even if it kills me…i am going to get estrella a
real christmas present and a real birthday present. *(beat)* my little
girl carries around this ugly little doll. cheap plastic. practically
naked and missing an arm. my little girl deserves better. i'm going
to get her one of those american barbie dolls. but not just that. i'm
getting her the whole set-up. the girl barbie, the boyfriend, the big
dollhouse. the

car. the whole thing. i already did the math. fifteen dollars for
each barbie. the boy and the girl. twenty for the car and the house
is eighty dollars. can you belive that? so much money for a doll?
(tabulating in his head) i believe… it should…i think it ought to
come to…i don't know, fifty just to send it… that's almost two
hundred dollars. *(to himself; worried)* two hundred! *(beat)* i don't
like the doll she has now. it's dirty. it's broken. dolls are supposed
to be pretty.

(extended beat)
*(oscar looks around for a few moments, hoping to see a prospective employer.
beat; proudly)*

i work hard. these are my tools. tools that i use to build and fix things. i don't steal or nothing like that. i am an honest man. it's not fair what people say about me and my friends. they treat us like we're animals and that's not true! they do not know how we feel...how much we miss our families. i love mexico, but there are no jobs in mexico. i am only doing what i have to do. i'm not hurting anybody. you make sure to tell people that. we are not criminals!

(extended beat)

(solemnly) criminals don't buy american barbie dolls.

MISS CONSUELO

by Guillermo Reyes

Author's biography

Who reads these bios anyway? But just in case… *For prurient interest only*: Read Guillermo's memoir, *Maria's Oscar* (to be published any day now), and you'll know all the secrets, which will no longer be secrets. Read, discuss and compare it to Rousseau's *Confessions* (impressive, ¿qué no?)

For dramaturgical interest only: he's written some plays, gotten them published and produced, and all that fun stuff. More name dropping: Felix Pire performed Reyes' monologue play, *Men on the Verge of a His-Panic Breakdown*, in both L.A. and Off-Broadway and he went on to be cast in *Twelve Monkeys* with Brad Pitt (ooooh!). Bobby Cannavale starred in *Chilean Holiday* at Actors' Theatre of Louisville and he later starred in *Fast Food Nation* and other films.

Recent plays include *We Lost it at the Movies*, developed at Arkansas Repertory Theater's 2007 Voices at the River Project and at Arizona State University Mainstage; *Mend* performed at the Sands Theater in Deland, Florida in February, 2008; *Farewell to Hollywood*, a rewritten version of an earlier play, debuted at Bloomington Playwrights Theater in September 2006. *The Suspects*, premiered at the Guthrie Theater in Minneapolis in April 2005, and the historical comedy about Thomas Jefferson, *Sunrise at Monticello,* premiered at Playwrights Theater of New Jersey in October 2005. *Men on the Verge* won the Best World Premiere Ovation Award of Los Angeles, and then the New York Outer Critics' Award for Best Solo Performance. It was published by Dramatic Publishing Company, and *Men on the Verge 2* was published by Gestos at the University of California, Irvine. A recent award: Premiere Stages awarded his historical comedy, *Madison,* first prize and produced it in Summer 2008.

Reyes received his Master's Degree in Playwriting from University of California, San Diego. He's currently Associate Professor of Theater and Film at Arizona State University in Tempe and head of the playwriting program. He's a member of the Dramatists Guild. Drop the playwright a message at reyes1@asu.edu.

Introduction

Miss Consuelo started as a short story that I wrote and published in *The Americas Review* (University of Houston) in early 1990 while still a graduate student in the MFA playwriting program at University of California, San Diego. In Los Angeles, I met Joseph Megel, the artistic director of a local theater troupe, Words Across Cultures, which, in addition to producing plays, also did readings of poetry and prose. Joseph directed a reading of the short story with actors, and shortly thereafter said, "there's a play in there." The story of an immigrant woman aspiring to become a romance novelist touched a nerve—romantic, comedic, wistful—with enough people in the audience to inspire me to adapt my own story. Joseph's encouragement also proved invaluable.

Seven years later, Joseph produced and directed the play at Playwrights Theater of New Jersey where he had become artistic director in the meantime, and received enthusiastic reviews including a *New York Times* notice that read, "Mr. Reyes has the deftness to channel his daftness and the flair makes an old gimmick (of the author typing away while characters talk back) newly fun." When I founded *Teatro Bravo*, I decided it was time, in the Spring of 2002, for Joseph to come out to the desert and direct *Miss Consuelo* for Phoenix audiences. No disappointments there. Joseph brought his own deftness at juggling my jocularity with great flair. He produced the laughs, and audiences were blessed with graceful performances, including Aniuska Garcia as the title heroine, and Cecilia Rosales-Torres as the passionate protagonist of the novel, Teresa Bella de las Galbas, who juggles two boy toy lovers while looking stunning in a dizzying array of outfits. DeAnna Robbins gave us her best Beverly Hills matron, and the youthful, amiable Alette Valencia, her niece, Perla. The young talent, Jorge Moreno, went on to get his own TV show in Mexico, and George Cole established himself as our local Lothario while playing Victor.

Consuelo combined two immigrant journeys – my mother's and my own. Consuelo represented my Chilean mother's aspirations while also representing the writer in me. Consuelo---*c'est moi*, as Flaubert might have said. My mother gave birth to the short story when she suggested she could write better *telenovelas* than most of the ones that were being aired on Spanish TV. I dared her to prove it, and she came up with the heroine of an avocado plantation in Spanish California and got stuck. You take it from there, she said, you're the writer. I did, by presenting my version of Consuelo's imagination and letting Teresa get frisky and kinky along the way.

My mother didn't get a chance to see this production of *Miss Consuelo*. In early 2001, she was diagnosed with breast cancer and, in the Spring of 2002, she was in her final months at a hospice in Portland, Oregon. She passed away that summer, but she'd left behind this rather fitting legacy of comedic mayhem.

Guillermo Reyes
Phoenix, AZ
December 2007

Production History

Miss Consuelo was initially developed through a series of readings at Words Across Cultures and the Bilingual Foundation of the Arts in Los Angeles, and the San Jose Repertory Theater in San Jose, California.

Miss Consuelo was originally produced at Playwrights Theater of New Jersey in Madison, New Jersey, in November 1997, directed by Joseph Megel, and produced by John Pietrowski with the following cast:

MISS CONSUELO	Marie Barrientos
TERESA	Laura Spaeth
PERLA	Zabryna Guevara
VICTOR and ENSEMBLE	Manuel Santiago
LEOPOLDO and ENSEMBLE	Isaiah Cazares
BETTY AVISHAM and ENSEMBLE	Elizabeth Corley
PROFESSOR CALDWELL	Joseph D. Giardina
MARCO and ENSEMBLE	Jesse Ontiveros

The Teatro Bravo production of *Miss Consuelo* was staged in April 2002 at Playhouse on the Park in Phoenix, directed by Joseph Megel with the following cast:

MISS CONSUELO	Aniuska Garcia
TERESA	Cecilia Rosales-Torres
PERLA and ENSEMBLE	Alette Valencia
VICTOR and ENSEMBLE	George Cole
LEOPOLDO and ENSEMBLE	Jorge Moreno
BETTY AVISHAM and ENSEMBLE	DeAnna Robbins
PROFESSOR CALDWELL and ENSEMBLE	Marcus Smith
MARCO and ENSEMBLE	James Garcia

For performance rights, contact: Bruce Ostler, Bret Adams, Ltd., via email at, bostler@bretadamsltd.com.

Characters and Suggested Doubling

ACTOR 1: CONSUELO CHAVEZ, Mexican woman in her 40s-50s, comic, full of *joie de vivre*, a bit deluded in her attempt to become a novelist even though she hasn't mastered the English language.

ACTOR 2: TERESA, fantasy protagonist of Consuelo's romance novel.

ACTOR 3: PERLA, Consuelo's niece, INDIAN PRINCESS, VALLEY GIRL, ROOSEVELT WOMAN, MODEL #2, and WAITER

ACTOR 4: MR. CALDWELL, THE NASAL GUY, and RICARDO THE GABRIELINO

ACTOR 5:   BETTY AVISHAM, LEONA THE TROTSKYITE,
           MODEL #1, and VILLAGE SHA-WOMAN
ACTOR 6:   AKBAR, JANE BRACKNELL, MODEL #3, LEOPOLDO,
           PIZZA BOY, and MARCO
ACTOR 7:   VICTOR, 50s, Leopoldo's father and Consuelo's romantic
           flame, AHMED, and JAIME IXTIQUOATL DE LA RAZA

Setting

Los Angeles, California, 1994, shortly after the Northridge/Reseda earthquake.

NOTE: Consuelo is a real woman with an accent. Not a TV stereotype of the accented Latina, but the real thing. If I've provided a few hints about her accent by spelling some of her dialogue such as "foorious pashions," it's not meant to box in an actress and a director into pronouncing it that way. I'm more interested in the real, lively, somewhat eccentric but always grounded, human being that Consuelo is. The accent is not the most important element of her speech, and a hint of it is better than a thick mess of sounds that prevents the actress from creating a true character.

Miss Consuelo
FIRST ACT

(One continuous act, bare sets, constant change of setting suggested through narration, lighting and minimal props.

Late at night in Consuelo's apartment as she types on an ancient typewriter. She's a Mexican woman in her 50s, perhaps stocky, very "proletarian"-looking. She struggles with the typing. She struggles in her mind with the wording of each sentence.

Enter the actor who'll later play LEOPOLDO who becomes NARRATOR of the moment. He opens his script and begins to read)

LEOPOLDO: "Miss Consuelo…a tale by Miss Consuelo as narrated by Miss Consuelo's characters in Miss Consuelo's imagination. Late at night, Consuelo bangs into her 1950s manual typewriter – oblivious of the '90s, oblivious, in fact, of any trace of present day reality. Enter Teresa…"

(Teresa enters, elegantly clad.)

LEOPOLDO: "She's a prototypical heroine of a romance novel."

TERESA: I am Teresa Bella de las Galbas, mistress of the avocado. I was born naked, naked as the willow and just as weepy. I emerged into the universe out of nothingness, like Venus out of his shell. *"His"* shell?

CONSUELO: *(Struggling with English.)* Oh. Like Venus out of her shell – that's it, Venus out of her shell! Caught the mistake, *órale* [= "right on"]!

TERESA: *Órale!*

CONSUELO: Not you. Me – *órale*; you go on.

TERESA: In this novel, I shall narrate to you my countless affairs with royalty, senators, dictators, billionaires and a few pizza delivery boys – pizza delivery boys?!?

CONSUELO: Yes, where is he?

(Leopoldo/Young Pizza Delivery Boy appears. He is, of course, right there already, as played by Leopoldo.)

LEOPOLDO/
PIZZA BOY: Pizza! Pizza!…

(Teresa stands aside looking as Consuelo turns to the boy.)

CONSUELO: *Ay, al fin* [= "at last"]! Almost midnight. I was hungry, *m'ijo* [= "son"].

PIZZA BOY: Say, I am under thirty minutes, ain't I?

CONSUELO: Oh, sure, sure, *m'ijo*, you deserve big tip, too. Here's a penny jar; take what you need.

(She hands him some pennies for the tip.)

PIZZA BOY: Say, could I get fifteen percent on this here tip, heh?

CONSUELO: Oh, just take the entire penny jar. I am now an *artiste*, I have no use for savings.

PIZZA BOY: Say, did you say you were a...?

CONSUELO: They call me Miss Consuelo, *la Novelista*!

PIZZA BOY: Did you write *Like Water for Chocolate, House of the Spirits*, or "Take it to The Limit one more Time" – never mind, dem's are lyrics. Can you do lyrics? Are you versatile enough to do lyrics?

CONSUELO: *(Confused.)* I am just, ah, Miss Consuelo.

PIZZA BOY: I'm asking because I'm not just a pizza boy. I dabble in epic verse myself.

CONSUELO: You are writer, too, *m'ijo*!

PIZZA BOY: I recite – and my dad says I talk too much, and I have trouble finishing anything I start –

CONSUELO: Then let me help you; welcome to Miss Consuelo's Literary Salon.

TERESA: Yeah, right.

(Teresa exits, having stolen the pizza.)

CONSUELO: You are my second guest here –

PIZZA BOY: Who was the first?

CONSUELO: I am, but never mind. What do you write?

PIZZA BOY: I've tried just feeling my way through words, you know, feelings.

CONSUELO: Feelings.

PIZZA BOY: But nah, it don't work, but still, I think it's a great thing to be a person of letters, yeh. I myself hang out at the Onyx Coffee House on Vermont. I watch people doin' poetry readings and get into this metaphorical mode in those 3 a.m. lulls, hey? Are ya with me? Say, you're a foreigner. Where ya from? I'm a Brooklyn Cuban myself –

CONSUELO: *Oh, un cubanito! Qué bien, m'ijo!* [= "Oh, a nice Cuban boy. Lovely"]!

PIZZA BOY: But very Brooklyn – mambo in the subway type.

CONSUELO: I write it down, "mambo in the subway type." I write everything for my writing class; I interview everyone on the bus *y todo*. *Vamos* [= ". . . and everything. Come"]. Speal your guts. This is one of my assignments, due two months ago, an interview with a troubled soul. Help me out, talk.

LEOPOLDO: Oh, okay. I'm Leopoldo. Leopoldo Caceres, make that Cathereth. Very Spanish, you try it. Cathereth, Cathereth, say it with lisp.

CONSUELO: I have trouble with accents.

LEOPOLDO: Even in Spanish?

CONSUELO: No Castilian accents, *por favor*, and no lisps either. Move on.

LEOPOLDO: Get me some beer then and I'll show ya.

CONSUELO: You teenage alcoholic, *m'ijo*? My teacher like his characters

perverse and lost in the world. Tell your troubles to Miss
Consuelo.

LEOPOLDO: No, you tell me. How can I get started, Miss Consuelo?

CONSUELO: What? Started in what?

LEOPOLDO: Give a beginner some advice here. Don't hold back on the big
secrets of the craft now!

CONSUELO: Oh, I wouldn't –

LEOPOLDO: I admire yer spunk, yer sense of effort, what a typewriter, it's
got character. How do I begin, Miss Consuelo?

CONSUELO: Oh, I say just…follow your *pasión*.

LEOPOLDO: Yes. "*Pasión!*" Kinda makes sense, with an accent on the "o"
and everything.

CONSUELO: The word "*pasión*" always had an accent on the "o," *m'ijo*.

LEOPOLDO: But the way you say it, it kinda has a ring to it, it sounds good,
it's the titillation of the muse –

CONSUELO: I don't teetillate, I don't do things like that.

LEOPOLDO: So that's all I gotta do, follow my "*pasión*"?

CONSUELO: Alright, don't get carried away now.

LEOPOLDO: Well, I'm gonna go home and start something…I am honored to
meet my first true woman of letters.

*(He kisses her hand. Teresa is back by now, has seen this, and is especially moved
by this part.)*

CONSUELO: My goodness.

LEOPOLDO: I will write my own Cuban-American epic, "From Havana to
Topanga!"

CONSUELO: An epic! You?

LEOPOLDO: You meet the finest people out here in the Hollywood Pit
Gardens.

*(They wave goodbye. Pizza Boy exits, changes to Leopoldo who continues as
Narrator.)*

LEOPOLDO/
NARRATOR: Teresa returns holding a tray of avocados, maybe mangos
depending on the season.

TERESA: Five more minutes, I would have put the boy to work on the
plantation, helping me breed future generations of *Californios*.

CONSUELO: No, the world is full of temptations and it is my duty as Miss
Consuelo to resist!

TERESA: Admit it, he was cute! *¿Si no, para qué escribes romance, a ver,
dime* [= "if not, why do you write romance, tell me"]?

CONSUELO: I am the only romance writer in the world devoted to hot,
passionate, but clean romance.

TERESA: *Que* clean *ni que nada* [= "Don't give me this clean business"]!
Vamos, write me a dirty passion scene now!

CONSUELO: No, I have decided now that you, *la protagonista*, are a virgin.

TERESA: What? Don't I get to fornicate at all in this?

CONSUELO: No, no fornicate for you. But good quote, *malvada* [= "evil
one"]! Professor Caldwelk will love that one. Miss Consuelo *al
ataque! (Types.)* "Don't I get to *fornicar…?*"
*(Transition to Caldwell's office at the city college where he's finishing reading parts
of Consuelo's epic.)*

LEOPOLDO: In Caldwell's office. City College.

CALDWELL: "…Don't I get to fornicar…" *(With American accent.) Forni-
carr?*

CONSUELO: Oh, I fix typos later. You read.

CALDWELL: I'm done, I think. Is this it?

CONSUELO: So then you give me that honest opinion you always like to give
in class to make students cry, but don't be too honest with me,
OK? Be gentle, *Calvo.*

CALDWELL: "Romance of the Guacamoles" – I like the title.

CONSUELO: *(All flattered.) Ay…oooy…sí pues.* [= "oh…ah…yes, well"]. Tell
me more.

CALDWELL: The truth is, Consuelo…

CONSUELO: You can call me Miss Consuelo, Professor *Calvo.*

CALDWELL: That's Caldwell.

CONSUELO: And that's Miss Consuelo.

CALDWELL: Consuelo Chavez is a perfectly fine name for a writer. Why
would you want to be known as Miss Consuelo of all things?

CONSUELO: Because Miss Consuelo is my thing, you know, my own
trademock, as they say. I want the reader in Mad-moy-selle or
Cosmo-po-lee-tan to look at the contents in the magg-zeene and
say, "Oh, yes, another story by *la legendaria,* Miss Consuelo."
You heard of *Querida* Abby, right?

CALDWELL: Who?

CONSUELO: Abby.

CALDWELL: Oh, "Dear Abby."

CONSUELO: That's not her real name, *Querida* Abby, see? So I come up
with Miss Consuelo for my trademock. Now let's talk about my
story, Mr. Calvo. Let's not meenz words either.

CALDWELL: To tell you the truth, I don't think it's your forte.

CONSUELO: What? You say roa-manz is not my forte, Mr. Call-back? Why
roa-manz is my life! All those fancee dresses the heroine wear
on page 3 1/2? Why, I've wore them!

CALDWELL: You have?

CONSUELO: Oh, yes. We go way back.

*(The Models invade the stage, Leopoldo becoming one of them. Teresa joins the
fashion parade, not to be outdone.)*

MODEL #1: All those years ironing dresses for top Hollywood actresses.

MODEL #2: All those years admiring top fashions from a distance –

MODEL #3: Consuelo's hands all over the silk –

MODEL #1: The mink.

MODEL #2:	The leather.
MODEL #1:	Paris on the *Quatorze Juillet*.
MODEL #2:	Tokyo Industrial Wear.
MODEL #3:	Santa Monica S&M.
MODEL #1:	All of them inspiring Miss Consuelo –
MODEL #2:	To flights of fancy!
MODEL #3:	And romantic literature!
CONSUELO:	Actually…I inherit the dresses from my greatgrandfather who buy them for his mistress, the Empress Carlota.
MODELS and TERESA:	Yeah, right!

(Models disband, looking haughty, as if walking off a fashion parade. Leopoldo exits with them.)

CALDWELL:	Look…Wardrobe is irrelevant.
CONSUELO:	No clothes, no fantasy, I say.
CALDWELL:	I believe we're all naked corpses inhabiting a hollow shadowy existence.
CONSUELO:	Wow!
CALDWELL:	Write it down! The storyteller's task is to endow his readership with horrid tales of middle-class perversion. We're all perpretators of existential genocide.
CONSUELO:	Really? *(She writes this down.)*
CALDWELL:	Look, maybe you have worn these ruffles, I believe you, and maybe romance is your life, as you say –
CONSUELO:	Oh, yes!
CALDWELL:	But still you haven't convinced me, Consuelo, that the story is close to you at all.
CONSUELO:	But I tell you –
CALDWELL:	I mean close to the essence of your minimal existence, of your angst-ridden soul, of your agonizing sense of immigrant selflessness.
CONSUELO:	Oh? I'm supposed to feel all that?
CALDWELL:	Of course! You spend too much time on all these lovers and their struggles to win Teresa's love, but not enough on their real feelings as men and women living in the post-nuclear world of Kafkaesque alienation.
CONSUELO:	What? Slowly.
CALDWELL:	What I'm really trying to say is stick to what you know! An old dictum, I'm not even sure if I believe it, but it applies to you students, if not to me – write it down!
CONSUELO:	Look, maybe I don't want to know all that kaka-esque thing!
CALDWELL:	Well, surely you know about your family in Mexico, and the long pre-Columbian history of that nation, the colonization, the reign of Maximilian, the Treaty of Guadalupe, the tragedy of annexation, the indignities of having to cross a border on your bare feet, illegally, I hope.

CONSUELO: I come to Los Angeles legally, Mr. Calvo! I am U.S. citizen
            now. Look!

(She pulls out citizenship papers, all dog-eared and looking like old dollar bills.)

CALDWELL: Congratulations then, now you're an official part of the
            American underclass!
CONSUELO: *(Skeptically.) Gracias!*
CALDWELL: In which case, we need to know about the inequities of your
            labor, your lack of health insurance!
CONSUELO: Oh, who want to know about all that, Mr. Call-wack? My
            heroine Teresa Bella de las Galbas is jest, how do you say, a hot
            potato, a sexee chick, and my readers want to know all about her
            pashion, her foo-rious pashions, she's all alone in that avocado
            plantation, *la pobrecita!* – and my reader want to know what
            happen to her, and so do I, Mr. Camm-wack! Why can't you
            help me write her story, not mine!
CALDWELL: Okay, fine!
CONSUELO: Fine!
CALDWELL: How long have you been studying English, Consuelo?
CONSUELO: Never mind Englitch, I teach myself the language of romance.
CALDWELL: I thought so. In that case, I recommend a good solid course in
            Basic English Grammar –
CONSUELO: Basic?!?
CALDWELL: Yes, basic! This open enrollment business does you a disservice;
            you're not really prepared to be in city college, not that many of
            our American students are either, but anyway…*(He hands her
            back the manuscript.)* I made some corrections – let me rephrase
            that, I made many corrections; I want you to go back home and
            retype the entire thing, for starters, then we'll worry about the
            furious passions.

(Consuelo picks up manuscript and walks away from Caldwell.)

CONSUELO: *(To herself.) Virgencita!* He bleed all over my *novela.*

(Consuelo reads the neverending comments.)

CALDWELL: *(As if reading his own comments.)* Unconvincing introduction…
            too many jewels around the heroine's neck…not enough
            "oomph" here…watch the run-on sentences, this part's
            unreadable altogether…what's the point of these kisses in
            this scene; how do they contribute to the Kafkaesque alienation
            of the modern world? I want it retyped in neat orderly fashion
            and I also want you to buy a new ribbon for your typewriter.
CONSUELO: A new ribbon for my 1956 typewriter?
CALDWELL: Yes. And this is it, Consuelo. Your last chance.
CONSUELO: Last chance, Mr. Call-dung?
CALDWELL: I warned you when you failed to turn in the interview –
CONSUELO: Oh, that's because I interview so many people –

CALDWELL: I only asked for one interview, to concentrate on one at a time, then you're two months late with the assignment, and you end up turning in a novel –

CONSUELO: Because this is creative writing class, ¿qué no?

CALDWELL: You're not ready to write an entire novel!

CONSUELO: I decide that!

CALDWELL: Fine, then finish your novel! Prove me wrong, and then you can stay in my class. Otherwise, you fail the class and you can't return.

CONSUELO: I never fail –

CALDWELL: No, because you never finish anything. Do you want to stay in my class or not?

CONSUELO: Well…yes.

CALDWELL: Fine, then you have three weeks to do your rewrites – which is plenty of time for a 20-page novel, which reads more like a film outline if you ask me –

CONSUELO: Really? Film?

CALDWELL: Whatever it is, I want it finished!

CONSUELO: Ok, Mr. Calm-well, I do as you say, but I'm sure the moment I feex the grammar, you'll fawl for Teresa. She's hot and sexee, and if you still don't fawl for her, what can I say? Your lawss. I accept your challenge, Camwack!

(Other Student/Valley Girl enters, a young woman from Simi Valley, all impatient and all eager to talk away, bubbly, and a non-stop gabber.)

VALLEY GIRL: Excuse me, I've been waiting all this time, and I do have an appointment, so I'm not just barging in – I've been dying to talk to you, Mr. Caldwell because –

CALDWELL: Yes, I've been dying to talk to you, too!

CONSUELO: Mr. Cald –

CALDWELL: Yeah, good luck, three weeks and don't forget the new ribbon. *(To other student as Consuelo on the doorway listens in on the conversation.)* Young lady, I've read your story collection –

VALLEY GIRL: *(Not letting him respond.)* And? And? And? Tell it to me straight because I really respect the alienated style of your teaching technique which has really connected me to the darkness of my pitiful existence –

CALDWELL: Please! Please! Young woman, your stories are so… catastrophic!

VALLEY GIRL: Really? What did you think of my story, "The Commuter Who Couldn't Shoot Straight"?

CALDWELL: Disgusting and perverse, utterly fatalistic.

VALLEY GIRL: I didn't think I had it in me to be so disgusting and perverse, but you really know how to bring that out in a student –

CALDWELL: How about some wine, dear? Would a '67 Merlot be alright? Blah, blah, blah…

(Consuelo moves to "out of office" playing area as Caldwell's and Student's voices fall off into a meaningless babble.)

CONSUELO: *(Looking in imaginary mirror.)* No one understand the language of romance.

(Staring at herself in a mirror, Teresa becomes her reflection.)

TERESA: Ah, if only you could fit into this body.
CONSUELO: But I do…I am you.
TERESA: Let's not compare. I don't age; I don't gain weight; I can express myself in various languages and accents. You are minimal.
CONSUELO: Oh, yeah? And I could tear you apart sheet by sheet.
TERESA: Look here…I say it's time for Miss Consuelo to go home, and tackle that only great ambition of hers: me.
CONSUELO: Yes, the romance continues!
TERESA: But, that evening, a man was waiting by the door of her apartment at the Hollywood Pit Gardens.

(She arrives at her doorstep carrying bags from a shopping spree. Standing there is Victor, a middle-aged Cuban man. She becomes flirtatious in her first line, and stretches her hand out to be kissed in very aristocratic fashion.)

CONSUELO: *¿Desea, señor* [= "What would you like, sir"]?
VICTOR: Are you Madame Consuelo?
CONSUELO: That is Miss Consuelo!
VICTOR: *¡Ah, sí, la Miss Consuelo!* I need to es-speak to you about a very serious matter. *¡Es muy, pero muy serio, señora* [= "It's very, very serious, ma'm"]!
CONSUELO: Look, my IRS extension form is in the mail, okay?
VICTOR: This is not about taxes, Miss Consuelo, it's about literature.
CONSUELO: What about literature, *señor?*
VICTOR: You are that famous writer, *¿qué no? – ¡no lo niegue! ¡no puede negarlo!* [= "aren't you? – don't deny it; you can't deny it"]! No, no, no!
CONSUELO: Ah, yes, I suppose I am.
VICTOR: Well, Miss Consuelo, I am concerned about the influence you've had on my son.
CONSUELO: Your son? Oh…yes, the –
VICTOR: Yes, the pizza pizza boy. I'm Victor Caceres, that's Cathereth! You say it.
CONSUELO: *Por favor,* I'd rather not. Please say what you have to say. *La Miss Consuelo* has many commitments.
VICTOR: I've never seen my son this way. That boy has been staying up all night typing this horrible free verse, and it's because of you, Miss Consuelo. You are an influence on my son.
CONSUELO: And that is a good thing, I hope.
VICTOR: I was suspicious; I came to see if there was more than that –
CONSUELO: More than what?

VICTOR: Whether my son had been seduced by some disreputable temptress. He said you have a salon where you receive gentlemen callers.

CONSUELO: Eeeeh! My Literary Salon is clean, virtuous, and *católico, señor*.

VICTOR: But now I see that you're only a mother figure.

CONSUELO: Well, what's wrong with that?

VICTOR: My Rosario passed away two years ago.

CONSUELO: *Pobrecita* [= "poor thing"]!

VICTOR: *Que Dios la bendiga* [= "God bless her"]. He needs a mother, which means I need a wife, but that's neither here nor there. The real reason I'm here is that I understand too well what he's going through –

CONSUELO: Do you?

VICTOR: The fact is he inherited his literary pretenses from someone –

CONSUELO: Such as –

VICTOR: Such as myself, Miss Consuelo! In my youth, I could imitate Lorca and Jose Marti like the rest of them. I recited my Havana passion poetry with a true flair like no other imitator. I'm in home repairs now. California is a good market thanks to the wonders of nature. We are the Cathereth family; we survived 700 years of Moorish oppression and 40 years of Communism; we now follow the FEMA money. But now something else has been stirring in my heart –

CONSUELO: Really? Tell me about your heart, *señor*.

VICTOR: And the truth is I can only write in Spanish, and I tried to enroll in a class at UCLA Extension taught in Spanish, but they canceled the course – not enough enrollment they said; but then there's you, a beacon of hope.

CONSUELO: Really?

VICTOR: You're my only *esperanza* [= "hope"], Miss Consuelo.

CONSUELO: Am I? In what sense? I barely know you – I demand dinner first, Starbuck's coffee at least.

VICTOR: I want you to…to tutor me, Miss Consuelo.

(She looks disappointed; she was expecting something more sensual, romantic.)

CONSUELO: I don't tutor. ¿*Qué se cree*? I don't deal with beginners –

VICTOR: Fifteen dollars an hour – ?

CONSUELO: *Señor* Cathereth*, por favor* –

VICTOR: That's not good enough for someone of your caliber, make that twenty dollars an hour –

CONSUELO: But I can't –

VICTOR: Oh, you can't take the time out to help a beginner now that you've become a hot-shot writer here at the Hollywood Pit Gardens.

CONSUELO: I put a stop to this –

VICTOR: Twenty-five dollars!

CONSUELO: I –

VICTOR: You're a tough bargain – !
CONSUELO: I don't bargain my talents –
VICTOR: Thirty dollars, Miss Consuelo, that's as high as –
CONSUELO: Forty!
VICTOR: Thirty-eight fifty –
CONSUELO: Done!
VICTOR: Good, good, Miss Consuelo! If you can inspire my son to stop
             doing pizza pizza delivery – when God knows I his own father
             could employ him – then you're an inspiration to us all. So
             here...

(He hands her a 300-page manuscript as if tossing a football.)

CONSUELO: I thought you were a beginner.
VICTOR: I give you two weeks. I want a written evaluation and kind, but
             helpful, comments. Start with the positive, then build to the
             negative.
CONSUELO: Two weeks, I have an important assign –
VICTOR: Oh, yes, your publisher is probably waiting for you to deliver
             your latest fun-filled epic.
CONSUELO: Sure, something very much like that.
VICTOR: Mine is called *Nostalgias*, very nostalgic.
CONSUELO: But two weeks –
VICTOR: Sure, two weeks. Let's say we meet for dinner then. My treat, of
             course, 8 p.m., the Mambo Palace of Burbank, next to Disney.
CONSUELO: Really? The Mambo Palace?
VICTOR: Will that be alright for *la prestigiosa* Miss Consuelo?
CONSUELO: It will do for now. I will have to find the right outfit.
VICTOR: A woman like you, I'm sure, will make any old rag look
             luscious!
CONSUELO: Really?
VICTOR: Like what you've got on now. It'll be a night to remember,
             Señorita Consuelo!

(He kisses her hand. She's left mesmerized. He exits.)

TERESA: Romance, she wrote.
CONSUELO: It's only a business transaction.
TERESA: Admit it, Miss Consuelo has met a man of great potential for the
             first time in years.
CONSUELO: I can't think about that, I have a deadline. Let's see, I have
             thirty-five minutes before going to the airport to pick up my
             niece; I can do some polishing – *(She crosses to typewriter.)*
             Sí, y ahora...(She sits at typewriter)
             Time for "Romance of the Guacamoles"!
TERESA: "The mansion is built, the carpenters and the adobe bricklayers
             are gone...Why am I so alone?"
CONSUELO: "...she has been alone for the past six weeks – no months – "
             No, make that "six years. *La pobrecita* has been alone for six

years, she ages and could turn any day now into a *solterona* – "
Ooops, no Spanish. Oh, how you say *"solterona"*? Dictionary,
where are you?

TERESA: A spinster!

CONSUELO: Spinstress! That's it. "So there she sits –

TERESA: …in my solitude which has lasted six whole years. By the
candle light, every night I look out into the landscape of the Old
pre-Anglo California and await for the ship that will wreck and
bring in some horny sailors…"

CONSUELO: *Oye* [= "Hey"], you watch your language, okay?

TERESA: Don't stop me; I'm on a roll!…But, hark, someone knocks at
my window and it's past midnight. Why, it's, it's…

(Enter Ahmed with torn shirt)

CONSUELO: It's Ahmed! The field hand imported from Cairo. He pulls the
window open and slips into the room –

TERESA: In one facile movement! *(Ahmed growls.)* His dark Arabic chest
is exposed and the blaze in the chimney reflects on his firm
nipples. He has torn his shirt crossing the barbed wire fence that
protects Teresa from the animals. He's bleeding a little. I like
that!

AHMED: During the day, Miss, I feed your pigs. At night, let me feed
your passion!

CONSUELO: He pulls her up into his arms, sweeps her off her feet, he throws
her on the bed and presses his lips into her….into her…

TERESA: Into her what?

AHMED: Don't be shy now.

TERESA: Say it! He presses his lips into her…

CONSUELO: No! Wait…they stop; someone's in the room; they turn and see
standing right in front of them…it's…

*(Akbar played by the same actor who plays PIZZA DELIVERY BOY enters also
wearing a torn shirt and his Pizza Delivery Boy Hat.)*

TERESA: It's the pizza delivery boy!

CONSUELO: No, it's Ahmed's twin brother, Akbar!

(He discards the hat.)

AKBAR: No, I am the real Ahmed! That's my twin brother faking my
lovemaking!

AHMED: Such things cannot be faked, brother. No, I am the real Ahmed!
Can't you tell, woman, by the deftness of my maneuvering?

AKBAR: I am Ahmed! Don't you recognize my firm nipples?

AHMED: You call those nipples! These are nip –

TERESA: Excuse me, but there's only one way to find out who the real
Ahmed is.

CONSUELO: And that night, she sampled the love of the two brothers…but
only with dry kisses –

TERESA:	Dry kisses?
AKBAR:	Damn!
AHMED:	You heard her, brother. This is a virtuous novel available at your local supermarket or any place where fine literature is sold.
AKBAR:	I want to locate her g-spots –
CONSUELO:	No! "That night, she discovered the truth – and the truth was that – "
TERESA:	If two avocados ripen just as well, why not throw them both into the salad?
AKBAR:	You Spanish girls learn fast.
TERESA:	No, it's ancient Toltec wisdom.
AHMED:	*(To Akbar.)* Satisfied now?
AKBAR:	Whatever!

(Perla enters.)

AKBAR, AHMED, TERESA and PERLA:	– *Tía Consuelo! Tía Consuelo!*

(Confused, Akbar and Ahmed and Teresa exit.)

PERLA:	Aunt Consuelo!?
CONSUELO:	What? *¿Qué pasa?* Oh, my God! I must have fallen asleep – no, I was in a trance –
PERLA:	I had to take a taxi, that's all the money I had – is this Hollywood? It don't look like Hollywood!
CONSUELO:	Those are cracks from the last quake, *m'ija*…Let me help you!
PERLA:	That's okay. I got a chance to make some calls from the airport.
CONSUELO:	Calls?
PERLA:	Connections, of course.
CONSUELO:	You already have connections?
PERLA:	No need to waste time – I'm here to conquer! *(Disappointed.)* Oh, look, I guess this place will do for now. I have to make another call.
CONSUELO:	Honey, you just got to the United States. How many people do you know?
PERLA:	Look, Aunt Consuelo, I stay out of your life, you stay out of mine.
CONSUELO:	*Oye, a la tía no se le habla así* [= "Don't talk to your aunt that way"]!
PERLA:	I mean, of course, very respectfully stay out of my life –
CONSUELO:	Who are you calling?
PERLA:	Look –
CONSUELO:	Tell me.
PERLA:	I have some pen pals.
CONSUELO:	Pen pals? Writers? I'm a writer.
PERLA:	You don't understand. My favorite is Marco, here's his picture.

	He calls himself a Mexican-American from West Valley High. And he's ready for marriage.
CONSUELO:	Marriage? Honey, you come to study.
PERLA:	I'll study, but he's a U.S. citizen and my student visa will run out and I want to marry a citizen before it's too late. I'll get my papers, and then, of course, divorce him.
CONSUELO:	You can't do that.
PERLA:	It's not romantic, you mean? I'm not romantic; I want to be a palm reader. No nonsense palm reader. Have my own salon.
CONSUELO:	A salon? Did you say – ?
PERLA:	I inherited Aunt Chuchi's mystical powers.
CONSUELO:	*¡Que* mystical powers *ni que nada!* I bought you a sweet sixteen dress.
PERLA:	Well, I'm 17; I'm beyond such nonsense. Let me see your hand –
CONSUELO:	What? I don't want a palm reading –
PERLA:	Oh, a very fractured romantic line –
CONSUELO:	None of your business.
PERLA:	– ooh, avocado trees, what do they mean? A forest full of them…and, oh, here's the Treaty of Guadalupe Hidalgo – very historic lines – the San Andreas fault runs through your veins – very Californian – and a Saint Sebastian hole – very ominous! – spit on it now!
CONSUELO:	No. Miss Consuelo does not spit! What about Saint Sebastian?
PERLA:	He's taken the place of Saint Valentine. You must do something, Aunt Consuelo! I won't live with a roommate who bears the Saint Sebastian mark.
CONSUELO:	I'm not your roommate, *señorita*, I'm your host.
PERLA:	And a very nice one, too. I'll call Marco now. He's bought me a ring.
CONSUELO:	A ring? Does your mother know?
PERLA:	*¡Tía Consuelo!* You don't tell my mother about Marco; I don't tell her you don't live in prosperous American lifestyle.
CONSUELO:	What? I like my apartment.
PERLA:	You would.
CONSUELO:	Well, the carpets are being cleaned; maid's on vacation.
PERLA:	*(Dials.)* I have big plans though, I'll be the Heidi Fleiss of palmistry. Hello…Marco? Your Perla has arrived! *(She takes the phone inside.)*
CONSUELO:	Well…*(Consuelo's work continues.)* "And they carry her off by the moonlight…and she says…"
TERESA:	"I have finally found the gardeners who'll nourish both my passion and my avocados."
CONSUELO:	"End of Chapter 2."

(Lights down as she looks at her palm again looking for something ominous.)
(Perla narrates following –)

PERLA: Scene: At Betty Avisham's house in Bel Air. Mrs. Avisham lives in a grand style that inspires envy and emulation – maybe even theft! Of course, she cries a whole lot.

(Transition to Betty Avisham's house where Betty is holding a handkerchief as she cries slowly. Consuelo walks in, giving her a glass of water. Betty is a wealthy woman in her 40s/50s, actress.)

BETTY: Why? Why? Why?

CONSUELO: It's okay, it will be okay, there, there, there.

BETTY: I mean it's one thing for a lover or a husband to abandon you. You shed a few tears, you move on to the next, but when your servants leave you, that's real trauma! What have I done wrong? I don't know why you would even consider leaving me –

CONSUELO: I'm no servant no more.

BETTY: What? You mean, existentially you have outgrown this position, which is very understandable. You'll be my very well-paid companion who just happens to do windows.

CONSUELO: No, Mrs. Avisham, after twenty years in the U.S., I want to move on. I'm no immigrant no more, I'm a U.S. citizen by now, and citizens don't do windows.

BETTY: Who puts such radical bleeding-heart ideas into your head?

CONSUELO: Here is my citizenship certificate. I am no longer menial labor –

BETTY: Oh, you're moving up in the world.

CONSUELO: Yes, I'm unemployed.

BETTY: Progress indeed. But–

CONSUELO: I have enough savings to devote maybe six months to…to myself –

BETTY: But what will you do with all that spare time? Aren't you frightened of the boredom that could ensue?

CONSUELO: Oh, I have many plans.

BETTY: Tell me! Confide in me!

CONSUELO: After twenty years in the U.S. –

BETTY: Most people would buy a condo or something.

CONSUELO: That wood be nice.

BETTY: I've always worried about your lack of property values.

CONSUELO: Me, too. But after twenty years, I gone back to school.

BETTY: School?

CONSUELO: Community college!

BETTY: How nice. What type of husband are you trying to find?

CONSUELO: Miss Avisham, I am not in school to find no husband!

BETTY: What? Surely you're not…

CONSUELO: I am there to learn.

BETTY: As in learn learn?

CONSUELO: I better not talk about it more; I go get my things.

BETTY: Consuelo!

CONSUELO: Sorry, Miss Avichump.

BETTY: I wish I understood. *(Consuelo exits.)* If only I'd been born a farm worker's daughter!

(Alone, Betty notices Consuelo's school bag, something is sticking out of it. It looks like a script. Her curiosity gets the better of her.)

BETTY: "Romance of the Guacamoles" by Miss Consuelo?

(Enter Teresa, now splendidly attired in a new nightgown.)

BETTY: "She wore a radiant dress for the brothers' duel. It reflected into the air like a mirrored ball at a prom dance…" I think I own something like that. Anyway, "Akbar pulled out the knife…"

AKBAR: Silence, brother, she is my woman, and, by Allah, I will perish for her like a man must hunt for his prey.

AHMED: Will you shed the blood of a brother when she has agreed to share her love in equally rationed pieces?

TERESA: Yes, I'll have you both! Loving is sharing!

AKBAR: I am sorry! But I am a man of honor. I will not share my woman with anyone, not even with my beloved brother. So, if we are enemies, draw your sword, brother! This woman is worth our fraternal blood shedding through expensive California real estate.

AHMED: Put her down, brother. She is not your property. She is your employer. Put her down!

CONSUELO: *(Having come in by now.)* I said put that down, Miss Avichump!

BETTY: Oh, oh, I was so…enthralled. I was in a world of magic and passion like they don't write anymore.

CONSUELO: Really? You like it?

BETTY: It's so grandiose and so, so, so –

CONSUELO: Clean?

BETTY: Come to think of it, yes. It leaves everything to the imagination; it stirs the mind like nothing I've read recently – and the spelling is so creative. What is this, Consuelo?

CONSUELO: I don't talk about it; you just give it here!

BETTY: So, this is why you're going to school.

CONSUELO: I told you, I don't want to talk –

BETTY: I love those two brothers. Two of them. Twins, too! I like that. You've been keeping your talents from me. I want more of this romance; I want to feel those two brothers inside me!

CONSUELO: I have to go now.

BETTY: Talk to me. I am not just your ex-employer, but one of your wealthiest friends.

CONSUELO: No, I mean it, I really don't have time. I have enough savings for six months only.

BETTY: That's at least two million in savings.

CONSUELO: No, more like six thousand.

BETTY: My God, that's my daily allowance! You can't live on that; it can't be done.

CONSUELO: In six months, I must become Miss Consuelo or starve.

BETTY: Six months? To become a writer?

CONSUELO: Now you think I'm crazy.

BETTY: Not at all, dear…but, Consuelo, I have an idea.

CONSUELO: No, not one of your ideas, please. I better go.

BETTY: You must join the Beverly Hills Minority Workshop!

CONSUELO: The what?

BETTY: I meant the Beverly Hills Minority Writer's Workshop. It is headed by my only liberal friend, Jane Simone Bracknell, but I'm afraid the workshop is constantly in recess.

CONSUELO: Why?

BETTY: Because there are no minorities in Beverly Hills. They usually have to be imported from the outlying communities. Why, I must get in contact with Jane right now and tell her all about you, dear.

CONSUELO: No, please –

BETTY: Oh, don't be silly, it's a wonderful workshop, an attempt to attract fresh new voices into our sagging cultural landscape.

CONSUELO: Sagging? That's a new word.

(Consuelo looks it up in her little Spanish/English dictionary. Betty has dialed and is now holding a digital phone up to her mouth.)

BETTY: Jane? Of course it's me – no, you don't owe me anything, darling. Relax. Now listen, I think I got you some new blood for your workshop. Yeah, her name is Consuelo. She's Mexican, female and underprivileged. Exactly what you need for the arts grant to get approved. She's writing a novel, I believe – "Romancing the Guacamoles" –

CONSUELO: "Romance of…"

BETTY: I'm sorry, make that "Romance of the Guacamoles." I don't think it's a satire, Jane. So you'll set up the meeting, please?… Of course, I'll contribute to your husband's reelection campaign; just tell him to shut up about the environment, because I'm still drilling the backyard for oil, all right?…Jane, this means so much to me; she's not just my ex-maid, but one of my very best friends. Yes, next week! *(Hangs up.)* It's set.

CONSUELO: What is set?

BETTY: You are now a member of the Beverly Hills Minority Writer's Workshop.

CONSUELO: But you really think I'm ready to –?

BETTY: With those two brothers – oooh, I think you are ready to play ball! Next thing, you'll be accepting an award for best original screenplay.

CONSUELO: Screenplay? Did you say screenplay?

BETTY: Imagine getting paid for writing dialogue without having to complete full sentences.

CONSUELO: That's it. I do a screenplay adaptation of my own novel.

BETTY: Of course, screenplays are cranked out in a week in this town.

	I've acted in my share of them.
CONSUELO:	It must be a ceench!
BETTY:	The simplest thing on earth!
CONSUELO:	Nothing like it!
BETTY:	As long as it moves, as long as it has action and –
CONSUELO and BETTY:	Essential moments of grand passion.
CONSUELO:	Yes, a screenplay. Teresa Bella de las Galbas will at last find a public that can appreciate her…¡Pasión!
BETTY:	Bravo! Bravo! I say, let Miss Consuelo return to her natural habitat – Scene: Back to Consuelo's apartment. The saga continues!

(Betty leads her back to the playing space behind the typewriter, and stays there to contribute to Voices. Transition to Consuelo is back to her typewriter in her apartment. She begins to type with much excitement, but all these Voices begin to haunt her – all other cast members appear, circling around her.)

CALDWELL:	It's due in two weeks –
VALLEY GIRL:	It's not grim enough!
VICTOR:	*(As Consuelo stares at the 300-page manuscript.)* I want my novel read and evaluated!
LEOPOLDO:	But she's my inspiration, *Papi.*
VICTOR:	She's my tutor now!
TERESA:	Romance! Romance!
AKBAR:	Don't be shy now.
BETTY:	I'm drilling for oil!
TERESA:	More, we demand more!
ALL VOICES:	More more more!
CONSUELO:	*Yaaaaa* [= "Enough"]!

(Perla enters, sees Consuelo frozen at typewriter.)

| PERLA: | *Tía Consuelo…* |

(Consuelo turns, sees Perla looking all pretty, wearing the dress she bought her.)

CONSUELO:	You look so…¡inocente!
PERLA:	Marco's graduating from Valley High.
CONSUELO:	Oh, really?
PERLA:	He's working part-time at his parent's Happy Greetings Card Store at the mall.
CONSUELO:	They have a store, so what?
PERLA:	But you're a woman full of dreams, aren't you?
CONSUELO:	Yes, I am. But sometimes, I wonder – there is only one member in my Literary Salon. There is only one chair. It's just me and my dreams, Perla.
PERLA:	Look, okay, Marco is the best I can do right now. He's got pimples and drinks milkshakes instead of cognac, but at least he's in the glee club, so don't judge me!

CONSUELO: I'm not!

PERLA: When am I gonna make it, Aunt Consuelo? When am I gonna make it big in America?

CONSUELO: *(Sarcastically.)* Maybe by the end of the month?

PERLA: Oh, okay! *Tía Consuelo!* You are an inspiration! *¡Una gran inspiración!* I'm glad I'll be staying with you forever!

CONSUELO: Forever?

PERLA: I'm never going back thanks to you!

CONSUELO: What? *¿Qué dices* [= "What are you talking about"]?

PERLA: I'm gonna have a great time, a great time in America! So I'm not going back to Mexico.

CONSUELO: No, don't say that – come back here, where you going?

PERLA: I'm gonna have a great time in America…in America…in America…in America…

(Perla drifts away in her pretty dress like Maria in "West Side Story" echoing her words, "in America, in America, in America." She spins around like Maria in the movie, but, outside, we hear a big THUD. Then we see some trash can lids come rolling in.)

CONSUELO: You okay?

PERLA'S
VOICE: I'm okay!

(Consuelo is left looking exhausted in front of her typewriter. The best she can do is furiously attack her typewriter as she hears Caldwell's voice.)

CALDWELL: Remember: Two weeks or you're out!

CONSUELO: *(Very needily.)* Screenplay! Go!

TERESA: That does it, twins – No more fighting between brothers!
            – It's obvious our love has grown too crowded! Ricardo the Gabrielino Indian awaits me by the cliff.

AHMED: An Indian?

TERESA: You've forgotten that you are mere servants.

AKBAR: Servants!

TERESA: I demand the magic we once had.

CONSUELO: Yes, magic!

TERESA: So that's why I'm leaving to do a study of indigenous mating rituals. I'm sorry, twins. I'm going to lead my life without you. That much is clear!

(Teresa exits, Akbar and Ahmed look heartbroken as they run out crying.)

CONSUELO: So let's see… *(She goes back to typing.)* "She meets Ricardo the Gabrielino Indian by the cliff." *(She sees Caldwell again in her imagination.)* You, you're the Gabrielino Indian. Get in there. Anyway, "He takes her to the village. He makes her walk ten miles to their village on her heels."

TERESA: Stop, please stop.

RICARDO: We're not there yet, *señorita.*

TERESA:	I say it is time to stop and listen to the mating call of the owl.
RICARDO:	Is that all you Spaniards think about? I mean, wait for the fertility rituals for god's sake.
TERESA:	What? I refuse to worship false gods. I have come to this land to tame the wilderness in the name of the Church and of my Queen, *Juana la Loca.*
RICARDO:	We don't follow orders from Spain. Out here you are a guest of the Gabrielinos. You are my guest, Teresa, you are my woman.
TERESA:	Then for once treat me as your woman, warrior chief. Take me into your nest.
RICARDO:	I'm trying to…but I think our screenwriter wants to censor this scene…look at her!
TERESA:	What? I'm turning 40 and I'm still a virgin?
RICARDO:	Ignore her!
CONSUELO:	No! "Suddenly they see in the horizon…"
RICARDO	It's the chaparral, it's burning out of control!
TERESA:	Oh, no! It will destroy the village.
RICARDO:	It's those Santa Ana winds – I bet you Spaniards brought them with you.
TERESA:	Sure, we Spaniards get blamed for everything! You're so P.C.
RICARDO:	And you're so Eurocentric. Oh, no, the fire is all around us!
TERESA:	Who will rescue us? *(Consuelo looks uncertain.)* I said, who will rescue us?
RICARDO:	How about if we just do a little mambo?
TERESA and CONSUELO:	What?

(Consuelo looks at the watch.)

CONSUELO:	I'm late for the Mambo Palace!

(Music plays. Teresa and Ricardo turn into dancers during this transition to the festive atmosphere of the Mambo Palace. Victor is sitting by himself, waiting for Consuelo. The Waiter or Waitress comes in, a tough-talkin' guy or tough-talkin' dame.)

WAITER:	Looks like you waitin' for somebody, mistah.
VICTOR:	For a very special lady. Have there been any messages?
WAITER:	Yeah. The lard delivery's late, but I don't see why that's any-a your business.
VICTOR:	I mean, from *La Prestigiosa Miss Consuelo.*
WAITER:	Consuelo? That dumpy immigrant who writes chick flicks?
VICTOR:	You know her?
WAITER:	We had her back in the kitchen; she spent most of her time jotting down in her journal. We want our immigrants free of American dreams, the dishes need to get washed, you know.
VICTOR:	You mean you had the audacity to fire her?
WAITER:	She walked out; I hear she went into the maid business.
VICTOR:	Now she's a full-time writer with her own salon.

WAITER: You don't say. Hey, I'm writing a screenplay, you think I could take lessons?

VICTOR: You'll have to take a number. As for being dumpy, there she is.

(Consuelo arrives, dressed up, looking quite impressive in an evening outfit. People stop and stare; Consuelo plays the movie star.)

CONSUELO: Good evening, my good people!

VICTOR: Why, *señorita Consuelo*…my lovely tutor!

CONSUELO: I'm sorry I'm late, I was just finishing a screenplay adaptation of my unfinished novel. *Encore du Champagne.*

WAITER: We're a Cuban place, we don't do no fancy –

VICTOR: You've got champagne. Do as you're told.

WAITER: Whatever.

(Waiter exits.)

CONSUELO: Busy life.

VICTOR: I understand, three-picture deal, and I am only a simple repairs entrepreneur!

CONSUELO: And tomorrow I join the Beverly Hills Minority Writers Workshop.

VICTOR: That is impressive! Waiter… She is a workshop member now.

WAITER: Yeah, good for her!

(Victor takes her hand.)

VICTOR: These are the hands that create magic!

CONSUELO: Oh, sure –

VICTOR: And my hands can repair any quake damage on your walls –

CONSUELO: Any time, *señor.*

VICTOR: Then let us do the dance of survival, Miss Consuelo! The night wears on and we have not done the cha-cha-cha!

CONSUELO: Then what are we waiting for, *señor? ¡Maestro!*

(Cha-cha-cha music plays and Victor bids Consuelo to get up and dance with him. It's very romantic. Teresa dances in the background in what turns out to be a spectacular number – Teresa and all the men in her life; Consuelo with her one. Then suddenly Victor stops.)

CONSUELO: What's wrong? *¿Qué le pasa?*

VICTOR: It's time for you, Miss Consuelo, to tell me the truth.

CONSUELO: The truth? Right now?

VICTOR: About the novel, Miss Consuelo – Right here, on the dance floor, Consuelo. Declare your love –

CONSUELO: Love?

VICTOR: For my craft, for my imitation poetry, for everything that I express as an exile, an *emigré,* all that stuff. Declare it here in front of the strangers.

CONSUELO: Well…I haven't –

VICTOR: You haven't been able to appreciate its epic grandeur.

CONSUELO: Maybe not.

VICTOR: So you're telling me –

CONSUELO: I'm telling you…maybe you need to explore the *(Quoting Caldwell.)* "Real feeling of men living in the post-nuclear world of Kafkaesque alienation."

VICTOR: *(So stunned he has to use his Cuban Spanish.)* *¿Pero qué es eso, checa; estás loca en la cabeza, o qué* [= "What the hell is that, woman; are you crazy or what"]?

CONSUELO: *Señor Cáceres, por favor!* Please…you must find a way to make the story reflect your agonizing sense of immigrant selflessness, frustration and angst!

VICTOR: I'm paying you to give me this…?

CONSUELO: That's what creative writing teachers get paid to say, don't look at me.

VICTOR: Why…*basta ya!* Maybe some of us are not destined to be novelists then.

CONSUELO: That's right, and if you pay for the champagne, we can leave it at that. No hard feelings!

VICTOR: Hard feelings? *Mira tú* [= "Look here"]…I…I…

CONSUELO: What?

(He grabs her and kisses her.)

CONSUELO: *Oh. ¿Pero qué pasa aquí* [= "What's going on"]?

VICTOR: Perhaps I have been deceiving myself all along, maybe it's not literary advice I need, Miss Consuelo.

CONSUELO: I think I better go.

VICTOR: I'm too Cuban for you.

CONSUELO: I never said that.

VICTOR: But you thought it, didn't you? Didn't you? Why did you come?

CONSUELO: Because…

VICTOR: *(Suavely.)* More champagne?

CONSUELO: No, I can talk without getting drunk!

VICTOR: Then?

CONSUELO: I came because I want to dance with a man and feel sophisticated in real life, not just in my many best-selling novels. That's why, alright?

VICTOR: Excellent.

CONSUELO: I want to see stars and listen to *la banda* play, and maybe a comet will shoot right past us.

VICTOR: I could arrange that.

CONSUELO: *(Aggressively, almost defeatist.)* No, you can't!

(Something is seen and heard in the sky)

VICTOR: Look up there!

CONSUELO: Very good…is that your son in that plane?

VICTOR: For you, we rented the message plane. It says "be my tutor."

CONSUELO: But it's not a real comet then…It's not your fault, but nobody

can make these things happen, that's all. That's the trouble with
being *La Gran Miss Consuelo!* Sooner or later, you realize,
nothing is meant to really happen! I am not the best-selling
writer you think I am. I'm sorry. *Me voy…*I go now. I go!

VICTOR: *Señorita!*

(She runs out. Leopoldo enters as Narrator as Consuelo exits and Victor remains alone.)

LEOPOLDO: As she runs out with great urgency, he notices she has dropped
            something…

(He picks up a cheap Bic pen)

LEOPOLDO: It is her instrument of magic, available in packages of six at the
            local Thrifty's. He looks up at the sky with great determination.

VICTOR: Consuelo…

(The music plays as he sits and is all alone on stage.)

VICTOR: Oh, my grand literary poetess of the Hollywood Pit Gardens…
            she has become my own…obsession! But with the help of
            the Mambo Goddess, I shall conquer her love and we shall go
            around the world making quake repairs, she and I…This is war.
            I shall conquer!

(He sheds a few clown's tears as he holds on to her pen. Teresa, as one of the "mambo dancers," is surrounded by the rest of the cast, except Consuelo, as they inspect the damage and create a kaleidescope of colorful strange characters who've just witnessed Consuelo's own drama rather than vice versa.)

(Lights go down. End of ACT 1.)

ACT 2

(Lights up. A few hours have passed. Consuelo's apartment as the novel plays itself out; a light shining on the empty desk bearing the old typewriter. Teresa and the Chief are frozen in place. The action starts up again.)

RICARDO: The fire is all around us.

TERESA: Who will rescue us?

(Akbar and Ahmed come running in)

AKBAR: We are here, Teresa Bella de las Galbas!

AHMED: We are ready to perish for you and, oh, OK, for him, too, I
            guess.

RICARDO: Look at them, those two boys have organized the field hands to
            carry buckets of water from the Pacific Ocean.

TERESA: They have trained the California condor to make water drops.

AHMED: This way, Teresa, Chief…

AKBAR: Hurry.

(They run to a "safe spot.")

AHMED: We are safe now; the Santa Anas have died down.

RICARDO: Young men, as the chief of the Gabrielinos, we shall name our land after you – what was your family name?

AHMED: Malihbu.

RICARDO: Then we will name the land Malibu, future home of Barbra Streisand.

AKBAR: Say, that's "Malih-bu."

RICARDO: Malibu will do! I'm the chief!

TERESA: Congratulations, my heroes. Too bad I have found my new life here in Malik-bu. Property values will rise now!

AKBAR: *(In fit of jealousy.)* You stay with them and I'll really burn down the village!

AHMED: Now brother, she has made her choice; we will remain alone and unwanted in the world.

RICARDO: Not necessarily. There is another prize. Here she is. The princess.

(Enter Princess played by Perla.)

RICARDO: She should be married at her age.

AKBAR: What's her name?

RICARDO: That is her name. She should be married at her age.

PRINCESS: Which one is mine, dammit?

RICARDO: Well, that is a problem, there's one too many.

AKBAR: And I do not share.

TERESA: Yeah, we've already been through all that.

RICARDO: Well, there is someone else.

(Village Sha-Woman or Berdache appears, played by Betty Avisham; she snarls a lot.)

RICARDO: There she is – She likes it with a fist. Yes, that is her name. She's the meanest, tawdriest, nastiest woman in the village. The men really like her.

PRINCESS: She's actually a man.

AKBAR: Oh!

RICARDO: Quiet, Princess, these outsiders have incredible hang-ups –

PRINCESS: She's only a berdache, a kinda kinky faith healer. Can you dig that?

AKBAR: We refuse to practice sexual perversion.

AHMED: Well, actually, I've always wondered what it might be like –

AKBAR: Brother! You're bi-curious.

(Coming in, and listening to the last couple of lines.)

CONSUELO: No, please, nothing kinky!

PRINCESS: Oh, no, the prude is back. I'm outie.

AHMED: She never lets us do anything kinky!

TERESA: Tell me about it.

AKBAR: I'm horny.
RICARDO: Yeah, well, join the club.
CONSUELO: Out! I'm gonna do this.
TERESA: We were doing quite well without you!
CONSUELO: Out! Out! All of you. You people don't understand the importance of wholesome romance.

(They all groan as they exit. Perla enters with a sense of urgency.)

PERLA: *Tía Consuelo*…where have you been? I've been waiting –
CONSUELO: I can't talk now, *m'ija*. Callwelk is going to kill me if I don't finish my assignment –
PERLA: But I needed to tell you that –
CONSUELO: He expect a full draft of my adaptation or he throw me out the class –

(She notices Perla is packing.)

CONSUELO: What are you doing?
PERLA: It's Marco, *Tía Consuelo*.
CONSUELO: Who – the boy from the Valley?
PERLA: We're going to Vegas.
CONSUELO: Vegas? <u>Las</u> Vegas, you mean.
PERLA: We're young, we don't <u>do</u> definite articles.
CONSUELO: What? *¿Qué dices?* I don't unders –
PERLA: He's infatuated.
CONSUELO: But you don't have to go.
PERLA: Look, Aunt Consuelo, don't lecture me right now please. I've been in the United States here three weeks – see? It's past midnight – three weeks exactly – and it's time to move on and stop being just any other immigrant. I'll be a citizen in no time.
CONSUELO: How? It took me twenty year, *m'ija*.
PERLA: Marco and I are getting married.
CONSUELO: *Cómo* [= "What"]?
PERLA: *"Cómo"* is what I said. But I've gone from shock to denial to full acceptance – especially since it was my idea! Here's the ring, don't ogle too much.
CONSUELO: But my sister, your mother, sent you here to study.
PERLA: I've graduated quickly into the full swing of life then.
CONSUELO: I don't allow!
PERLA: Wait till you meet him before you don't allow.
CONSUELO: Good for nothing –
PERLA: He owns a van.
CONSUELO: I don't care if he – what type of van?
PERLA: His dad gave him a Honda mini-van for his graduation. I told you they're uppity Latinos from the Valley.
CONSUELO: I've been here almost twenty year and I never meet a man with a van –
PERLA: And you admit this!

CONSUELO: You don't talk to your *Tía Consuelo* that way! Now, tell me, *m'ija*, do you love him?

PERLA: We've been writing each other letters for three years now. I've followed his development from first love to final love.

CONSUELO: But do you love him?

PERLA: *Por favor, Tía Consuelo*, you want everything on the third week.

CONSUELO: See what I mean? I, as *la Miss Consuelo,* refuse to allow marriage that is not steeped in *pasión.*

(The doorbell rings)

PERLA: He even rings the bell, he doesn't just bust the door in, which would be very masculine if you think about it, but no…

CONSUELO: *Ya cállate, loca* [= "Shut up already, you maniac"]! Let me handle this.

(Consuelo goes to open the door)

CONSUELO: Look here, *jovencito* [= "young man"]!

(She opens the door. But she's stunned. Standing in front of her is a very nice-looking, clean-cut, innocent, naïve young man. She almost feels sorry for him at first sight.)

MARCO: *(Faintly.)* Hi.

CONSUELO: Oh…

MARCO: You're Aunt Consuelo, aren't you?

CONSUELO: Yes – I mean no, I'm not your aunt.

PERLA: Come in, my darling. *(To Consuelo.)* You should have seen him on the dance floor, he's as dorky as they come.

MARCO: I don't dance ballroom style very well, I admit.

CONSUELO: Can you do the mambo?

MARCO: No, no tropical dances, ma'm.

CONSUELO: What type of Latin boy are you?

MARCO: Well, I'm from Woodland Hills.

PERLA: Aunt Consuelo used to clean houses there, didn't you?

CONSUELO: Quiet. Look here, *señor* Marco –

MARCO: Call me *"m'ijo."* I mean, that's Hispanic, isn't it?

CONSUELO: Look, boy. My niece just arrived from Mexico.

MARCO: I know, and she's everything I've ever dreamed of!

CONSUELO: But you barely know her.

MARCO: In my letters – which she has kept and cherished, haven't you, Perla – ?

PERLA: *(Not too certain.)* Ah, yeah, sure.

MARCO: – I have revealed my soul to her in those letters, Aunt Consuelo. My mom likes her a lot, too. The entire family thinks of her as a daughter already. That's what three years of letters can do. People just don't write like they used to. You're a writer, Miss Consuelo, surely you can appreciate the power of romantic correspondence.

CONSUELO: Yes. But my spelling is unromantic sometimes.

MARCO: Well, get spell-check. Computers do the work for you, oh,
            but the inspiration, oh, yes, the inspiration can't be faked by a
            computer. I love your niece, Aunt Consuelo.

PERLA: Wait! Wait for me to get there for you to say that...*(She rushes
            to their side.)* Say it again.

MARCO: I have waited for her all my life. I love her.

PERLA: You do believe in the power of romance, don't you, <u>Miss</u>
            Consuelo? Remember romance. You write it, Aunt Consuelo,
            and you practice it, too, don't you?

CONSUELO: Yes, mostly, but...you're both so young.

PERLA: My mother married at 15, remember?

CONSUELO: Yeah, and your father turned out some *borracho mujeriego.*

MARCO: I gather that's not a good thing.

CONSUELO: No, and I came to the U.S. to avoid marriage of that kind.

PERLA: And you've done that very well; now look at you, poor thing, a
            spinster.

CONSUELO: I'm just fine with no man. I survive!

PERLA: Well, survival is not good enough for me!

MARCO: Don't talk to your auntie that way, honey. I agree, Miss
            Consuelo, the path toward love is filled with obstacles. That's a
            metaphor, I think. Some of us make mistakes, and the rest of us
            (Bragging.) relish in the jackpot. My parents sell greeting cards;
            we love little sayings like that. At any rate, I understand your
            apprehension, but if I ever make your niece unhappy or if I take
            to drink or adultery, I will seek counseling.

CONSUELO: What about her? She needs counseling.

PERLA: If he makes me unhappy, he'll just have to buy me my own
            mini-van. *(Laughs.)*

MARCO: *(Laughs.)* She's a hoot, this one! A real hoot!

CONSUELO: At her age, I had a chance like this, to marry a man who work
            for the Mexican government, a man who owned land, and
            wanted to run for governor, maybe president –foolish dreamer, I
            told him!

MARCO: What happened to him?

CONSUELO: He became governor and president.

MARCO: And you turned him down?

PERLA: She could have been First Lady of Mexico – dems are the
            breaks.

CONSUELO: Well, he's wanted now for corruption in office; he's a man on
            the run. Serves him right.

PERLA: At least he made it big. You believe in big dreams, don't you,
            Miss Consuelo?

CONSUELO: Well...At the time, I made fun of dreams. I didn't realize you
            can't do nothing without them...

MARCO: *(Like a psychoanalyst.)* When did these dreams start?

CONSUELO: When I became citizen...I said I have to do something,

something different now…I didn't know you had to start so
much younger. But I have to do it; I have to try.

PERLA: Well, that takes care of the novel, but what about marriage?

MARCO: You mean romance, Perla?

PERLA: For her, marriage – you're not getting any younger, *tía!*

*(They hear singing outside. It's Victor singing some romantic song like "Feelings"
or "Sabor a mi.")*

MARCO: What is that?

CONSUELO: Oh, no.

PERLA: Is it…what I think it is? *(She opens door.)* Yoh, troubadour! Get
in here!

VICTOR: I have come for her, *la prestigiosa Miss Consuelo.*

CONSUELO: *(To Victor.)* Look here, you –

VICTOR: Calm down, Miss Consuelo. I have only come to return the pen.

CONSUELO: Pen?

VICTOR: The pen – ?

CONSUELO: Well, keep that cheap old thing.

VICTOR: Now, Miss Consuelo, this simple instrument is responsible for
the Magic of creation.

CONSUELO: *(To Perla and Marco.)* You were going to Las Vegas, *¿qué no?*

VICTOR: Nobody moves until I say what I have to say – *(To Perla and
Marco.)* Good evening, miss, sir –

MARCO: Howdy.

PERLA: Good evening. They call me Perlita Bonita.

MARCO: Can I call you that?

PERLA: Yeh, yeh, whatever.

VICTOR: It is an honor, *señorita.*

CONSUELO: I have homework, you know.

VICTOR: I won't be long, I promise. I admit it now. It's not just the search
for disaster relief money that has brought me to these shores, it
was my search for personal fulfillment.

MARCO: That's sweet.

PERLA: Quiet.

VICTOR: I have come here to embrace risk. *El riesgo del amor* [= "the
risk of love"]. Remember that, children, *el amor es sólo un
riesgo* [= "love is only a risk"]. Old lyrics from a bolero.

MARCO: Perfect for greeting cards. Could I borrow that?

VICTOR: Of course. He's an original; I like him.

CONSUELO: Victor…we said I only become your tutor.

PERLA: Aunt Consuelo, a little word of advice – ?

CONSUELO: I don't take advice from you, or greeting card from you or
anybody else! I'm tired of this. I don't practice romance, OK?
Miss Consuelo can't practice romance.

MARCO: But you're the guru of romance.

PERLA: You must do research for your novels.

VICTOR: You must live out your fantasy for it to end up on the page.

CONSUELO: Look, I don't dream being no First Lady of disaster money, okay? No more disaster in my private life, I say! No more. I have an assignment to finish. I have the Beverly Hills Minority Workshop tomorrow.

VICTOR: Let me escort you to your workshop in my Cordoba with Corinthian leather.

CONSUELO: No, I don't ride no Cordoba, I am happy with my '73 Chevy. That's it.

PERLA: But Aunt Consuelo –

MARCO: Aunt Consuelo, I'm disappointed –

CONSUELO: Well, you go make mess of your lives, now it's my turn to do what I have to. Mr. Cathereth, I have priority, see? *(Shows him the old beatup typewriter.)*

VICTOR: That old thing's your priority!

CONSUELO: Younger than you, I bet!

VICTOR: Romance is all about age then!

CONSUELO: No, it's about typing! And typing fast! I need to be alone with this, my only friend, and all my other friends, Teresa, Akbar, Ahmed, Ricardo. I will become Miss Consuelo, resident artist of the Hollywood Pit Gardens, if it kills me! It's the only thing in my life I won't mess up. Everything else don't work! Is that all clear, *señor*?

VICTOR: Alright...*muy bién*...but don't say I didn't try. I'm Mr. Cathereth, proud descendant of Queen Isabella...*con permiso* [= "excuse me"] ...

(He exits.)

PERLA: How could you?

MARCO: That wasn't romantic, Miss Consuelo.

CONSUELO: No, maybe it wasn't, but the work need to get done! Now out, out, *váyanse, váyanse* [= "go, go"], go ruin your life and leave me alone to mine.

PERLA: But *Tía Consuelo*...

CONSUELO: Out!

MARCO: It breaks my heart, honey.

PERLA: Yeh, yeh, let's go to Vegas. What a character! We'll be together, she'll remain alone.

(They exit. Teresa enters; she looks mournful.)

TERESA: That was nasty. If you can do that to Mr. Caceres –

CONSUELO: – that's right, if I choose, I can white out your *chi-chis* [= "boobs"]. Anyway, we're behind on our work! Come on..."alone in her room, she is alone ten more years! She's an old hag now. The spider webs cover her from head to toe... Ricardo the Indian abandoned her without consummating their *fornicación*.

TERESA: *(As an older woman.)* "I am Old Teresa, mistress of the avocado! The land lies fallow, broken, barren, and inert---I am a 70-year-old virgin. I had a faaaaaarm in Malibu, named after the two men I loved. The Santa Ana winds tore through the earth and threatened our prosperity. I had a faaaaaarm in Malibu..."

(Lights change. We hear a phone ringing. Enter Caldwell in quick cameo. He's holding a phone as if Consuelo has called at midnight. He's wearing pajamas.)

CALDWELL:	Hello...who is this?
CONSUELO:	...And that's why I'm going to be a little late –
CALDWELL:	What do you mean you're going to a minority workshop now?
CONSUELO:	The Beverly Hills Minority Writers Workshop –
CALDWELL:	That's the stupidest thing I've ever heard of.
CONSUELO:	You don't understand!
CALDWELL:	Look, the assignment for my class is due early tomorrow morning! – and it's already tomorrow morning – so you can't go fooling around with the screenplay adaptation of a novel that hasn't even been written yet.

(Valley Girl sticks her head out.)

VALLEY GIRL:	Come to bed, Jean Paul Sartre!
CALDWELL:	Coming, Simone de Beauvoir!
CONSUELO:	What?
CALDWELL:	Never mind. I was trying to engage in existentialist copulation when you rudely interrupted –
CONSUELO:	I don't know what you're talking about, but I prove you wrong one day! I become sensational! Overnight!
CALDWELL:	If the assignment is not turned in the way it should be, you're gone from this class overnight. You decide!

(He exits.)

CONSUELO:	*¡Pinche viejo* [= "Stupid old man"]!
TERESA:	As the morning dawns...
CONSUELO:	The screenplay adaptation is done. It's time to face the workshop!
TERESA:	She's wide awake now, and we're all ready at last to face the Beverly Hills Minority Writers Workshop.

(The Workshop members approach with chairs.)

CONSUELO:	Excuse me? Is this the war-shop?

(Jane Bracknell, played by same actor who played Akbar, comes to greet her in a major gender-bending type of doubling.)

JANE:	There she is: *c'est toi!*
CONSUELO:	What?
JANE:	Hello, I'm Jane Simone Bracknell, I'm a descendant of the great Bracknells of London, owner of the Rodeo Tanning Express, full-time liberal and originator of the workshop.
CONSUELO:	*(Trying to enunciate.)* So kind of you to let me come.

JANE:	No, it was about time we found you.
CONSUELO:	Anything I can do to help your sagheeing cultural landscape.
JANE:	Let's not get personal, dear. And over here –
ROOSEVELT:	I'm Debonnaire, one of the remaining original Roosevelts. Welcome to the workshop, *herr-mana* [= "sister."].
TROTSKYIST:	Leona, president of the Beverly Hills branch of the Socialist Worker's Party.
NASAL GUY:	*Mee casa es su casa.*

(Everyone turns to a lone man, sitting with arms folded and looking quite above it all.)

JANE:	And this is –
JAIME:	*(Icy stare.)* Jaime Ixtiquoatl de la Raza.
JANE:	He's actually half-Scandinavian, half-Chihuahuan.
JAIME:	All the same, I'm a proud member of "the cosmic universal race," with an emphasis on my heroic Aztec roots. I've been sent here by the University Committee on Ethnically Rigid Affairs to guarantee the purity of the process. You may proceed.
JANE:	Thank you, Jaime! I'm so relieved we may proceed! Time to get the script; give it here, Consuelo. And it's got such a nice shoddy look to it.
ROOSEVELT:	So underprivileged!
TROTSKYIST:	So pure!
JANE:	So proletarian!
ROOSEVELT:	What's the title?
JANE:	Yes, tonight's underprivileged screenplay is called "Romance of the Guacamoles."

(Everyone laughs, but the laughter ceases when everyone notices that Consuelo herself is not amused.)

JANE:	Quit your oinking, it's not a comedy! Now, Deb, you get to read –
ROOSEVELT:	I get to be Teresa Bella de las Galbas –
TROTSKYIST:	I'll be Ahmed.
NASAL GUY:	I'll be the avocado tree.
JANE:	I'll be the twin brother Akbar. Ooh, I get to play a man!
JAIME:	I'll pass, but you may proceed without me. I'll be here taking notes, and I'll pass judgment later.

(The group starts the reading.)

ROOSEVELT:	"I am Teresa Bella de Las Galbas. I was born naked, naked as the willow and just as weepy…"

(The following lines are read as if they were in the script.)

NASAL GUY:	And for the next two and half hours, the script about the grand Teresa –

JANE: – was read slowly, patiently, as the readers strained to read from the depleted mileage left on the ancient ribbon of Consuelo's 1956 typewriter.

TROTSKYIST: There was even an attempt on their part to give their lines feeling.

ROOSEVELT: Nobody complained.

JAIME: Nobody groaned.

NASAL GUY: Nobody dared to snicker.

TROTSKYIST: No one offered a reality check.

TERESA: *(Appears in chains.)* "And that is how today, I still wear this chain around my neck, to remind me of the devastation of my life with the identical twins, Ahmed and Akbar, and forever into my late age…I shall wear it…*(Fades out.)*

ROOSEVELT: I shall wear it, carrying the burdens of their furious passions for me until I die.

ROOSEVELT: "The And." A-n-d?

(Stunned silence.)

JANE: *(Wiping a tear away.)* Well, that was so…romantic. They just don't make them like that any more. *(Jane places her in the Hot Seat.)* Now you sit there still like Saint Sebastian and wait for the arrows to hit.

CONSUELO: What? San Sebastian? An omen.

JANE: Any comments from the peanut gallery?

ROOSEVELT: Me! Me first! … Well, let's face it, it's not Hispanic enough.

CONSUELO: What?

ROOSEVELT: Where's the levitation scene?

CONSUELO: The what, honey?

TROTSKYIST: Support your premise, woman!

ROOSEVELT: I mean, I've read "One Hundred Houses of the Chocolate Spirits." So, you know, more magical realism! That's Hispanic, isn't it?

TROTSKYIST: I say, fuck that shit, man! Romance is the language of a dying class structure and should be depicted only with the understanding that it serves an oppressive need for homely, average-looking women in need of sexual fantasy, which should be banned altogether in an ideal post-revolutionary world – but as long as we live in a decadent capitalist society, let's enjoy it and use it for masturbatory purposes, so onward, sister, let your fingers do the walking!

CONSUELO: It's a clean novel, thank you very much.

JANE: Next –

ROOSEVELT: Wait, wait, I also think it needs more character motivation, a better exposition, and a more delightful denouement that can guarantee a deconstructionist and minimalist approach to the romance genre. It's otherwise okay.

NASAL GUY: Look. Let's face it, I've been in the Industry long enough to know if the story's gonna be done at all in Hollywood, it needs to de-emphasize its ethnicity. *(He's booed.)* Don't get me wrong, I'm with ya all the way, I want ya to make it big, but you can't listen to these amateurs who know nothing about the biz. You're not gonna sell no Trotskyism to the studios.

ROOSEVELT: Such opportunism!

THE
TROTSKYIST: Philistinism.

JANE: Appealing to the lowest common denominator.

THE
NASAL GUY: Look, take it or leave it – but here's my rec. Get Jennifer Lopez to play the oversexed Teresa, throw in a little lambada number to get a top-ten theme song out of it, play it on MTV all day, and now we're cooking. Spice up the young Indian princess and cast a major Latina actress like Winona Ryder, and you nail down the teenage market…throw in a speech denouncing the treatment of the Native American, and you get the campus p.c. crowd, not to mention the book tie-in that will make this required reading on all major campuses – Sharpen up the dialogue for the avocado tree! Yes, as a form of narrator/ spiritual guide and you nail down both the New Age crowd and the avocado growers in one fell swoop. *(Going on without listening to anyone.)*…Make sure there's a statement about the high cost of fire insurance in Malibu and you get middle-class audience identification…and whatever you do, make sure that the Indian chief doesn't smoke pot. War on drugs, you know – decaf is in, stimulants out. You get a family picture for everyone with a little sex and ethnic music thrown in, and it's a relevant pic for our times. Here's my card, I'll help you pitch it; who's your agent, Miss Consuelo?

CONSUELO: Ah…I'm registed with the Hollywood Maintenance Agency.

JANE: Then trade cards, you two, We have one more reaction…

(There is silence again. Everyone turns to Jaime, who has been sitting quietly waiting to pounce. He rises augustly out of his chair, nearly making it tumble on the wooden floor of the classroom.)

JAIME: It's trash!

JANE: Now, Jaime!

JAIME: Sit down, Jane, you liberal trollop.

JANE: Why, I never – !

JAIME: Somebody should tell the woman the bad news: A Mexican woman should express herself in relationship to her class, her gender and her ethnicity, as defined by the nearest university committee on underprivileged affairs. In other words, she should be writing minority fiction preferably published by the Aztec Shoestring Press. And even if she refuses to comply with the rules, she needs to learn how to write a full sentence. Why can't she write in Spanish anyway?

CONSUELO: I do, *m'ijo*, but I choose to –

JAIME: I myself have published a book of poems "The Mixtaquaachipan-Svenska Letters" in the language of my Aztec ancestors, Nahuatl, and in Swedish. I've won many grants for it from NEA panels and other people who can't even read Nahuatl nor Swedish but they know it's "relevant." Impressive, *¿qué no?* But her...look at her!

CONSUELO: What about me?

JAIME: She is a phoney through and through, not a real minority at all, an assimilated person, brown on the outside, white on the inside like a coconut. I declare her incorrect!

(Everybody else except Jane points at her, calling her, "Incorrect, incorrect!" Consuelo's terrified; nobody's ever declared her incorrect.)

JANE: Now please, we must hear the author explain her own work, it's only fair, I should think. Sit down, Jaime, and put away that incomprehensible book of poems where I don't have to see them. *(Jaime sits down. Consuelo is left speechless.)* We're all listening, sister, we're all yours. Just exactly what were you trying to say with the amusingly entitled, "Romance of the Guacamoles?"

CONSUELO: Look, it's all very simple! Ah...yeah.....*sí, pues* [= "yes, well"]...You know...Romance. Lots of it! And mix it around like *menudo*, you know? *Menudo?* It's edible. Ah, how about Danielle Steel, Judith Krantz, Dolores del Rio, Corin Tellado, no?...OK then, Kafka, Kafka-esque? Alienation? Jean Paul Sartre? Professor Caldwell. Better not. *¡Ay, Diós mío. Mi corazón!*

ROOSEVELT: I think that means "heart" in Spanish!

JAIME: Why can't she say it in Aztec?

(Consuelo runs out horrified. Blackout. Lights up. Consuelo stands holding her bag, her bus transfer and wearing a maid's uniform. Teresa stands next to her. Ahmed and Akbar come join her later.)

TERESA: So this is the future. There's not much in store for it, is there? It's been a week since the disaster at the Beverly Hills Minority Writer's Workshop, *pobrecita!*, and you've decided to –

CONSUELO: – to never write again.

TERESA: What's to become of us, or more importantly, me?

CONSUELO: I go back to cleaning now, and burying myself in work. You out!

(Teresa leaves looking rejected. Consuelo crosses to the bus stop.)

CONSUELO: Time to wait for the bus now, under the rain, all the cars of L.A. passing me by. The bus comes and I get on.

(Two men follow her into the bus. It's Akbar and Ahmed.)

CONSUELO: You again?

AKBAR: Surely you'll go home to add a new chapter.

AHMED: My nipples are sagging.

CONSUELO: So that's what "sagging" means.

AKBAR: What?

CONSUELO: Never mind. You're both history now, *jóvenes* [= "young men"], out of my life *por puro pendejos*.

AKBAR: Can we do our final scene please?

AHMED: It won't take long…we have to leave some time or another.

AKBAR: It's the final farewell.

CONSUELO: Alright, but don't take long, I get off a couple of stops from now and you don't follow.

AKBAR: Come on, dude…

(Consuelo watches as Akbar and Ahmed play out this final scene.)

AHMED: So brother, I truly am sorry for the things I said.

AKBAR: Me, too. To think that for the love of a California temptress, I almost shed the blood of brother.

AHMED: Oh, brother, I am not a man who shows his feelings, but I feel the tears now –

AKBAR: Oh, brother!

AHMED: Brother!

(They hug.)

CONSUELO: *(Derisive tone.)* Oh, brother!

(They pull apart.)

AKBAR: The ship awaits me, I am headed for Panama. There is a canal waiting to be built, and you?

AHMED: I'm headed for Santa Monica to attend a workshop on self-esteem. *(Looks at Consuelo.)* Self-esteem?

CONSUELO: I'm a little rusty, OK?

AKBAR: Goodbye, brother! No matter how far, we'll be brothers for life. *Akhi lel hayat* [= "brothers for life"].

AHMED: *Akhi lel hayat!* But look…*(Talking to Consuelo.)*

AKBAR: Look, Santa Monica and Vermont! There's the campus of the Los Angeles City College.

CONSUELO: I don't go near.

AHMED: Maybe a little surprise visit with Professor Caldwell could recharge the creative batteries.

CONSUELO: Oh, no, he don't want to see me.

AKBAR: Maybe it's time to tell him off.

CONSUELO: What?

AHMED: To tell him he has ruined your life.

AKBAR: Time to ruin his day!

AHMED: Let him know how you really feel!

AKBAR: Give him all the immigrant angst he deserves.

CONSUELO: Bus driver! I get off here!

(Consuelo finds the Caldwell offices full of boxes. Mr. Caldwell is half-way finished with his packing.)

CALDWELL: Consuelo.

CONSUELO: *(Sharply.)* Hello, Caldwench! So…I don't turn in the assignment! It's a statement!

CALDWELL: I'm sorry, Consuelo, I have some…

CONSUELO: What happened? You FIRED? I hope so!

CALDWELL: I'm celebrating actually.

CONSUELO: Really? Why? You have no right.

CALDWELL: I got a job at UCLA. I'll finally be teaching real students – I mean nothing personal, but you know, they'll be pre-selected students, none of this open enrollment shit. I've done time in the city colleges! And I got the job just as I'm finally getting my collection of stories published by Simon and Schuster. See? Look at the cover!

CONSUELO: Oh…yes…*Drowsy Nausea* by Theodorus Caldwell. Congratulations. They're probably boring.

CALDWELL: They're supposed to be! That's why *The New Yorker* has already called to ask for reprint rights; they'll publish excerpts of my modern tales of middle-class perversion in their special issue of "Summer Angst" edited by John Updike. My attempt to plagiarize his lethargic, boring style has finally paid off.

CONSUELO: Good for you, I guess –

CALDWELL: See? There are big exciting changes happening in my life, so how's your writing coming along? How's "Romance of the Avocados"?

CONSUELO: "Guacamoles." – I don't write that no more anyway. Look, I have a complaint.

CALDWELL: What? About me?

CONSUELO: My niece is gone –

CALDWELL: How is that my fault?

CONSUELO: I don't know, but I blame you for everything!

CALDWELL: That's not fair, is it?

CONSUELO: Nothing is fair! So take responsibility; be a man about it! And you, you, just sitting there talking about alienation and Kafka and *Drowsy Nausea* and *pendejadas* like that! I say it is time to tell you in English that you are full of it, Mr. Caldwell, and you gonna make a lousy UCLA professor and I hope students start a hunger strike and burn your *Drowsy Nausea* after you assign it to them to read because it has nothing to do with real people living in the real world of immigrant angst and alienation!

(Silence. She looks surprised at herself.)

CALDWELL: I have taught you well.

CONSUELO: No, you don't!
CALDWELL: You sound successfully alienated, even pissed off!
CONSUELO: That's right.
CALDWELL: You're angry!
CONSUELO: Damn right!
CALDWELL: So what are you gonna do about it?
CONSUELO: I don't know, have the Mexican Mafia come knock you off.
CALDWELL: No, maybe finish your novel? Huh? How's that? You got the strength and the anger for that?
CONSUELO: What?
CALDWELL: I thought you did. I thought you had it in you. You were one of the few motivated students I had.
CONSUELO: Really? *(Suspiciously.)* What you mean?
CALDWELL: Most students who take my class come with pseudo-literary ambitions, I usually have to break them out of that habit. You came here with romance. That's trite, tacky and lowbrow, but at least it's something to work with.
CONSUELO: I'm special, you mean?
CALDWELL: Damn right special, Consuelo. After the grammar gets fixed, the grades go up, maybe you can follow me across town.
CONSUELO: Across town?
CALDWELL: That's right. UCLA –
CONSUELO: UCLA? People like me are only invited to come clean the place! They even did away with affirmative action in that *pinche* school.
CALDWELL: Too bad. But listen, it's UCLA: The Creative Writing Program. I'll be the head of it, including the man handing out the scholarships.
CONSUELO: Scholarships, huh?
CALDWELL: Only if the grammar gets fixed. How about it, huh? Consuelo, our very own transfer student. Interested?
CONSUELO: What about the Simi Valley girl?
CALDWELL: Oh, that bimbo left me for a surfer dude who reads John Grisham!
CONSUELO: I'm sorry.
CALDWELL: That slut's not getting any of my scholarships, though may she get the clap from him, bitch! But now there's you –
CONSUELO: Leave me out of this!
CALDWELL: It won't be the same without you, you'll bring new life to academia, a fresh new voice.
CONSUELO: I've heard that before –
CALDWELL: Finish school, Consuelo, and don't let anybody tell you you're too old!
CONSUELO: You gone crazy, Caldwelk, you gone crazy! It never gonna happen, never, you're dreaming, dreaming, I won't dream no more, Caldwell, I don't have the energy for it. Out of my way! I am just a lowly immigrant in post-nuclear state of modern

existence! Excuse me.

(She goes running as Caldwell laughs, all in a day's work.)

CALDWELL: See you in the big leagues, Consuelo. I know you'll make it. I'm
            outta here.

(Narrator picks up.)

LEOPOLDO/
NARRATOR: It was time to get back home to the Hollywood Pit Gardens.

(Consuelo crosses to her apartment. She sees Perla sitting on the stoop outside.)

CONSUELO: Perla?
PERLA: *(Quietly.)* Hi.
CONSUELO: Forgot the keys, *m'ija?*
PERLA: Sorry, I left them behind thinking I wouldn't need them again.
            Marco gave me the "hee-hove."
CONSUELO: But why? A pretty girl like you?
PERLA: All I did was ask about the family assets, landholdings, stocks,
            real estate.
CONSUELO: Perla, you shouldn't…
PERLA: A wife has a right to know.
CONSUELO: You already divorced then?
PERLA: No, we didn't even get to the chapel. He dumped me by the
            Hoover Dam.
CONSUELO: And what you do all these weeks all by yourself, *m'ija?*
PERLA: I met an engineer at the dam who might be interested in
            divorcing his wife and abandoning his five children just for me.
CONSUELO: Don't tell me, he bought you a ring.
PERLA: No, he wanted more time to think about it. People are so slow!
            My first month in America, and I can't even break up a marriage
            yet!
CONSUELO: Well, you're not going to.
PERLA: I mean how do you deal with failure? What's your secret?
CONSUELO: I'm no failure!
PERLA: I see: denial. That should work for a little while.
CONSUELO: You treat your Aunt Consuelo with respect!
PERLA: We are all failures, nothing's ever gonna happen! We won't
            have a palm reading salon, and you'll never be a romance
            writer!
CONSUELO: I have many things.
PERLA: I demand results!
CONSUELO: One day you'll get them!
PERLA: But you never have!
CONSUELO: Oh, you never know. I am a new woman now.
PERLA: How?
CONSUELO: I am different from the immigrant who arrived from
            Guadalajara. I am a citizen, I write English, bad English, but I

	write. And I still have Spanish, not great grammatical Spanish, and in this neighborhood I've learned a little Armenian, Korean, and Cuban –
PERLA:	Cuban?
CONSUELO:	Sure, and I don't need things to be perfect or like a dream any more; I just want to come home and make tea for you.
PERLA:	For me?
CONSUELO:	For my favorite little niece.
PERLA:	Am I really your favorite? It's okay to spoil me.
CONSUELO:	You already are, *mi pobre zonzita* [= "poor dummy"]. How about tea now? Let the night begin.

(Victor enters. He's wearing repairman clothes.)

VICTOR:	Not so fast, Miss Consuelo.
CONSUELO:	What are you doing here?
VICTOR:	You don't return my phone calls, you don't –
CONSUELO:	Oh, I've been very busy with –
VICTOR:	Out on a book-signing tour, I know.
CONSUELO:	Please! Please stop that! Victor, I am not *La* Grand Miss Consuelo. I told you. I am just a simple woman now. Call me Consuelo. Little Consuelo. Average Consuelo.
PERLA:	*(To Victor.)* Say something.
VICTOR:	I have a surprise for you. *M'ijo, entre* [= "Come in, son"].

(Leopoldo enters)

PERLA:	We haven't met –
LEOPOLDO:	Where have you been hidin'?
VICTOR:	In a minute. Tell Miss Consuelo the news.
CONSUELO:	What news?
LEOPOLDO:	I won first prize in a poetry contest.
CONSUELO:	Really?
LEOPOLDO:	Oh, yes. It was the Toluca Lake Rasquachi Poet's Prize for best poem written in a badly lit coffee house. It's gonna be published in their quarterly review.
CONSUELO:	Well…congratulations, I guess.
VICTOR:	You inspired him, Consuelo.
PERLA:	She inspired me, too, to come to the U.S. and to overstay my visit.
LEOPOLDO:	*(To Perla.)* You need a place to crash?
VICTOR:	Later, and tell her – he's been offered a full scholarship.
CONSUELO:	A scholarship really?
LEOPOLDO:	UCLA wants me to enroll in their Creative Writing program, I'll be studying with Professor Caldwell.
CONSUELO:	You poor thing. I mean, congratulations.
LEOPOLDO:	*(Sounding like the voice of Caldwell haunting her.)* And it's a scholarship that's open to students of all ages.
CONSUELO:	Why you say that?

LEOPOLDO: Because –
CONSUELO: Stop haunting me, Caldwelk!
LEOPOLDO: What? Dad! What did I say?
PERLA: Aunt Consuelo, he's only informing you about opportunities available to everyone.
CONSUELO: Not now.
VICTOR: Don't you realize, Miss Consuelo, what you have done for us? You're the last of the big time dreamers!
CONSUELO: I am, aren't I?
VICTOR: I've always understood your fantasy, and I know now I've met my match: *la* Miss Consuelo.
PERLA: So you like her alter ego?
VICTOR: No lower egos for me, I say! I want to woo that alter ego; I want to make love to it.
CONSUELO: Kinky.
PERLA: I'm a Mayan Princess.
LEOPOLDO: Really? And I'm a Cuban-American poet –
CONSUELO: That's enough, please! It's good that you got a scholarship, Leopoldo. I hope life takes you places but the rest of us, oh, we just have to carry on with our little lives the best way we can now.
VICTOR: No, forget that, my son and I…we just came from the epicenter.
PERLA: Where? Northridge?
VICTOR: Reseda! We got some condos to fix, big new contract –
PERLA: Contract?
CONSUELO: Choose your words carefully in front of the child.
LEOPOLDO: It's only a FEMA contract.
PERLA: Turn the words around and it spells "fame."
LEOPOLDO: *(Coming on to Perla.)* I'm Leopoldo, by the way, and I like surfing the Net for babes.
PERLA: Hi, there.
VICTOR: How can I reward you, Miss Consuelo? How about a soccer game?
CONSUELO: I don't play soccer.
VICTOR: No, I mean – it's the World Cup.
PERLA: The World Cup, Aunt Consuelo!
LEOPOLDO: Clash of the Titans!
VICTOR: Bolivia meets Burundi! Interested? Maybe we could all…
PERLA: A double date, it's a done deal, Mr. Cathereth!
LEOPOLDO: Sounds good to me, too.
CONSUELO: Wait a second now!
VICTOR: Then how about dinner for four in Pasadena after the game – Saturday night?
CONSUELO: This Saturday?
VICTOR: It can be Mexican, we already did Cuban.
LEOPOLDO: Come on, Miss Consuelo.
PERLA: *Tía Consuelo!* Come on.

CONSUELO: Look…Maybe *"The Guadalajara en un Llano, México en una Laguna"* Restaurant – longest title, best enchiladas.

VICTOR: Why not?

PERLA: Onward to final victory!

CONSUELO: Alright…we will proceed with this dinner, but it will be a polite engagement. The new average Consuelo takes her time. We will explore all possibilities, and negotiate them, but no commitments need to be made until further notice. Is that understood and acceptable to you gentlemen?

VICTOR: Yeah, but I like the old wild Miss Consuelo. The one with the salon.

CONSUELO: All in due time, I say. Let the passion and the romance flourish day by day…if it's going to happen at all. I am open, but realistic about the chances…so please…here's my hand, you may kiss it, it's average and dry, nothing special.

VICTOR: I'll decide that.

(He kisses Consuelo's hand, and makes Leopoldo follow suit with Perla's hand.)

LEOPOLDO: Later, princess.

PERLA: Later, young heir of the repair empire.

VICTOR: Till Saturday, *preciosa.*

CONSUELO: Saturday, *señor.*

(Leopoldo and Victor exit.)

PERLA: At last, a government repair deal! In my first month in America!

CONSUELO: Alright, inside.

PERLA: No, I have to go buy a dress.

CONSUELO: What about – ?

PERLA: Forget tea, Aunt Consuelo. You must never rest in the pursuit of the American Dream! "I like to be in America, OK by…"

(Perla runs out toward the street. A car screeches. Perla shouts in, "I'm OK." She runs inside the apartment.)

CONSUELO: Clowns, fools, all of you. *(Surveying the room.)* This is it…this is all there is and I am okay.

(Teresa enters.)

TERESA: You can't be too sure about that.

CONSUELO: You are in the past, too. Like all my silly dreams. You will vanish from my memory –

TERESA: Just wait. *Ya verás* [= "You'll see"].

(Snoring is heard.)

CONSUELO: What is that?

(Teresa draws a curtain, which reveals Betty Avisham sleeping on her couch.)

CONSUELO: Mrs. Avichamp!

BETTY: Oh, Consuelo, such lovely dreams I was having – those two

	brothers.
CONSUELO:	What are you doing here? How did you – ?
BETTY:	I paid the concierge to let me in.
CONSUELO:	Who?
BETTY:	The manager, whatever you call that person with the wooden leg. Now listen, where on earth have you been? Don't you return phone calls? My friends at the workshop, they raved about you –
CONSUELO:	They did what?
BETTY:	Or maybe they "raged." No, actually they said they were "overwhelmed."
CONSUELO:	They hated me.
BETTY:	Which didn't prevent them from passing on your concepts to the higher-ups, the executives, the head honchos themselves.
CONSUELO:	Really?
BETTY:	My dear, you and your salacious tales of California history are the talk of the town –
CONSUELO:	I don't believe –
BETTY:	With those two sensual brothers, how could it fail? You are the buzz.

(Ahmed and Akbar enter.)

AHMED:	We are the buzz!
CONSUELO:	The bus?
ALL THREE and BETTY:	The buzzzzzzzz!
CONSUELO:	I got it!
TERESA and BOYS:	We're back.
BETTY:	Now dress up like one of your heroines and come with me. We have a meeting, I'll be your representative, manager and confidante.
CONSUELO:	What? A meeting with whom?
BETTY:	A man so important in Hollywood, he wants his name kept confidential in case of any leaks. We are being listened to, I feel it.

(Teresa and Brothers look at one another.)

CONSUELO:	Nobody is listening.
BETTY:	You'll take notes, accept changes as told, and be ready to throw the entire concept out the window if the deal is right.
CONSUELO:	What if I don't want changes –?
BETTY:	It's not what you might want, my dear.
CONSUELO:	Now, wait, wait, Miss Avisham. I thank you but –
BETTY:	No need to do that, not yet.
CONSUELO:	But maybe I do need to finish my schooling.
BETTY:	What?

CONSUELO: You know, so I can really learn to finish a full sentence.
BETTY: That could jeopardize a Hollywood career, my dear.
CONSUELO: Well, Mr. Caldo was right, I must learn my grammar first.
BETTY: Why? Whatever your faults as a writer, you have reached an acceptable level of mediocrity necessary to make it in Hollywood.
CONSUELO: I have not!
BETTY: One does not turn down a meeting.
CONSUELO: Well, I do! I want my education.
BETTY: Consuelo, you must sell a screenplay first before you're entitled to such a sanctimonious attitude.
CONSUELO: I'm not acting sanc-ti-monical. But you listen here, Avichamp, if you want to help me –
BETTY: Of course I do, it's what I've been trying to do all afternoon---
CONSUELO: Then you help me with grammar and spelling.
BETTY: Me? I?
CONSUELO: You went to *Vomitar* College, right?
BETTY: Vassar, dear, not *Vomit-tar.*
CONSUELO: Time to put your expensive education to work; stop being such an Avichump!
BETTY: Me? Why?
CONSUELO: You are my friend, right?
BETTY: Friendship does not extend to humiliating encounters with grammar.
CONSUELO: You my friend or not? You said I was one of your best friends, or was that all just fake, like the jewels?

(She struggles to say it, has a little tear in her eye.)

BETTY: Well…my, I, yes, yes, oh, yes, have my friendship, have it all…
CONSUELO: Good.
BETTY: – and I suppose I could put my education to work again –
CONSUELO: That's right.
BETTY: And my considerable discretionary income.
CONSUELO: Yes!
BETTY: We'll need a dictionary.

(Teresa's ready with the dictionary; the boys bring the typewriter.)

CONSUELO: There you go.
BETTY: We'll, of course, buy you a laptop.
CONSUELO: No, my typewriter stays! It's been my friend.
BETTY: It's the modern world; we'll throw that old thing out as soon as…!
CONSUELO: Wait, I'm beginning to feel them.
BETTY: Feel them?
CONSUELO: They are here, around us…Ricardo comes back.
TERESA: Yes…he comes back.

AKBAR	
and AHMED:	What?
TERESA:	After twenty-five years, Ricardo comes back.

(Ricardo the Gabrielino Indian enters. He's older, feeble.)

TERESA:	Ricardo…after all these years –
RICARDO:	You have waited for me!
BETTY:	*(Moved.)* Oh, she has waited for him!
CONSUELO:	"Yes! He takes her into his arms, and the two, old bodies come together and levitate! They copulate in the air as they turn to earth, wind, and fire, and in the sky the entire village sees their bodies as they turn into Santa Ana winds that send a ball of fire covering the land."
RICARDO:	That's it. She did it.
TERESA:	I had magic realist sex!
AKBAR:	That was gross.
AHMED:	I thought it was hot!
CONSUELO:	I go to confession now. *(Crosses herself.)*
RICARDO:	Don't you see? It's a breakthrough!
BETTY:	It's your first sex scene, my dear, your talent has matured!
CONSUELO:	As long as it's in good taste.
BETTY:	As long as it remains romantic, sensual, playfully joyous, but never graphic!

(A bell rings. Leopoldo/Akbar plays messenger followed by Ahmed.)

CONSUELO:	What's that?
AKBAR:	It's the future calling.
AHMED:	A world of endless possibilities.
TERESA:	It's a scholarship from UCLA.
CONSUELO:	No, it can't be.
RICARDO:	"Romance of the Guacamoles" on its way to a publisher.
TERESA:	Miss Consuelo: the darling of the intellectuals.
BETTY:	I will be your sponsor, your patron, your Catherine de Medici.
CONSUELO:	What?
AKBAR:	Magic realist genre: a wave of the future.
RICARDO:	Followed by the sequel: *Romance of the Piñata Makers*.

(Perla comes in dressed as a Piñata.)

PERLA:	"Love me inside and out."
BETTY:	Yes, I will be a patron of the arts at last. I will have a purpose in this world.
CONSUELO:	The future is calling!
TERESA:	And who turns it down?
RICARDO:	Not Consuelo!
CONSUELO:	No, not Consuelo! The grammar gets fixed.
PERLA:	The romance flourishes.
CONSUELO:	The world awaits me.

AKBAR: The future has called.

BETTY: The future is here!

TERESA: Only in America could a humble woman aspire to so many endeavors.

ALL: *(Except Consuelo.)* It's Consuelo Chavez! Oooh, Consuelo Chavez.

CONSUELO: Miss Consuelo: Simple Worker and Novelist.

End of play

PLACES to TOUCH HIM

by Guillermo Reyes

Author's biography is on page 129.

Introduction

Places to Touch Him originated with a dare. My friend, Jorge Huerta, while directing the original production of my gay-themed play, *Deporting the Divas,* complained that I avoided sex in my plays, that my characters might endlessly talk about it, but rarely could they be seen performing more than just a shy kiss, if that. In short, he called me a prude. He was right, to a certain extent. My dramaturgical diffidence prevented me from writing something more than a brisk scenario of bodies coming together, which is cut miserably short by one of the characters in a scene in *Deporting the Divas.* I had shied away all this time from overt, explicit sexuality because....I don't know. Catholic upbringing? Discomfort with the obligatory frontal nudity that beset most gay-themed plays in our times? Plain distaste for anything too overt? Prudeness? This new play would attempt to defy the psychosexual hang-ups that inhibited my imagination at the time, and were products of a history of both indiscretion in my family and inhibitions simultaneously. But I'll leave the confessional style to my autobiographical narrative, *Maria's Oscar,* which explains this paradox in greater detail.

Places to Touch Him became my way of dealing with one man's awakening to his sexuality, to obsession, and, yes, to plain carnality all within the milieu of Phoenix where I had come to learn a thing or two about my sexuality – for various reasons I won't go into right now. A lawyer, and aspiring politician, seeks to run for the city council at the same time that he's developed an obsession for a young man who eventually becomes a stripper. This politician is considered safe and asexual, completely non-threatening to mainstream voters. But this relationship will clearly threaten his asexual image. This scenario becomes an excellent excuse for a lovely set of dance numbers, in which Domingo, the object of affection, first shows off his skills as an amateur stripper, and a second number in act two when he's become more of a pro, not to mention a more private act in which he entangles our hero/politician in a provocative three-way with a waiter. Can the politician maintain his personal life private, and can he afford to fall in love when the issues of the local Latino community have heated up and deserve the attention of serious politicians?

Actor Andy Alcala drove down from Portland, Oregon, to portray Cesar, the politician, and Alonso Minjares transferred from Tucson to provide the heat with a powerful presence on stage (and washboard abs, to boot) as the provocative Domingo. *Places to Touch Him* became our hottest ticket, (our most successful production until *The Women of Juarez* broke box office records) and clearly a sensual piece that still eschewed frontal nudity but teased us with suggestive sexuality appropriate to the play's themes. (Jorge Huerta could finally absolve me of my sins of denial.) Bisk Consoli managed to pull off an upset, meaning that he was cast when another actor dropped out. Bisk, tall and handsome, seemed like a "compromise" when first cast. The role of the aide, Matt McMurphy, was written for a man whom one might imagine as a less square-jawed presence on stage and more of a round-bellied one. But Bisk provided the acting skills that helped him come across as needy and love-starved and we bought it, so did the audience and the critics. Clay Wright, himself a local boy from an LDS family, provided the errant oversexed Mormon boy with great sagacity. As a director and writer, I enjoyed the best reviews I had gotten with a local production. This show hit a nerve of some kind. An older gentleman came up to me to thank me for it. For what exactly? He said it was close to his story. (Lucky him, I suppose, though he didn't provide details.) Another friend asked me if I knew about the rumors of a former Phoenix mayor who had allegedly done such and such – I did not. I was a recent arrival to the Phoenix scene. When the play was produced in San Diego by the Diversionary Theater, the mayor of a local municipality called to ask if the play was based on him. I didn't know there was a closeted gay mayor in a small city near San Diego. I assume inside many of us there's a dutiful and earnest man such as Cesar awaiting a romantic liaison with a sensual partner (and also a recklessly fun and irresponsible one) such as Domingo. If this play touches that nerve, then let it be the most sensual, most provocative touch of them all.

Guillermo Reyes
Phoenix, AZ
December 2007

Production History

Places to Touch Him was originally performed in Phoenix, Arizona, at Teatro Bravo in September 2002 at the Playhouse On the Park, written and directed by Guillermo Reyes with the following cast:

CESAR... Andres Alcala
DOMINGO .... Alonso Minjares
MATT.. Bisk Consoli
JOSH .... Clay Wright
DANCER ....Alfredo Cazarez

For performance rights, contact Bruce Ostler at Bret Adams, Ltd., bostler@bretadamsltd.com

Characters

CESAR: Cesar G. Gutierrez, 38, well-known lawyer, renowned community activist, potential politician and unsuccessful gay man.

MATT: Matt McMurphy, mid-30s, Cesar's best friend, also a lawyer and political consultant with a win-at-all-costs mentality. Otherwise, charming.

DOMINGO: Domingo "Domino" Lopez, 30, but looks younger, working class young man trying to educate himself, but carrying the baggage of the past, and lots of other unconfirmed rumors about him. He's a sexual magnet, but also seems to want to project empathy and humor, and wants to be liked for something other than looks.

JOSH: Josh, waiter, 20s, cute, from Mormon background, but now
         openly gay.

Setting

Phoenix, Arizona, present time.

A multiple set, creatively used, sparsely furnished, to give us a sense of the Phoenix
Saloon (the name of the main bar), Cesar's office, an outdoor place for a rally in the
desert, a backstage room for the Saloon, and Cesar's apartment.

Places to Touch Him
ACT 1 - SCENE 1

(A neighborhood gay bar in Phoenix, present day, early evening, happy hour time.)

MATT:	So…this was just one kiss?
CESAR:	A specific, well-executed kiss.
MATT:	Where exactly?
CESAR:	On the lips, of course.
MATT:	Oh, okay, we've got one kiss on the lips –
CESAR:	Entire civilizations have fallen over one kiss.
MATT:	No, that usually involves a kidnapped virginal bride under the auspices of some jealous Greek God.
CESAR:	Well, I'm talkin' Aztec God –
MATT:	If you're referring to Domingo Lopez, I can assure you this kiss meant nothing to him.
CESAR:	And you have inside sources to verify – ?
MATT:	I don't want to spend our happy hour on this.
CESAR:	Let me show you this one scene –
MATT:	No. I've spent the last five years watching dramatizations of your failed love life. Excuse me, but no. I need you to concentrate on the city council race –
CESAR:	Business and happy hour don't mix.
MATT:	I'll be gentle; you'll like it.
CESAR:	I doubt it.
MATT:	Listen –
CESAR:	I'm not –
MATT:	Listen! The voters want to see a confident, youthful, energetic homosexual. In Phoenix, you're more likely to lose because you're a Democrat than because you're gay, so you need to focus now on how to execute something other than a kiss. Hey, other Tex-Mex cowboys will come along –
CESAR:	He isn't Tex-Mex, more like Arizona-Mex.
MATT:	*(With a "whatever" gesture.)* Hmmmm.

(Josh brings them a second round. Cesar ignores him; he's in his own world. Matt pays him and tips him. Josh smiles and walks away.)

MATT:	Thanks.
JOSH:	No prob. *(Exits.)*
MATT:	You didn't even notice him; you didn't even say thank you.
CESAR:	Sorry.
MATT:	You're not being sociable with a potential voter.
CESAR:	I am not in campaign mode right now, I'm thinkin' of – *(Sigh.)* ahhhh –
MATT:	Physical beauty is overrated.
CESAR:	Because we don't happen to have it?

MATT: Speak for yourself, Cesar G. Gutierrez! We are beautiful, albeit on the brink of maturity, and if other men don't appreciate our sometimes-imperceptible-but-nonetheless-very-much-in-evidence loveliness, it's their fucking loss!

CESAR: Well, I'm tired of being their loss. I want to kiss somebody who is not a "compromise," who actually makes me feel unstable and overjoyed, passionate, yet tremulous and insane all at the same time. That's Domingo Lopez.

MATT: Mr. Domino himself.

CESAR: Mr. what?

MATT: Friends and foes alike call him "the Domino."

CESAR: Why?

MATT: Because we are all chips; in his game, you've just become one of the falling pieces of it, congratulations. More tequila?

CESAR: No! I think people don't give him enough credit. Let me show you –

MATT: I said no dramatizations!

CESAR: Shut up and look. Same setting: the Saloon. On a cool November evening…slight rain outside, enough moisture on the window panes to keep you in a state of longing – *(He sighs.)* –

MATT: Moving on.

CESAR: Yes, moving on –

(Change of lights to signify a flashback. Cesar crosses over to the other table to do this scene. Domingo enters wearing cowboy hat and outfit, looking all virile and sexy.)

CESAR: Over here.

DOMINGO: You came.

CESAR: You sound surprised.

DOMINGO: I been stood up before.

CESAR: Who would do that, to you of all people? *(To Matt.)* Am I sounding desperate?

MATT: I'm just watching, remember? More tequila, Josh, please.

DOMINGO: Hey, I kinda like this place, it's different for me. It's very… middle-aged.

(Matt gives Cesar a look.)

CESAR: Ah, you mean to say it's a little more subdued than that nightclub you go to.

DOMINGO: No, I mean the old trolls who come here – except you, of course – they make the place look lame.

CESAR: Lame. Of course.

DOMINGO: But we can talk here at least and that's great. I say places like this are disappearin', the world's gettin' louder as if the *pinche* bar owners don't want us to talk, like they want us to drown in their noise.

CESAR: Yet you changed into a rather provocative and loud outfit –

DOMINGO: I'll end up at the Mexican cowboy bar as usual where the men don't talk, they just move to the beat of the *norteño* music. Sweat is also good, it's the poetry of the masses.

CESAR: Can I order you anything?

DOMINGO: Not right now, 'night is young. I really just wanted to talk to you, Mr. Gutierrez.

CESAR: Cesar, please.

DOMINGO: Yes, Cesar.

CESAR: It was a great conference; I'm glad I met you.

DOMINGO: Prominent *vatos* like you sharing their success stories with those of us still strugglin', quite an honor, Mr. Gutierrez, ah, Cesar.

CESAR: You're a bright student; I'm sure you're going places.

DOMINGO: I didn't want to go back to school but my grandmother said get off your ass, *pendejo*. In so many words. The alimony and child support were kicking in, too.

CESAR: You are marr – ?

DOMINGO: Was married. Two boys. One unfulfilled ex-wife. I needed more schooling to keep up. Besides, I've gotten to know professional men –

CESAR: Good, we're a source of inspiration. *(He gives Matt a look. Matt looks back skeptically.)*

DOMINGO: A successful Latino lawyer, a gay Latino lawyer, too, man. A good example to all the bent boys and girls from *el barrio*.

CESAR: I'm sure you've had other role models.

DOMINGO: Not really.

CESAR: Come on, somebody –

DOMINGO: My old man did what he could, but he was undocumented and worked as a dishwasher until he retired. I can't blame *el jefito* for his poverty. He's back in Sonora, with cancer.

CESAR: Sorry.

DOMINGO: Yeah. *(To Josh.)* I'll take water. *(Back to Cesar.)* You got an ex-wife or anything?

CESAR: I've never been…with anyone.

DOMINGO: You're not a virgin, are you?

CESAR: No. I meant I've never been with anyone who's lasted. I'm just…self-reliant.

DOMINGO: Nobody does it alone. Come on, you must have had role models, real ones.

CESAR: Ah, let's see, Cesar Chavez.

DOMINGO: Someone closer to home?

CESAR: My dad then.

DOMINGO: See? I knew it.

CESAR: He got his education thanks to the GI bill and since then he hasn't let anyone in the family avoid an education. He's a professor down in Tucson, U of A. Chicano literature.

DOMINGO: Good. See? I didn't even know they had Chicano poets until I went back to school.

CESAR: Well, we do.

DOMINGO: Nobody taught me nothin'; our people are not supposed to write anything, according to the school system 'round here.

CESAR: Well, let me write this down then –

DOMINGO: What?

CESAR: Alarcon. Homoerotic, Chicano poetry.

DOMINGO: A book about Mex-Sex?

CESAR: Mex-Sex?

DOMINGO: Mex-Homo-Sex. You know…let's say, two Mexican macho men in their cowboy outfits on top of each other, naked but wearing their cowboy hats always. Man, that's hot. What's your kink?

CESAR: I – I don't have a "kink."

DOMINGO: Get one.

CESAR: Just like that. I walk into a store and ask for one?

DOMINGO: You know what I mean – waddy you like?

CESAR: Foreign films –

DOMINGO: No, no, that's not what I'm asking. For instance, I like lots of bends and twists –

CESAR: And that would be – ?

DOMINGO: You get those two Mexican cowboys, very macho, very masculine, but they're holding hands, then they're kissing, then their clothes are off, and I'm in the middle, a couple more join in. One man in front, another in back, about two dudes hanging around down in my crotch, lots of entanglements, and you can't tell whose leg is whose –

CESAR: That's –

DOMINGO: An orgy, men are touching me all over, and I'm their sacrificial virgin – oh, but don't worry, my imagination's way ahead of the reality. I'm a Catholic boy from *el barrio,* I only do group sex on Lent…That was a joke.

CESAR: Of course –

DOMINGO: And you're not laughing.

CESAR: Look, it's not that type of book so –

DOMINGO: Alright, time to try…

(Domingo reaches out and gooses him. Cesar jumps, surprised. Matt looks over amused.)

CESAR: What was that?

DOMINGO: Too much conversation; 'time to grab something.

CESAR: My rump? *(Domingo's tasting his drink.)* My drink, too?

DOMINGO: My germs, yes! And next time I won't be so gentle.

CESAR: *(After a beat.)* I'll get the check.

DOMINGO: Now you're uncomfortable.

CESAR: You have very interesting ideas, but –

DOMINGO: They're not ideas; they're impulses.

CESAR: Clever distinction, but –

DOMINGO: Why did you come here?
CESAR: Why did you?
DOMINGO: Come on, you tell me, you're the famous guy; I'm an assistant
           manager at a burger joint; why are you so curious about me?

(Cesar sits down.)

CESAR: Well, don't call yourself "nobody."
DOMINGO: I am.
CESAR: You have things to contribute to society, I'm sure; your children
           need you and you must learn to value your achievements
           without having to compare yourself to others, which is really an
           insidious aspect of this system which ignores the contributions
           of working class people such as yourself, especially the
           contributions of immigrant workers without whom the economy
           would collapse. You need to resist and overcome the self-hatred
           taught in our educational system, which is run for the promotion
           of the corporate class in their eternal need to create clones for
           their old boys' network. Anyway…ah, I'm sorry.
DOMINGO: Don't be. That gave me a woody.
CESAR: Alright, look…I've been wondering since yesterday, since the
           start of the conference – whether or not it was my imagination –
DOMINGO: What?
CESAR: Whether or not you've really been…flirting, or just playing
           games or what?
DOMINGO: Before I say anything else, you gotta know up front, if you don't
           already, I have a reputation –
CESAR: No, really? I'm so surprised.
DOMINGO: Come on, I know people talk about me. What have they told
           you? Give it to me straight.
CESAR: How about you tell me?
DOMINGO: I have to be careful –
CESAR: Of what?
DOMINGO: Sexually inactive people can be very resentful.
CESAR: On their behalf, I give you permission to brag all you'd like –
DOMINGO: I'm not bragging, I just do alright with men, you know. Sue me.
           Hah, you're a lawyer, get it?
CESAR: Got it. What else?
DOMINGO: I may be a father; I have responsibilities; I have this whole other
           side to me, but I go home with strangers, do some pot, maybe
           coke, tequila, whiskey, and creative sexual positions. Can you
           handle that?
CESAR: Yes, I could. Well, the last part, not the drug part.
DOMINGO: You're too good for that.
CESAR: Just not my thing, that's all.
DOMINGO: Fine, I need a change of pace myself. I told you, you are the first
           man who's ever caught my attention because of brains.
CESAR: So I don't inspire lustful thoughts of incredible sex?

DOMINGO: We can work on that.

CESAR: I don't think I have to work on it, I am sexually...alive, I am.

DOMINGO: No need to convince me, you want my heart and soul, or just my butt, you choose.

CESAR: Look, alright, somebody with your looks doesn't normally talk to someone like me.

DOMINGO: What? Why you say that?

CESAR: It's true. This type of thing never happens to me.

DOMINGO: You're a successful man.

CESAR: In certain areas, yes, but –

DOMINGO: You're only, what? Forty-five?

CESAR: Well, no, 38 actually.

DOMINGO: Ooops, sorry. Hey, I'm 30.

CESAR: You look 20.

DOMINGO: My luck. People think I'm a kid; I get cruised by kids in a college full of them, but I've been there and done that. I'm ready to move on –

CESAR: To what?

DOMINGO: I don't know yet...I want somebody to be there for me.

CESAR: In what sense?

DOMINGO: Look, I don't know when it's gonna be right for me – a relationship of some kind, I mean, but I'll know it when the time's right –

CESAR: Well, we're not getting any younger, Domingo!

DOMINGO: I'm trying! But you see maybe because I have a reputation, people assume I will leave them first and they leave me first, so it never works out. I want somebody to be courageous enough to stick it out, to be man enough to be there for me. I know I'm not easy, and that I come with a lot of baggage, but that's where *el coraje* comes in, don't you think? I want somebody to be patient, to stick by me, to take me in slowly and gradually, to have some patience. I want it, I want it real bad. I do. Do you believe me?

MATT: Now wait a second –

CESAR: Don't interrupt – the kiss is coming up.

MATT: Excuse me, this is not the same Mr. Domino whom I know and love to hate –

DOMINGO: I admit I've made my mistakes.

CESAR: He admits he's made mistakes.

MATT: The Domino I know would never admit to such a thing.

CESAR: Then you don't know him –

MATT: Trust me, I do.

CESAR: What does that mean?

MATT: I don't want to say anything I might regret.

CESAR: About?

MATT: Why don't I let you get to your kiss first?

CESAR: I'm not sure I can. Tell me what you know.

MATT: Please, don't let me interrupt. Josh, darling, I hope you're running a tab.

(Cesar gets back to Domingo with some misgivings.)

DOMINGO: So where is he?

CESAR: Who?

DOMINGO: The man willing to woo me; I like the word, to woo. It's clean and fast, and you can even say it while giving a blow job. Woo. See?

CESAR: Yeah, I'll have to try that some time, thank you. So…you're getting ready to settle down, huh?

DOMINGO: Perhaps.

CESAR: Why?

DOMINGO: Because…I'm kinda scared…

CESAR: Of what?

DOMINGO: I – I'm a lot more like you than you think.

CESAR: In what sense?

DOMINGO: I have never had a lover either. I mean somebody who lasts. See? You complain about not enough men, I've probably had too many. Quantity can keep your ego going, but how long can it run on that alone? I mean, look, I have one gray hair back here, wanna see it?

CESAR: One gray hair, wow. What you young people have to put up with.

DOMINGO: I have another one in my crotch.

CESAR: I –

DOMINGO: But you can't look at that one yet.

CESAR: I really wasn't asking to –

DOMINGO: Besides, I yanked it out this morning. Do you dye your pubic gray?

CESAR: I don't care to – just shut up about that, okay? Thanks.

DOMINGO: Sorry. I'm just saying, let's face it, the days of being young, attractive, and hopelessly irresistible are coming to an end. Man, how have you coped with it?

CESAR: Assuming I'm there.

DOMINGO: You're not?

CESAR: Domingo, I've never been young, attractive, and hopelessly irresistible. So I'm not there yet, nor will I ever be because I wasn't there to begin with.

DOMINGO: I see.

CESAR: You're not even going to offer words of encouragement, "you're not that ugly, Cesar," that type of thing?

DOMINGO: Each to his own self-image, *pendejo.*

CESAR: You're cruel.

DOMINGO: If you have something to offer, Cesar, just show me *y ya, cabrón!* I better go.

CESAR: No. Please stay. Stay.

(Cesar looks around, a little scared, then pulls over and kisses him. Domingo allows himself to be kissed, then kisses him back. It lasts a couple of seconds. They stop, Domingo looking at peace, Cesar looking all around self-conscious of kissing in public.)

DOMINGO: That was bold; it was ruthless.
CESAR: You like that, huh?
DOMINGO: You've got my number, *(Purposely mispronouncing.)* Ceasar.

(Domingo exits. Cesar turns to Matt.)

CESAR: See?
MATT: I must admit.
CESAR: Admit what?
MATT: You made him sound sincere, like he meant it –
CESAR: He did, he does and, besides, he said he wasn't going to be easy.
MATT: Alright, alright, I see –
CESAR: Surprised, huh? I did good. I'm the man.
MATT: Don't gloat. So you've called him?
CESAR: Yeah.
MATT: And now you're going out again?
CESAR: Well, not yet.
MATT: Why?
CESAR: He hasn't called back, that's why.
MATT: In how long?
CESAR: Ah –
MATT: A week?
CESAR: A month.
MATT: A month?
CESAR: Alright, five weeks. Make that seven.
MATT: And you've kept this to yourself all this time?
CESAR: Yeah. I didn't think you'd understand –
MATT: Doesn't matter. I must be kept abreast of everything! Now where is he? What's his problem?
CESAR: I'm sure there's a perfect explanation –
MATT: And you're still waiting?
CESAR: I am.
MATT: Well, don't.
CESAR: I want to. I've never been kissed by somebody that handsome.
MATT: What? I remember a perfectly fine kiss between you and me –
CESAR: That was a long time ago, Matt.
MATT: I know that, but I'm just saying, I resent the insinuation that somehow I'm not –
CESAR: You're not! I'm sorry but you're not – you have your own appeal, but you're not quite like him! Face it, he is…fantasy! And for once, I want to sense what that's all about. Why should beauty be forbidden to me? Why has it always been inaccessible to me? As if I were cursed somehow.

MATT: Fine! You're entitled to your stupid fantasy.

CESAR: Doesn't sound like you mean it.

MATT: I don't. I told you, I know more than I should –

CESAR: What do you know?

MATT: I'll show you –

CESAR: Just tell me, only *I* do re-enactments.

MATT: Fine! Look, he gave me a ride –

CESAR: And?

MATT: I get into his van and he has a twelve pack in the back seat, and two open cans of beer on the coffee cup holders. He was sipping from one of them while he drove. That's right. He drank while he drove! Not to mention the fact that he had already downed about five shots of tequila at the bar.

CESAR: Then what happened?

MATT: Nothing.

CESAR: No accidents, no police search?

MATT: Nothing like that, no, but –

CESAR: He tried anything?

MATT: No, I tried, but he wasn't interested.

CESAR: So now that you've been turned down, he's a jerk.

MATT: I'm resentful, but he was already a jerk.

CESAR: You're resentful that he's shown an interest in me.

MATT: No. I'm used to it –

CESAR: Waddy you mean?

MATT: Up on stage, you impress people –

CESAR: And not down here?

MATT: People like to hear your wisdom up there, and it gets attention; people find it sexy. I've had to compete with that always.

CESAR: What? You're jealous?

MATT: No, I just take care of you. You have great potential. Some people can be attracted to you and you don't even realize it.

CESAR: Who are all these people? Why don't they come forward?

MATT: You don't notice because they don't all look like Domingo, that's all. You're hard on yourself because you don't look like a model, but you're also hard on everyone else, and that's cruel. It also makes you vulnerable to his charms, and I don't like to see my candidate looking vulnerable.

CESAR: I'm not a candidate yet.

MATT: But you will be. He could be sincere but, chances are, he likes the idea of fucking somebody important.

CESAR: I won't let anything affect my campaign.

MATT: So you'll announce finally?

CESAR: I'm exploring it.

MATT: I want us to get beyond that. I don't like to work for losing candidates; I've already spent a lifetime in Arizona losing to Republicans, times are-a-changin'!

CESAR: Onward to victory, Lady MacBeth!

MATT: A simple request: No bimbo eruptions, Cesar, please!

CESAR: Domino – I mean Domingo is not a "bimbo."

MATT: You haven't seen the worst side of him.

CESAR: And if I do, Matt, it's my business.

MATT: No, it's our business.

CESAR: No –

MATT: And the business of the people of Phoenix, particularly the Latino community, which has not been fairly represented in this town.

CESAR: The Latino community can survive without me. Maybe I don't need politics any longer –

MATT: You live for polit –

CESAR: Maybe it's time for me to live for something else.

MATT: Cesar, darling, this is Matt you're talking to –

CESAR: I need somebody in my life; I need to do more than press hands on a campaign trail; I need hugs that become long embraces, even an all-night friction of flesh and bones, blood and sweat, all the human fluids coming to a boil –

MATT: Oh, my!

CESAR: That's right, something hot, intimate, something I can claim my own. I want to do things I've never done before: I want to walk hand-in-hand with my male partner into a nightclub and dance the night away; I want to wake up in the morning and grind coffee beans for somebody, I want to come home and have somebody nag me about the laundry, and I would just love a simple moment of recognition – recognition, yes, I want people to suddenly turn around and notice – wow, he has a boyfriend. I want to feel the pride that goes with that, and yes, the vanity of it, too. Why is it too much to ask for after thirty-eight long, long years, that somebody should be there for me? What is it about me that says he's meant to be asexual? Is it written on my forehead? You tell me.

MATT: Look, personally, I am just used to the idea that you're just a unit, alone, and unencumbered.

CESAR: A eunuch, you mean?

MATT: You can keep your balls; nobody has to touch them, that's all.

CESAR: That's what I'm talking about.

MATT: I think everyone in this city sees you this way: as the celibate gay politician. And for a campaign manager, that's a big relief.

CESAR: If you want to be my friend, not just my campaign manager, you will help me find a voice in this community and keep my personal life private. Better yet, help me keep my private life happening because so far, I haven't had much of one. So will you? Will you, please?

MATT: Well, yes, I'm eager to help…but why hasn't he called, Cesar?

CESAR: I don't know –

MATT: He's no longer interested –

CESAR: He sounded –
MATT: He sounded sincere; they all do. He had his fun with a
           prominent member of our community, then he moved on to
           some gay congressman or something.
CESAR: I have to go; don't call me any time soon.
MATT: I have to, Cesar!

(Cesar exits. Matt is left looking worried.)

MATT: Josh, refill, *pronto*!

(Quick transition to Cesar's law office.)

SCENE 2

(Two months later. Cesar is on the phone as he tries to get his desk organized.)

CESAR: I'm only in for the Border Patrol. Since I'm suing their ass, I
           figure I should take their calls…no, no one else, I've got Mary
           Ann on the other line about that rally she's organizing, and the
           mayor? I'm meeting him for lunch, no need to get back to him
           right now. Well, get back to Matt and tell him I could use his
           help on that case, but if he's too busy – what? Who? – No, I
           can't see anybody right now. I've gotta finish this call, I –

(Domingo walks in.)

CESAR: *(On phone.)* It's alright. No, don't hold calls; the gentleman in
           question won't be staying long…Mary Ann, let me call you
           back; I'll see you at the rally, and then maybe we'll talk about
           the campaign, you know, the whole works; I'll fill you in,
           nothing, trust me, nothing unusual, I just have to go, bye.
DOMINGO: *¡Chale!* Nice place, man.
CESAR: Where have you been?
DOMINGO: Mexico.
CESAR: And you couldn't leave a message? It's been three months.
DOMINGO: My father's dying. I think that's more important than our pride
           right now, *¿qué no?*
CESAR: How true is all that?
DOMINGO: Man! Don't tell me you don't believe me.
CESAR: Yes, I don't.
DOMINGO: His cancer's very advanced. I need a lawyer.
CESAR: I'm not it.
DOMINGO: Hear me out.
CESAR: I don't have to, Domingo. I'm a busy man. When you come see
           me, you call ahead; you make an appointment.
DOMINGO: Look, man, don't be a *chingón* right now, I need your help.
CESAR: I –
DOMINGO: Please.
CESAR: Five minutes.

DOMINGO   Dad, *el jefito*, man. They won't let him back in because he was
           living here illegally, and he has a minor criminal record – a
           misdemeanor, shoplifting, when he was 19 – but I say he spent
           all his adult life paying taxes and social security, man, not to
           mention contributing his cheap labor to the country. I say he
           returns to get proper treatment. He's too old to be crossing the
           border; he needs some sort of medical exception. I figured a
           lawyer can help me.

CESAR: You're right. Here. *(He scribbles something down.)*

DOMINGO: What's that?

CESAR: Mary Ann Dominguez, good friend of mine, also an
           immigration lawyer, hot, fiery Latina advocate, graduate of UC
           Berkeley Law School. Tell her I sent you; she'll be reasonable.

DOMINGO: Frankly, I wanted to ask for one of them freebies.

CESAR: *Pro bono?*

DOMINGO: Yeah, if it's all the same to you.

CESAR: Was this on your mind that first day we met?

DOMINGO: What?

CESAR: Yes or no.

DOMINGO: Man, if I'd been so calculatin', don't you think I would have
           already put out?

CESAR: The point is I don't trust you, Domingo.

DOMINGO: It's that friend of yours, ain't it? The one who tried to get a lift
           from me, figured I drink too much –

CESAR: I think I can figure you out by myself.

DOMINGO: Alright, I thought one of our idealistic attorneys, the type who
           dedicates his life to the community, would be eager to help me
           pero ni modo –

CESAR: That would be Mary. She's political, idealistic--

DOMINGO: I was also looking forward to coming back and picking up
           where we left off –

CESAR: You have family problems, maybe you should concentrate on
           that.

DOMINGO: That's exactly what I've been doing the past three months,
           hombre. I even had to take the semester off. I got behind on my
           work; I've had to drop my classes, postpone my education, and
           no, no love life right now, just *la pinche mano,* man. My father's
           an important obligation.

CESAR   Yes, well…I'm sorry. I need to get back to work.

DOMINGO: So I didn't return a phone call, alright, several phone calls. I
           should have called back, left a message, dropped an e-mail.
           I apologize. I told you I'm not calculating enough. I ain't the
           lawyer type around here.

CESAR: I'll level with you – I showed a side of me that I don't even
           show my family; I felt…vulnerable.

DOMINGO: Good.

CESAR: No, it's not good; I don't like the feeling. I don't do that.
            Ever. I'd had a couple of drinks, I was opening up to a perfect
            stranger, and that's all you are, a perfect stranger.

DOMINGO: I meant it though, I want to get to know you.

CESAR: I can't date someone like you.

DOMINGO: Like me?

CESAR: The real difference between you and me is not class, nor
            education; it's simpler than that. I return my phone calls.

DOMINGO: Alright, so I blew it. Forgive me.

CESAR: It's not really you. I – I'm an obsessive person.

DOMINGO: What does that mean?

CESAR: I…I fall in love with impressions, first impressions, fantasies,
            ideals; I shouldn't but I do. One kiss seemed already the
            beginning of something ideal, a love story maybe, a love that
            would change lives and set history on a new course. I'd like to
            experience all that, preferably with both body and soul. Other
            people have experienced it, why couldn't I? Why am I the one
            exempt from such a thing? Why couldn't that happen to me?
            That one kiss seemed to shatter the solitude for once, or so it
            seemed at the time…the ideal manifested itself in you somehow,
            on your face, your body, your lips; they became part of this
            story, this story that changes lives. It may sound ridiculous to
            you.

DOMINGO: No, no, it doesn't. But now you're getting to know me and
            you're already rejecting me.

CESAR: I certainly am.

DOMINGO: The reality's tough; I'm the son of illegal aliens, I have real life
            problems. I'm not fantasy. Yet, I seem to fascinate you –

CESAR: You fascinate me; you scare me.

DOMINGO: I don't blame you. My life's been scary and fascinatin'. In
            school, I had all the pressure to join gangs. All my classmates
            were doing it, gangs, drugs, selling and taking them; hell, it's a
            miracle I didn't go in that direction. I went with early marriage
            instead, 'figured it would help make me stable, reliable,
            dependable…that was my first downfall, because it meant
            supporting a family on fast food wages. I'm sure you've figured
            it out by now, that fast food wages don't support an entire
            family…well, you've dealt with enough *inmigrantes* to know
            that. That's what I liked about you to begin with. You seemed to
            know where I'm coming from. I couldn't get somebody better to
            listen. I didn't even know I was queer – well, I was hoping some
            of that high school experimenting was a phase; I believed it, I
            couldn't possibly be a *maricón*; hell, I'm masculine, the girls
            said so, my friends were the toughest sons of bitches, we played
            soccer, baseball, football, wrestling, how could I possibly be *de
            la otra cuadra?* Life surprises you, don't it?

Roberta is a Latin girl from North Dakota of all places – well, they moved there from Mexico to work for the meatpackin' industry; she came out here to study and get away from lame-ass boring parents stuck in that small-town routine of working for the Man and then dying young in some sorry-ass accident – "the machine cut off my hands, there it goes, oops," – she wanted a better future too, but unfortunately for her, she saw me and wanted me; I let it happen 'cause I needed it; I needed to prove myself a man. We both ended up workin' the Fatty Burger at midnight shifts.

My first male lover was someone who was also married just like me – he was my sister's husband. He and I would meet when the girls were out visiting family, baby showers, something really saintly and innocent like that. We were alone sucking each other off to wild abandon, *hijole*, that was hot, two family men sixty-nining each other and leaving stains all over the couch; we had to wipe 'em off with Mr. Clean Extra Strength. He decided to stay married. I decided to know myself. Somewhere along the line in that required humanities class, I must have read that Greek guy, that "know thyself" *vato* –

CESAR: Socrates, I think.

DOMINGO: Yes! He liked the boys; he liked 'em young. Bad influence, I suppose. But I don't regret it. It's been a shock to all my family, not to mention myself. I have what it takes to make a really good queer, I really do – very physical, sweaty and sexual, but very spiritual, too, Catholic boy with balls and full of traumas you wouldn't believe. Am I still scaring you? Hey, I got no tattoos, never went in that direction either, though the cops in Phoenix stop me all the time, and ask where are my tattoos – I think I get stopped just for that. So, still scared of me?

CESAR: No. Now I don't know what to think.

DOMINGO: Look, I'll go to Mary Ann what's-her-name, just let me –

CESAR: I don't think –

DOMINGO: Touch me. You were so eager to last time.

CESAR: I wanted to have you, I wanted to –

DOMINGO: Put your arm around me – like that, *así, mano, así* – and just take it easy, just feel that, will you? Make me feel warm, don't think of anything else, just think of what it feels like to be touching me here and now, that's all; it makes no difference where you've been or where I've been, this is all we've got right now. That feels nice, don't it?

CESAR: What do you want from me?

DOMINGO: See? You're not concentrating. Right now, this is all I want from you, your arms, please keep 'em there.

(Cesar begins to kiss his neck. Matt enters on the other side of the stage as if he's been watching all along and watches the last half of this scene.)

DOMINGO: See? You're rushing now. There'll be plenty of time for the smoochie stuff later.

CESAR: You'll be gone soon; I may never see you again.

DOMINGO: We haven't even dated and you're already feeling abandoned. You've already built an entire life for us together, haven't you? Haven't you fantasized it to death already? You've even imagined the breakup scene.

CESAR: And my heart's been torn to pieces already, yes.

DOMINGO: Man, I done nothin'. I am not your lover, so how could your heart possibly be broken, *pinche pendejo?*

CESAR: The real thing would be more excruciating then.

DOMINGO: I want you to listen to me. I want you to get to know me, just me. I am not your obsession, Cesar, I am a simple fast-food worker; one day I'll have a business degree, if I ever get through school; you forget I have to make a living while going to college with kids to support. I am really all of those things, and I think I do damn well, circumstances and all. When I really fuck up, you'll know it. This time, I haven't. You've got my number, I think it's your turn to come after me. To woo me, to court me, to make love to me – but don't go imagining things. I'm a man like any other; I need someone in my life, someone who cares about me, just me, not the image of me. I need to move past that already, I found one more gray hair right there, see? – and another one in –

CESAR: I don't need to see them all.

DOMINGO: I know…Well, thanks for Mary Ann's phone number, man, I'll use it. But as for us, homes, the ball's in your court, *y ya. Ahí te watcho,* homes. *(Exits.)*

(Quick transition to Scene 3 in the bar. Matt's been watching this re-creation. Cesar goes to join him as if he really needs a drink now. Josh, with the help of stage hands puts up new decor; the Saloon is clearly going through a suspicious transformation.)

SCENE 3

MATT: He actually quoted Socrates?

CESAR: In so many words. Man, he does something to me.

MATT: The more you talk about him, the less I recognize this guy.

(Enter Josh.)

JOSH: Can I get you anything else?

MATT: Another round.

CESAR: No! *(They both give him a look.)* Ah, well – alright, another round. *(To Josh.)* But tell me, what's going on around here?

JOSH: You're talking to me?

CESAR: Who else?

JOSH: You just sit there and ignore me most of the time, Caesar.

MATT: He pronounces it "seh-sarr" as in Chavez, not Julius.

CESAR: Let him pronounce it "Caesar" if he likes; it makes me feel like an emperor.

JOSH: Like you're always on top.

MATT: Hmmmm.

CESAR: Besides, I've noticed you all along, I've just had other things on my mind, ok? Don't take it personally. You're – ah – you're hot.

JOSH: Oh, okay. Thanks.

CESAR: Now tell me, what is going on with this place? What are you doing to it?

JOSH: Oh, you mean the special area we're adding for the strippers.

CESAR: What? Why?

MATT: You hear that, Josh? For him that's a problem.

CESAR: I'm just surprised, this place has always been the tamest Saloon.

JOSH: We're trying to compete with those new bars across the street. We're having an amateur contest; you're welcome to enter it.

MATT: That's a thought.

CESAR: I think I'll probably just leave – and never come back.

MATT: You sit.

JOSH: I hope you noticed my new piercing – back of my neck, really cool. It's the angel Moroni – in honor of my Mormon ancestors. *(No comment.)* Okay, I'll be back with your drinks. *(Exits.)*

MATT: What's wrong with you?

CESAR: This used to be a decent establishment for average deviants.

MATT: Well, I for one welcome the change of pace. Just finish up with the Lover Boy situation and we'll watch the show –

CESAR: Oh, I don't know about any shows, but he's consulted with Mary Ann. She's going to help him and, as for myself, I don't know, I suppose I'm stuck. I have to "woo" him –

MATT: Do you even know how to "woo?"

(Cesar laughs, Matt looks at him funny.)

CESAR: I'm sorry, inside joke.

MATT: Whatever. Now, look, here's my cell. Call him.

CESAR: Let a few days go by. I'll get to it. Really. Now, please, any news from the councilman?

MATT: Are you really up to it? Your mind is elsewhere.

CESAR: I want my mind elsewhere; tell me.

MATT: Well, the councilman intends to run for re-election.

CESAR: Fine then, he'll have me as an opponent.

MATT: Pitting a Hispanic candidate against an African-American one? I don't like it.

CESAR: I don't intend to play racial politics, I'll just attack his record.

MATT: The guy's just as liberal as you are, if not more so; I don't see the point. I've got a better solution. Wanna hear it? Of course you do, now listen…

(Enter Domingo.)

CESAR: No, look who's here. Domingo – ?

(Before he gets a chance to say anything else, Josh enters with the drinks, and Domingo plants a kiss on him, not just any kiss either, but something a lot more intimate than we've seen from him.)

CESAR: Oh….did you see that?
MATT: Uh-huh. He is so busted.

(Josh comes over with the drinks, followed by Domingo.)

DOMINGO: Look who's here. Cesar, *el mero mero,* homes. *(To Matt.)* Hi, I'm Domingo.
MATT: Actually, we've met –
DOMINGO: Oh, oh, you look different, you've obviously lost weight.
MATT: Come speak at my funeral.
CESAR: Take your compliments where you can get 'em, Matt.
DOMINGO: Cesar, *el vato* Cesar, *¿qué onda,* sweetheart?
MATT: Love it when you go ethnic on us, Domingo.
DOMINGO: *Chale*, homes, check out my new pecs.
JOSH: Okay, so we're running a tab now, or what are we doing?

(Matt hands him his credit card, Josh exits.)

DOMINGO: What's wrong, Cesar? This time you're the one who hasn't called.
CESAR: True, I haven't.
DOMINGO: So what type of greeting is this, *hombre?*
MATT: I think he's a little shook up about seeing you kiss the waiter.
DOMINGO: Oh, that. Why shouldn't I kiss him? I sleep with him.
CESAR: Oh?
MATT: Hmmmmm.
DOMINGO: For purely physical reasons. Thanks for bringing me here, I wouldn't have met him otherwise.
CESAR: Uh-huh.
DOMINGO: Now, I'm his favorite, he says.
CESAR: His favorite what?
DOMINGO: *(To Matt.)* You see the thing about Cesar is that he's possessive and yet the *vato's* never once asked me out. He's told you all about it, I'm sure.
MATT: Oh, yes, very nice reenactment –
DOMINGO: Reenactment?
MATT: Oh, just something between us, it was convincing, even touching.

DOMINGO: Until I'm in a serious relationship, I intend to have sex with anyone I please. I have been upfront with Cesar, but he still suspects the worst.

MATT: You're very good about confirming the worst.

DOMINGO: I see, so being sexually active is frowned upon in the uppity lawyer circles you people run in – or better yet, you envy it, since so many of you have trouble getting laid.

MATT: Don't look at me when you say that – I've done my share of lowlifes.

DOMINGO: Anyone below your tax bracket is a lowlife –

MATT: You can lay off the class struggle, Che Guevara, I come from trailer trash myself –

DOMINGO: You admit it –

CESAR: Okay, Okay! That's enough, the two of you, just shut up, please! You were on a roll there, but it's my life, thank you, so I think I'll just pass on having a life right now, I gotta go –

DOMINGO: You can't go. I need you for moral support.

CESAR: Support? Wait! Don't tell me. You – you're entering the contest!

DOMINGO: The winner gets to be special go-go boy on Saturday, that's an honor you know –

MATT: "Best Crotch in Your Face" goes to…

DOMINGO: A boy's gotta have dreams.

CESAR: What dream would this be – ?

DOMINGO: To aspire to more than just the minimum wage lifestyle.

CESAR: I'm sure Hollywood will come calling.

MATT: West Hollywood.

CESAR: Matt –

DOMINGO: I'll dedicate my dance to you, Cesar, maybe we'll finally have a real date.

CESAR: Why have a date when we can have an unveiling?

DOMINGO: For a homo, you're awfully square. I have to go prepare. But tell me you like me; I want somebody to like me.

CESAR: Lots of people like you, "homes," it's just that –

DOMINGO: And you?

CESAR: You know how I feel.

DOMINGO: Good enough, so tell me, you'll stay, please; it's the first time I'm trying something like this, and to tell you the truth, I'm a little scared. I know you can't tell because I'm so masculine and muscle bound and utterly perfect, but you know…

CESAR: I get the point.

(Cesar looks at Matt, then defiantly turns to Domingo, kisses him on the cheek and sits down.)

DOMINGO: I knew you would! Thanks, lover man. *(Exits.)*

CESAR: Maybe you could go now.

MATT: And miss Salome's dance, are you kidding?

CESAR: Don't call him that.

MATT: He wants your head on a platter, baby – the wrong one, too. This guy's out to screw with you big time, and he gets off on it. Can't you tell that?

CESAR: So he's not safe! I…I still ….like him somehow.

MATT: Yet, you're afraid of him –

CESAR: Not at all.

MATT: You haven't gone out with him, you are hesitating because your instincts are telling you to run while you can.

CESAR: You're telling me that, not my instincts.

MATT: So fine, stay then, watch him dance, I know I am. Watch a dozen old queens tip him 20 bucks for the pleasure of pinching his nipples. We'll then vote on whether he wins the contest, or the chance to become a "husband."

(Josh returns.)

CESAR: Josh –

JOSH: Another round? You usually have two, max.

CESAR: No, I was wondering, you mind if I ask you about Domingo – you – you and he – you don't mind talking –

JOSH: About six weeks now. We have gone through the whole range of color condoms, but he doesn't respect me in the morning. Why?

MATT: That wasn't shy at all, was it?

CESAR: I still don't understand –

MATT: Cesar's never heard of the word "fuck buddy."

CESAR: I've heard of it, but I've never really met one, you know.

JOSH: That's me, the official fuck buddy of the state of Arizona.

CESAR: Thank you for sharing.

JOSH: It's all part of my research.

MATT: Is that what you call it?

JOSH: I'm doing my dissertation at ASU on macho attitudes in gay Latino male psychology –

MATT: You don't say.

JOSH: Domingo's a classic case. Trust me, I'm the expert. I grew up in Douglas by the border, all my high school experimentation was done with men who spoke Spanish only, and who frankly didn't want to talk – except they shouted *gringo* as they came on me. Anyway, the show's about to start. *(Exits.)*

CESAR: Just when I'm ready to dismiss somebody as shallow, it turns out they're getting a Ph.D. in psychology, what does it mean?

MATT: That shallow people are getting higher degrees.

CESAR: I don't think –

MATT: Never mind him, I'm intrigued by the whole thing, you might as well pursue this –

CESAR: What? You're going to be supportive now? You're not going to say that I might get some negative publicity by dating some working class – ?

MATT: No, because I may not support your campaign this year anyway.

CESAR: What?

MATT: Don't get me wrong, Cesar, in the long run, I think you'll be a terrific candidate, intelligent and literate, and all that stuff, but –

CESAR: You're dropping me.

MATT: No. I met with the councilman –

CESAR: And he did what? Recruit you?

MATT: He's willing to endorse you next time around –

CESAR: Next time aro – what do you mean next – ?

MATT: You don't enter the race this year; you endorse the councilman for re-election, and in four years, he's willing to move on, and leave the seat open for somebody else to fill, with a nice endorsement thrown in if you agree to step aside now.

CESAR: And you've made these decisions without me.

MATT: It's not a decision, it's an offer; one I'd be prepared to take if I were you.

CESAR: If you won't be my campaign manager, I'll find another one. As for Domingo and me…well…that's my business, isn't it? After the dance, I'll ask him out; I'll take him back to my place, to the Jacuzzi in my complex, and well, you're not invited.

MATT: Don't be like this.

CESAR: You may go now.

MATT: Oh, no, I told you, I'm staying, I'm watching –

CESAR: From that table then, over there – better yet, I'll move over there.

MATT: I care about you, Cesar.

CESAR: If you did, you'd wish me happiness –

MATT: I do – but –

CESAR: But what? You think I'm not tough enough for politics, or for this game of relationships. You think I'm a child who needs to be protected from someone who might hurt me – hey, I'm ready, Matt, bring it on, because I've never been more ready in my life, for politics, for sex, for the politics of sex. If you want to stand in the way, I say you watch out because I'm here to cheer him on and take him home and get on with my life.

MATT: Before you do, I'd run a background check if I were you.

CESAR: Oh, that's great, before I go out with a guy, I have to have him investigated.

MATT: You're a public figure now –

CESAR: Whatever happened to trust?

MATT: Ask yourself why his stories are just so conveniently dramatic; oh, he was married to a poor girl who worked for the meat-packing industry, dad is dying of cancer, his poor kids –

CESAR: Why would he lie about all that?

MATT: He senses one day you'll be important, he wants to come along for the ride. Be on the safe side, check the facts.

CESAR: You mean you haven't done it already? I'm surprised you'd let
          your candidate be caught off guard.

MATT: I figured this one needs to come from you.

CESAR: I – I'm not listening to any more of this; I trust him, and I will
          date him.

MATT: You're scared; I would be. *(No answer.)* Okay. Enjoy the show.

(Josh enters, prepared to be the host.)

JOSH: Ladies and gentlemen, I beg your indulgence, and indulgence is
          something we're here to beg for, on your knees, baby. Welcome
          to tonight's new contest, the Mr. Saturday Night contest. The
          winner gets to party on down in his shorts for the Saturday
          crowd; that's quite a privilege here at the Saloon. Contestant
          Number 1, local boy from South Phoenix, and a former prom
          king from our very own Desert High. It's Mr. Domingo
          Lopez…

(Domingo walks out and starts his dance. He's a little self-conscious at first. But once the music starts, he begins to gain strength and confidence. He dances to Los Ilegales' "Baila" or MDO's "Es la cosa" or Shakira's "Suerte." He approaches Matt and makes him smell his boot, Matt looks away, not amused. Then he approaches Cesar and devotes the rest of his dance practically to him. Cesar is hesitant, not quite wanting to respond, but Domingo pulls down his shorts and ends up in a g-string. That'll do it. Cesar now takes the initiative and ends up hugging him in an intimate embrace as the dance stops practically in his arms. Matt walks out looking skeptical, even scared for his friend as lights go down.)

ACT 2 - Prologue to SCENE 1

(At the Saloon. Domingo teaches Cesar how to do a basic line dance. No words need be exchanged. It should be a mysterious, musical interlude of a moment, lit to suggest a dream reality even though it's very real. After a few tries, Cesar begins to get the hang of it even though he's still a little awkward, and he's wearing work clothes and looks out of place. Matt is looking on, also wearing work clothes, and doesn't seem to approve. Josh walks in and sees the men doing the dance and then pulls Matt over. Matt resists; he's too self-conscious and awkward, but Josh succeeds in getting him to the dance floor.

The four men end up doing the line dance quite well, and lights go down. The transition links the dance to the following rally.)

SCENE 1

(Domingo stands up in a spotlight; he's addressing a crowd in the desert town, Florence, AZ. He starts off looking shy and a little scared, but he gathers steam as he goes along.)

DOMINGO: Wooh! It's not just a rally, it's a line dance, yeah. Ah...my, ah, good friend Cesar Gutierrez, you know him as *el vato* Cesar, man with the quick feet? Community activist and potential future city councilman, the Caesar Man himself—well, he asked me to speak to y'all today, never spoken to this many people, but he wanted me to speak about some of the issues that you're all fighting for here in lovely Florence, Arizona, home of the detention center where Homeland Security locks up border crossers.

Look...You got more important people here today to speak about those issues, and I've got no statistics, I only know what I've known as the son of an "undocumented" worker. Fancy name, huh? When I was growing up they just called us *mojados!* Now, we're "undocumented." Lawyers, they want to make our lives a little easier by changing the name of things. I know something about lawyers...

I've got nothing against them, of course, my best friends are, you know...But the fact is...the *mojados* are way beyond getting wet, they've gone into dry cleaning now, their children have settled this side of the border, well, like me. My father died recently, cancer, they said; was he exposed to deadly pesticides in his first job as an onion picker? I don't know, it was long ago, but how could I rule it out? Dad grew up on a farm in Sonora. One year a drought hit, the crops failed, and the whole family went hungry; there was nothing to sell out on the open market; what was he supposed to do, worry that some politician in Phoenix was outraged about the border crossings? So he crossed over, that was the most realistic thing to do at the time, and the only thing that saved his life.

I'm not saying "open up the border," I'm just saying the border's been opened up already by hunger and that's a much more powerful force than anything we could do or say. I'm not a politician, I don't have answers, but I say come up with a policy that makes sense to all hard-working people both here and there, and to stop pretending we don't need each other. Thank you.

(Applause, he's surprised by it, but then he basks in it. Quick transition to Scene 2.)

SCENE 2

(Matt and Cesar in the midst of conversation after the rally.)

MATT: I suppose it was a fine move, letting him speak from the heart.

CESAR: But you're still not impressed.

MATT: Cesar…he's a stripper.

CESAR: Part-time stripper.

MATT: In politics, that's all the time there is.

CESAR: You said so yourself, he's good with average folk, and it was
         not a "move," it was a very spontaneous choice on my part.

MATT: I prefer to let my candidate speak.

CESAR: They've heard me speak; I share my forum now.

MATT: Just remember, he's something to get out of your system –

CESAR: We're back to that? Matt, you should know –

MATT: What?

CESAR: He's moving in.

MATT: Oh? I'm not surprised.

CESAR: Yes, you are –

MATT: Not at all.

CESAR: Admit it – and you're lucky I still speak to you.

MATT: Why do you if you don't listen to me?

CESAR: I listen to you. I am letting the election go by, waiting four more
         long years, see?

MATT: Not so fast, *amigo.*

CESAR: Matt!

MATT: You can skip this year's election, but I have it on good word
         that one of our current city councilmen is stepping down to run
         for mayor, which means –

CESAR: A special election, I know!

MATT: That gives you an extra nine months or so to enjoy the boy toy
         and then let him go.

CESAR: That's not how I –

MATT: You were thinking about it already, weren't you?

CESAR: No!

MATT: Then why did you have a background check done on him?

CESAR: What? You? You're spying on me!

MATT: Come on, your instincts led you to check the facts.

CESAR: So I did! But guess what?

MATT: What?

CESAR: The facts hold together. The whole story, Matt, everything.
         Dad's cancer, the ex-wife, the kids, the enrollment at
         community college. He hasn't lied to me one bit, so he's
         moving in because I can trust him. He'll be a fine companion for
         a political candidate. So thank you, once again.

MATT: I see. I assume he doesn't have to pay rent then.

CESAR: It's not that type of arrangement.

MATT: Careful, here he comes, the boy from *el barrio,* or should I call
         him the boy saint?

(Domingo enters.)

DOMINGO: Cesar, *¿qué onda?* man, we have to go celebrate. *(To Matt.)* Well, hello, I thought you were fired.

CESAR: Domingo, Matt is my friend – and there's not gonna be any campaign this year, so nobody's fired.

DOMINGO: Oh, too bad – I'm getting to like this.

MATT: More speeches like that, and you'll end up running for city council yourself.

CESAR: Don't give him any ideas.

DOMINGO: My sociology professor told me the first gay candidate for a city council in San Francisco was this Latino drag queen –

MATT: Wow. Queer History 101. Gone back to school, have you?

DOMINGO: Three units, sociology – better than accounting. Did Cesar tell you our news?

MATT: Cohabitation. Must be very economical for you, Domingo.

CESAR: Matt…

DOMINGO: You know, Matt, I liked you a lot better when you mentioned you came from trailer trash. Give me more of that, and a lot less yuppie scumbag, and we'll be friends totally.

MATT: I respect trash, I come from it, it has its place obviously. I just hope the voters can come to the same conclusion; they're not always that generous. Good show the two of you, I mean it.

(Matt exits and leaves them alone. Domingo hugs him.)

CESAR: The two of you are gonna have to stop meeting like this.

DOMINGO: He loves it.

CESAR: I hope we're not rushing into things –

DOMINGO: He's putting doubts into your mind again.

CESAR: No, I have my own doubts.

DOMINGO: We've been through this already. And by the way, you never gave me an exact figure –

CESAR: As long as you pay half the utilities –

DOMINGO: But I have to pay some sort of rent, I insist, otherwise *pinche pendejos* like Matt are gonna say –

CESAR: Fine, we'll come up with a figure –

DOMINGO: Nothing too steep though, no more than I was paying before.

CESAR: Fine.

DOMINGO: I'm a partner, not a dependent.

CESAR: Yes, yes, sure. Listen, before we drive back to Phoenix, there's just one thing –

DOMINGO: I told you we should go celebrate, buy some booze and other fun things –

CESAR: See? Moving in together requires me to spell out some of the rules.

DOMINGO: Yeah, rules, I know. No booze.

CESAR: Booze is fine; booze is also legal.

DOMINGO: So…moving in would require me to –

CESAR: To keep your drugs away from my home. Yes. I just don't want
            it near me, if it's all the same to you.

DOMINGO: It's only fair, it's not as if I did it every day –

CESAR: I'm not calling you an addict. But sometimes –

DOMINGO: I work, I'm dependable and I'm back in school. Look, you sure
            you want to do this?

CESAR: I said I did, as long as you accept those conditions. Do you?

DOMINGO: Fair enough, nothing at home.

CESAR: And about the stripping –

DOMINGO: You're asking me to give that up, too?

CESAR: Well, eventually you're going to have to…reconsider.

DOMINGO: I'll eventually get a degree, a better job in an office and a pot
            belly and nobody will want to see me strip.

CESAR: Meanwhile, you'll be discreet?

DOMINGO: How discreet can a stripper be, Cesar?

CESAR: I mean don't flaunt it.

DOMINGO: I don't need to go to no boring cocktail parties with stuffy
            people. My friends accept me as I am. Do you?

CESAR: You know I do.

DOMINGO: But hell, the people like me, you saw the crowds, and in this
            case I didn't even have to strip for them.

CESAR: People love you, Domingo; they just want you to be a little safer
            in everything you do.

DOMINGO: I've survived this long, let's go celebrate with the legal stuff,
            Okay? Okay? Smile at me, *pendejo.*

CESAR: I'm smiling, I just don't go for big smiles.

DOMINGO: Are you my lover now or not?

CESAR: I've been your lover for a while now; it's you I worry about.

DOMINGO: No, don't say that. Forget lover anyway, I'm your husband.

CESAR: Strong words!

DOMINGO: Not intimidated though, are you?

CESAR: No. I've faced more difficult situations than the prospect of
            "marriage."

DOMINGO: It's supposed to be a state of bliss.

CESAR: It's more like sailing and surviving the storm.

DOMINGO: You're a pessimist; I'm having fun. Now you're driving me
            back to the city and you're coming to see our new show –

CESAR: If only it were a private show.

DOMINGO: Don't be greedy, we are dedicating it to you. You'll see, the
            lights dim, in the shadows you see a few figures, and then it
            starts, oh, let me show you –

CESAR: No –

DOMINGO: Yes, what's the point of us having fun at the club if people you
            care about can't share it? Sound, lights, action!

SCENE 3

(We segue into Domingo at the Saloon. "Peek-a-Boo" by Siouxsie and the Banshees plays. Domingo and a couple of background dancers do a new strip that is a little more artful than the second one. Cesar watches. The strip ends in applause as Josh rushes out.)

JOSH: Applause for our lovely new boys!

MATT: Alright!

(There's a freeze. Quick transition as Matt enters into Cesar's office.)

MATT: Time for a reality check…

DOMINGO: Now what?

MATT: I need you to check out the Saloon before the cops move on it.

CESAR: What are you talking about?

MATT: Rumors that the boys are not following the rules –

CESAR: Which rules?

MATT: Cesar, you know what I'm talk –

CESAR: I really don't! So why don't you just come out and say it?

MATT: The customers are being allowed to touch!

CESAR: Touch what?

MATT: Don't be naïve. Looks like the gentlemen of the new Saloon are now having a much better time than we ever did at the old one.

CESAR: So this is about your regrets over missed opportunities.

MATT: I'm serious. My informers are in the vice unit.

CESAR: Since when do you have informers?

MATT: Don't question what I do; just trust me on this.

CESAR: Let the vice unit take care of it.

MATT: No, no, wait, this is where I – influential lawyer – come in.

CESAR: Why are you getting involved?

MATT: Why? Why am I getting inv – Cesar! Look, sooner or later they're gonna have to crack down like they did with the girly bars or otherwise the straight folks are gonna wonder why they're letting the gays get away with sleaze, but…but…but the mud can splatter all over, and I'd rather work on damage prevention now than damage control later, alright? Especially when there is an important political career looming in the horizon. And besides, there's more than just touching going on.

CESAR: You've got my attention now, go on.

MATT: I'm not naming names. I have no idea if Mr. Prince Charming is involved, but I need you to check it out before it becomes necessary for Vice to move in. They're sending us the message; clean up our own act, or they'll do it for us.

CESAR: As if we're responsible for everything that goes on in the gay community?

MATT: Move on it, Cesar, and don't think the information may not have already traveled across town –

CESAR: To whom?

MATT: To Mary Ann Dominguez.

CESAR: She's my –

MATT: She's considering running for the city council primary –

CESAR: Not against me. I'm her friend.

MATT: Friends in politics? Now there's a shifting notion. If you react now, the voters won't care; you reacted in time, they'll like that. If you let it go, your enemies can blow this out of proportion – candidate's lover involved in sex ring. It has a good ring to it.

CESAR: I don't believe she'd use something like that against me.

MATT: Mary Ann is a bitch! If you didn't know that, I'm happy to break it to you, and you made the mistake of introducing her to him. She knows all about you and him. She's capable of doing a lot of damage, but if she splatters mud, I'll splatter it right back.

CESAR: I don't want us involved in negative campaigning.

MATT: Good boy, your integrity speaks volumes, so leave the dirt to me –

CESAR: Matt.

MATT: See this?

CESAR: Your cell phone?

MATT: It's not just a cell phone, but a computer that faxes, reads and distributes e-mail. I can move information very quickly around the country with this, particularly damaging information. And, yes, I have a few things on Mary Ann Dominguez. If she escalates, I have first strike capability.

CESAR: Well, you've got Osama shaking, I'm sure.

MATT: If she's not scared of me yet, I'll make sure she gets there very soon.

CESAR: Hell, I'm scared of you now.

MATT: Good. Meanwhile, you'll do damage control where it counts: at home. *(Exits.)*

JOSH'S
VOICE: *(At the club.)* "And applause for our lovely new boys, gentlemen."

(We hear applause, transition into Domingo's space.)

DOMINGO: Cesar…

CESAR: We need to talk.

DOMINGO: There's a show going on, it's the best show we've ever done; we've got a Vegas choreographer now, you've gotta check it out.

(Domingo goes behind a divider to get dressed.)

CESAR: Wait a sec, you can strip in front of strangers, but not in front of me –

DOMINGO: Cesar, please, I'm shy.

CESAR: Right! Look, I need you to level with me – what is going on behind the scenes here?

DOMINGO: I don't unders –
CESAR: Domingo…the vice squad is onto it!
DOMINGO: I don't run the place, I just work here –
CESAR: Yes, you do. That's the problem. What have *you* been doing?
DOMINGO: Cesar, please.
CESAR: And how much of all this does Mary Ann Dominguez – ?
DOMINGO: I haven't seen her in ages.
CESAR: Are you sure about that?
DOMINGO: You think I'm backstabbing you with Mary Ann – I don't know anything about her campaign.
CESAR: How do you know about her campaign at all?
DOMINGO: Today's paper, hello.
CESAR: Since when do you read the paper?
DOMINGO: I don't believe this. You're paranoid.
CESAR: You can never be too sure. What's going on here seems perfect for an embarrassment of some kind; so what is going on?
DOMINGO: You sure you want…?
CESAR: Yes, the whole story, the truth.

(Beat.)

DOMINGO: …some lonely old man started it.
CESAR: Uh-uh.
DOMINGO: He came back stage and wanted to meet the boys and then soon enough he was offering money, so one of the strippers allowed him to suck him off right back here on the hard wooden bench – and soon enough everyone was doing it; management was getting a cut, and third-quarter earnings have been spectacular.
CESAR: I bet. What about you?
DOMINGO: I helped a really lonely man. I mean, he's always been there for me, listening to my confessions –
CESAR: Confessions? I don't want to know names or professions –
DOMINGO: I think celibacy is cruel anyway.
CESAR: I'll tell you what's cruel: they're called STDs.
DOMINGO: It's not like it's hard-core prostitution; it involves mostly a lot of touching –
CESAR: Thank you for the distinction. "Your honor, my lover's not a prostitute, he just does a lot of touching."
DOMINGO: No, honey, they touch me.
CESAR: Guilty nonetheless!
DOMINGO: Some men are in dire need of "touching" and we have something they want for entertainment –
CESAR: Let them get cable!
DOMINGO: *Chale,* man, our customers leave here with a smile of serene satisfaction on their faces. How I hate to see people caught up in their *pinche* solitude, *sabes?*
CESAR: So you've become the crusader –

DOMINGO: You should know all about solitude. You never had a boyfriend until the age of 38, for instance, so solitude had a claim on you and on your psyche, and my very presence has challenged that.

CESAR: You're mouthing off some ideology that doesn't sound like you; it sounds suspiciously like that, that, that sociology professor –

DOMINGO: I'm learning, I'm growing, and you resent that.

CESAR: Resentment is a proper thing for a lover, which brings me to the fact that you and I are supposed to be in a relationship.

DOMINGO: Fine, but I've technically become a sex worker now, so it's up to you to deal with it.

CESAR: A sex worker?

DOMINGO: Or a sex radical, call it what you wish.

CESAR: Whatever happened to your disdain for euphemisms? Why don't you just call yourself a slut?

DOMINGO: That's low.

CESAR: It's truthful.

DOMINGO: My sociology teacher warned me about you –

CESAR: Oh, has he?

DOMINGO: He says you're conventional and you'll whitewash your entire campaign to appeal to middle-class voters.

CESAR: I see, now I'm a sellout.

DOMINGO: He says I can always go stay with him if you become unbearable –

CESAR: Wait a second, you and he – you're having an affair? – wait, of course you're having an affair; you're a slut; you are exchanging favors with your sociology teacher; you give him head, he gives you a brainwash –

DOMINGO: Look! He's been very good to me and he's taught me to challenge myself and think less conventionally.

CESAR: What is sociology anyway? It's a pseudo-religion like scientology.

DOMINGO: You're showing your ignorance, Cesar, or you're just jealous.

CESAR: Alright! Here's more conventional wisdom for you: I need you to promise that you are being careful and that you are practicing safety.

DOMINGO: I protect myself always.

CESAR: Good!

DOMINGO: Although he does want me to try barebacking.

CESAR: What? Sex without a condom?

DOMINGO: I haven't done that yet, but in his new book he urges gay men to return to "the raw essence of erotic power – "

CESAR: How about me punching him in the face without a glove?

DOMINGO: See what I mean? You are influenced by straight people's attitudes towards our sexuality.

CESAR: It's not a matter of what straight people might think; people are dying!

DOMINGO: But there comes a time and place when sex needs to be about risk!

CESAR: When I drive, I demand air bags.

DOMINGO: But even they can't save you some times. Oh, how did he put it? "A condom blocks out the Dionysian impulses of post-structuralist surrender – "

CESAR: Could we just…ah…just get the Greek Gods out of this argument?

DOMINGO: And, let's see, "gay sex should be about confronting the limitations of the straight marital state and gay men should not be in a rush to emulate it."

CESAR: So…so…so you get an A in sociology, now what? What does it mean for us, huh? Us two?

DOMINGO: You tell me, I'm not the one who has a problem with this.

CESAR: Alright, new house rules: maybe you need to move out.

DOMINGO: Maybe I do. When?

CESAR: You could make an effort to struggle more for our relationship.

DOMINGO: I don't feel like it, I'm pissed off at you, Cesar; 'thought you had more of a visionary spirit.

CESAR: You want me to respect your choices? Well, you could at least communicate them to me without me having to spy on you. You were obviously ashamed about this; you were obviously not willing to talk about it. You want respect, you have to earn it, and becoming a fantasy boy for old men in need of sucking go-go boys is not my idea –

DOMINGO: Fine.

CESAR: Fine what?

DOMINGO: I'll move out.

CESAR: Domingo…How are the kids doing?

DOMINGO: What do you care?

CESAR: I've gotten attached to them.

DOMINGO: Send them Christmas gifts.

CESAR: I don't want us to break up –

DOMINGO: Oh, so we'll stay together for the kids, that's quite conventional, isn't it?

CESAR: I'd like us to be adults and work through this…Don't go.

DOMINGO: If I stay, you'll have to live with the consequences of my choices.

CESAR: Then you'll have to forgive me for trying to change your mind, but I won't kick you out, and I won't let you go without a struggle.

DOMINGO: Fine, fine –

CESAR: And the Saloon will be raided tomorrow night, and you – father of two – better not be anywhere near it, if you want to stay out of jail.

DOMINGO: I'm earning more money than ever, and I'm saving now, and that feels great.

CESAR: Think of the long-term rewards of school –
DOMINGO: Education won't pay the bills that need to be paid now.
CESAR: Let me pay.
DOMINGO: And have your friend Matt ridicule me? No, I'm paying my
            bills, I'm helping my kids, I've started their college fund and
            everything –
CESAR: At the expense of taking so many risks?
DOMINGO: Yes! I will not be treated like a wetback –
CESAR: Nobody's treating you like –
DOMINGO: I will not make the wages of one, and I will not get stuck my
            entire life working at some half-ass job only to find out my
            insurance won't cover my cancer treatment or whatever it is
            that'll strike me down the road. I won't be a pawn of the system
            like my father was, I won't go begging for charity. So it's not
            "respectable," so it won't get me invited to one of Matt's dinner
            parties, oooooh, it's my loss. I'll have the ninety-nine cent
            special at McDonald's and I'll save my money for my kids. That
            is who I am right now. In the future, fine, I'll be a middle-aged
            guy with a business degree; let's talk dinner parties then, why
            don't we?
CESAR: I just want us both to be safe, and I want you to think twice, I
            mean, is this any type of career – ?
DOMINGO: It clearly wouldn't make sense for you, no.
CESAR: I mean for anybody.
DOMINGO: I told you, I will not return to the minimum-wage lifestyle.
CESAR: How will you explain this to your children?
DOMINGO: The same way I've explained it to you. I am not ashamed,
            Cesar. Shame is a very relative term when people are perfectly
            willing to tolerate illegal immigrants so that their lettuce will
            be cheap. Contrary to popular opinion, illegal aliens are very
            popular in this country; business people are fighting hard to get
            our labor.
CESAR: Look, you're not an illegal alien, although what you're doing
            sure is illegal.
DOMINGO: Sometimes, I don't see the distinction. I'm tired of the
            hypocrisy –
CESAR: Okay, you're preaching to the choir, but our relationship is more
            than just about cheap labor!
DOMINGO: You're the one treating me like a criminal.
CESAR: Look, truce! I'll sleep in the guest room tonight.
DOMINGO: I'll sleep away from home.
CESAR: Your choice.
DOMINGO: It certainly is.

(Domingo exits.)

SCENE 4

(Matt and Cesar at the Saloon next day.)

MATT: Alright, so how much do these boys charge?

CESAR: Please.

MATT: I'm curious. Before they raid the place, we might as well try their services.

CESAR: Matt, please.

MATT: Alright. Look…I'm sorry for you it's come to this.

(Josh enters with their drinks.)

JOSH: Hi.

MATT: How much, Josh?

JOSH: How much for what?

CESAR: The drinks.

JOSH: Oh, of course.

MATT: What did you think we were asking for?

CESAR: Yes, we hear this place has gone through a lot of changes since we used to frequent it.

JOSH: Exciting changes, I think. For the better, too.

CESAR: Fine, you probably won't be needing my tips then since you're all doing so well providing other types of services.

JOSH: Whatever!

(Josh exits.)

MATT: I think he's become one of them, too –

CESAR: It's like the Stepford Wives; they've become a secret cult of male sluts.

MATT: Sounds good to me. Too bad a lot of our friends are going to jail because of this change in management.

CESAR: Mismanagement. I tried to warn that stupid owner, but that old queen seems to think he can bribe the vice squad, too.

MATT: At least we're lawyers, we can defend them.

CESAR: Not me.

MATT: When is the raid supposed to happen?

CESAR: Yesterday, but I guess they decided it'll be an unpleasant surprise any day.

MATT: I'm sure Domingo took the warning; he won't be stupid enough to get caught.

CESAR: I think he will be; I think he is.

MATT: You'll get through this.

CESAR: Don't say that.

MATT: Cesar, face it, this relationship is practically over; you can't go on like this.

CESAR: I love him, don't you understand that? I care about him, I share
         my life with him.

MATT: He obviously doesn't share his life with you, so…hey, another
         adventure in the Wild Wild West.

CESAR: When's he going to come out here?

MATT: Tell you what, let's not stick around to watch the show, or
         the raid, or whatever's supposed to happen. I was kidding
         when I said I wanted to check out the merchandise. I'm dating
         someone, you know.

CESAR: Really? You?

MATT: Don't act so surprised.

CESAR: Sorry.

MATT: Just another lawyer, boring patent and contractual law, but he's
         well-read and likes the classics, and has me reading the latest
         translation of *The Odyssey* so we can compare notes.

CESAR: I got the new Fagles translation.

MATT: Really? Me, too. He gave it to me. I kinda like a man who
         pushes the classics.

CESAR: Good for you. We do sound kinda boring, don't we?

MATT: Well-read, you mean, people who can carry a reasonably
         intelligent conversation.

CESAR: Boring!

MATT: That's him speaking, not you.

CESAR: You're right, but sometimes I wonder –

MATT: So he gets laid more often, that's not an achievement.

CESAR: I beg to differ. I mean look at you, you haven't been with
         anyone since – ?

MATT: Since you, so?

CESAR: That long?

MATT: I thought I wouldn't recover, but I have –

CESAR: We had a very quick thing, wasn't even an affair –

MATT: But at the time it meant everything to me.

CESAR: I…I didn't realize.

MATT: But trust me, recovery is possible. My only symptom left over
         is the continuous bout of bitchiness that besets my otherwise
         pristine personality – I'm sure you've noticed it.

CESAR: Nope, I haven't noticed a thing.

MATT: And I do have to admit one thing –

CESAR: What?

MATT: I give the creature a little bit of credit –

CESAR: That's big of you!

MATT: I interpreted that night with Domingo in a more extreme way
         than warranted –

CESAR: What do you mean?

MATT: I admit, my way of telling it was perhaps…biased.

CESAR: Why? Domingo's proved himself to be an extreme person.

MATT: Yes, the drinking part was true, but he probably wasn't as drunk or as obscene as I made him out to be. But he – he just scared me. It blinded me to his other side –

CESAR: Such as?

MATT: The fact that he can be charming, and he is much more powerful and dangerous that way. He's got a certain appeal to him, and if only I weren't so, so stupidly cautious about everything – face it, I was trying too hard to prevent you from going there –

CESAR: All of your warnings have come true, how could I resent you for that?

MATT: Because for your sake, I also wanted it to be true; I wanted you to find "perfect love," if such a thing is even possible for anybody.

(Matt touches his hand and keeps it there for a few seconds until Cesar pulls back.)

CESAR: Alright, that's enough, I don't want to see that part of you –

MATT: Look, you want to go do the sing-along *Sound of Music?*

CESAR: I don't know, Matt. Let Julie Andrews sing, everybody else shut the fuck up, you know.

MATT: Just testing.

CESAR: Subtitles are for foreign movies anyway.

MATT: There's a really good Rene Clement retrospective –

CESAR: Which film? Don't tell me. *Forbidden Games?* One of my favorites.

MATT: One of the great film classics of all time! Wanna go see it?

CESAR: Tonight?

MATT: Right now.

CESAR: Okay. Let's blow this joint, and let the chips fall where they may! Come on.

(They exit as lights go down.)

SCENE 5

(At Cesar's apartment, later that night, Cesar walks in.)

CESAR: Hello? Domingo? You home?

(Josh walks out wearing a bathrobe, looking quite drunk)

JOSH: Oh, it's Cesar.

CESAR: I know my name, thank you, what are you doing here, Josh?

(Domingo walks out, also wearing a bathrobe.)

DOMINGO: Look who's home? You kept us waiting, so we got started without you.

CESAR: You disappeared from the club.

DOMINGO: You told me to.

CESAR: I mean without telling me –

JOSH: *(To Cesar.)* Were you the one who told? Our friends got arrested because of you.

CESAR: Excuse me, I was trying to prevent this incident from happening –

DOMINGO: He tried, it's true.

JOSH: Oh. I'm sorry, I wanted somebody to blame.

DOMINGO: He's not to blame personally, but everything he stands for is.

CESAR: Oh, yes, the sociology lesson again, thank you.

JOSH: Guys, why don't we all just, like, disrobe and relax?

CESAR: *(To Domingo.)* What did I say about drugs?

DOMINGO: You think he's under the influence? That's just his personality.

JOSH: Not so. Hey, I'm half way through my dissertation; I finished my chapter on Foucault, let's celebrate –

CESAR: Domingo, get Josh out of here.

DOMINGO: The circumstances have changed, we're unemployed, we want to forget. You wanna join us for sex?

JOSH: Yeah, join in, don't be shy.

CESAR: Josh, just, ah, you know, mum's the word, be a good boy. Okay? Good boy. *(To Domingo.)* The understanding is – or was – in my house, everything's –

DOMINGO: Everything's off limits. Your whole life is off limits.

CESAR: Now you take your special friend, and go to his place, leave me out of it.

DOMINGO: You owe us a little more time, Cesar –

CESAR: I do, huh?

DOMINGO: We want your company; we want you.

JOSH: We're in the business of pleasing gentlemen of caliber, just like you.

CESAR: That's very lovely.

DOMINGO: Have a drink and loosen up, darling! We're celebrating the end.

JOSH: The end of the good times.

DOMINGO: The end of everything! Celebrate it with a big bang; are you man enough for that?

CESAR: Maybe it's time to pay attention again to your studies –

DOMINGO: Man, what are we learning exactly? How to perpetuate the system of solitude, each to his own tv set?

CESAR: How about learning a craft that allows you to earn a respectable living?

DOMINGO: Enough of that, now you drink, drink, and be merry; we'll sing you a song, Josh has a lovely voice –

CESAR: How about cuts from *La Bohème* ?

JOSH: How about you cum in my mouth?

DOMINGO: Josh, you nasty boy, that wasn't very nice. Nasty!

JOSH: I was being naughty, not nasty!

CESAR: How about I go into my bedroom now and read *The Odyssey*?

JOSH: Why?

DOMINGO: Nothing's wrong with reading, Josh.

JOSH: But in order to do what? Reading should be selective, and it shouldn't substitute for life.

CESAR: We wouldn't want indulgence to interfere with scholarship.

JOSH: You're getting the hang of it. Hey, I've never fucked a nerd before.

CESAR: Who's the nerd? I'm a lawyer.

JOSH: Wear a cowboy hat at least, Cesar, give us some fantasy.

DOMINGO: Say, I read parts of *The Odyssey* in my first semester in city college myself.

CESAR: And you learned nothing –

DOMINGO: What makes people feel more alive anyway? Drink up!

JOSH: Drink it all down, Cesar.

DOMINGO: If you're gonna go into that bedroom, you'll need to take us both with you, Cesar.

JOSH: You're the man of the house, act like it, honey.

DOMINGO: You could read to us out loud from *The Odyssey* in a new translation by Robert Fagles, as published by the Viking Press, don't think I haven't noticed. I pay attention to details, Cesar.

CESAR: If you were to spend a little more time actually reading the book than the front cover, you'd be doing a lot better.

DOMINGO: But how are you doing? You have all the means of civilization, comfort, culture, appliances, and you're not happy, homes. You have me now and you're scared still, scared of my sweat on your face.

JOSH: Scared of a three-way, man.

CESAR: Not scared, I'm just naturally cautious.

DOMINGO: Then we'll just proceed without you, man. Come here, Joshie, come over, be a good boy. Good boy. *(To Cesar.)* You can think of it as a private show, just for you; you think you're so mature and so establishment, and so afraid of offending the voters –

JOSH: Fuck the voters, man!

DOMINGO: Shut up, Joshie, be a good boy, this is my little speech to the future congressman, or whatever it is that he wants to be. *(To Cesar.)* Josh is nice and warm in my arms, and he's all hot blood circulating through his veins into his wee little brain, which he more than makes up for when the blood inflates his huge penis.

JOSH: Yeah! It's big.

DOMINGO: And he's blood and flesh and I've got him now in my arms, and you're too afraid to have him and you'd like to have him, too, don't you? Have us both for that matter at the same time, because fantasy is not forbidden to you, you're not above it. You're not superior to anybody else. We want to celebrate that with you, Cesar, because you've been alone for way too long and we want the solitude to stop here and now. Josh and

I…*(Kisses Josh.)* we're right here for you and we want you to be happy for once.

CESAR: My happiness doesn't require numbers; one lover will do.

JOSH: Monogamy sucks.

DOMINGO: And so will you in a minute, Cesar, just watch! *(Domingo kisses Josh, and they start making out heavily in front of him.)*

CESAR: That's very lovely, boys, you put on a nice show. Stop that. I'll call the cops –

JOSH: 'been there, done that.

DOMINGO: Shut up!

CESAR: Alright! I understand, 'trying to teach me a lesson in conventionality versus impulse, the discourse of Dionysian instinct versus Apollonian rationality, all very Nietszchean, or is it Ayn Rand? And, yes, I've read the books, and I'm tired of the discourse, too, but I think there is such a thing as discretion and good taste, so why am I watching this? Alright, I've learned my lesson…But I still come down on the side of romance, yes, romance, boys, what you're doing is not romantic.

Because there's nothing as romantic as the nurturing power of intimacy, which I thought was possible here among us – not us, the three of us, I mean between us, Domingo and myself as one-on-one lovers…But I suppose under the influence of drugs and booze, all that is left is animalistic drive. It's a lovely sight the two of you and I've never quite been in a situation like this; I've always been monogamous, or for that matter just manual, but here, I think you're asking me to leave that aside and experiment with polygamy…boys, please! Make room!

(He gets in between them on the couch and purposely sits down between them. The two boys start groping him and kissing him as the lights go down.)

SCENE 6

(The morning after. Cesar comes out wearing a robe.)

CESAR: Domingo? Good morning?

(He gets no answer. He goes to pour himself some water. Domingo comes in, fully dressed and groomed.)

DOMINGO: You're up. You were out cold.

CESAR: Where are you going?

DOMINGO: Josh is waiting for me; I put my stuff in the car. I'll be staying with him.

CESAR: I see.

DOMINGO: I'm no good for you, Cesar.

CESAR: I knew that when you moved in –

DOMINGO: I'm serious.

CESAR: I am, too, I knew what I was getting into.

DOMINGO: You thought you did. Hey, I'll drop by occasionally and give you a good blow job, it'll be great as always –

CESAR: Domingo, only a couple of months ago you were talking about how you wanted somebody there for you. Did you mean that or not?

DOMINGO: Hey, I'm having so much fun at the club and I am learning so much more than I ever thought I would; men still want me, and they want me in bigger numbers than ever – But, as I said, I'm your friend, Cesar, hell, I'm your official fuck buddy –

CESAR: It's not only about sex. Domingo, this is your home.

DOMINGO: That's not enough to keep me here. Josh wants to go traveling, too; I've never really been outside the States visited a few family members down in Nogales, and that's it for my international travel so far. I'm saving up for Europe and maybe all of Mexico afterwards, South America, and, of course, all the men over there who are dying to meet us. See what I mean? It's impossible to slow down when life is getting ever more intense. And no, I can't devote myself to you, Cesar, to your happiness, or to us. That's it, I can't devote myself to us, the idea of us.

CESAR: What will you do now that the club's shut down?

DOMINGO: It'll come right back in a different shape and form, thanks to our great lawyer, Matt McMurphy, who is negotiating with the vice unit.

CESAR: He should stay out of it, and mind his own business.

DOMINGO: Oh, Josh and me – we've got plans, we've got a few leftover clients who need their escorts, we'll be just fine with an independent client base. See what I mean, Cesar, you are made for more important things, like getting elected and saving the community from itself.

CESAR: I'd settle for saving you from yourself.

DOMINGO: No, don't think that way. You will be a great leader for the Phoenix community, and now that you've learned line dancing, you can have a social life. Go dancing, Cesar, meet somebody who'll make you happy, who'll be loyal to you alone, somebody clever and well-read who won't be taking off when you least expect it.

(There's honking outside.)

DOMINGO: Don't you honk at me, white boy!

CESAR: You listen to me –

DOMINGO: Cesar –

CESAR: Just listen. You walk out that door, and you'll be living off strangers, you'll be on drugs, you'll be in trouble. Maybe you can glamorize it now, the excitement of it all, but deep down inside, you wanted a life of stability, you did, and you wanted it with me, admit it –

DOMINGO: Briefly maybe –
CESAR: See? You admit it.
DOMINGO: I was still in awe of you then –
CESAR: And you're not now?
DOMINGO: I've learned something about myself –
CESAR: That you have the intelligence and the beauty to reach for
          something bigger than that life.
DOMINGO: – that I'm not there yet!
CESAR: You are.
DOMINGO: No, Cesar, that's you. You have the intelligence, the education,
          and yes, even the looks for it. The man you wanted to transform
          was not me, it was you, all along. And it's there, you're all
          there, trust me. You have what it takes, in your own stuffy way,
          to be a lover and a politician, even a guy who goes line dancing.
          You pass the test, I assure you –
CESAR: Well, thank you but –
DOMINGO: I'm the one who fails the test. Please don't say anything – I'm
          just a difficult person, harder on myself than anybody else –
CESAR: Don't give up.
DOMINGO: You can do wonders, my dear, and you can do it without me.
          Josh and me – we'll be alright really, I promise. Don't be angry
          at me whatever you do. I'll always remember you for all you
          tried to do for me and my kids. It made sense; you're my hero,
          always will be. I'll even vote for the first time and I'll vote for
          you, of course, not for Mary Ann Dominguez. Please, let me go.

(Domingo kisses him on the cheek. Another honk.)

DOMINGO: Coming, I'm coming!

(Domingo exits. Cesar is left alone, lights go down.)

EPILOGUE

(Cesar speaks to the masses.)

CESAR: Tonight, we've made history, and I'm proud that you've elected
          me to represent you on our city council. I want to thank the
          people of this diverse community for their support. I think new
          leadership for a new millennium requires a dialogue among all
          the communities and I'm glad that you've appointed me as that
          spokesperson. I can do the job, and I will devote all my time,
          and I do mean all my time, to this endeavor. I have everything I
          need right here, and I thank you.

*(Cesar receives the applause and goes out to greet his fans and shake hands.
Enter Domingo who is about to follow him when Matt intervenes.)*

DOMINGO: Look, bitch, I just want to say hello to him, Okay? As a citizen,
          as a voter.

MATT:	He doesn't want to see you.
DOMINGO:	Let him tell me that.

MATT:	He doesn't answer your phone calls, does he now? I have built a good network of security around him.
DOMINGO:	So you keep him alone where nobody will touch him.
MATT:	To help him stay away from temptation.
DOMINGO:	I'm graduating at the end of the semester; I want him to come to my graduation.
MATT:	I'll give him your message along with the many other requests for public appearances.
DOMINGO:	If I could just –
MATT:	I'm sorry but you'll need to leave.

(Enter Cesar.)

DOMINGO:	Cesar, please…Cesar?
CESAR:	It's alright, Matt –
MATT:	It's not alright, we've worked very hard, and we've been lucky so far –
CESAR:	I can handle it, Matt. Leave us alone, please.
DOMINGO:	Yeah, you go ride on your broom now, okay?
MATT:	Five minutes, and then you have to go pose with Grandma.
CESAR:	I look forward to it. Thank you, Matt.

(Matt gives him a look and exits.)

CESAR:	I really haven't got much time, Domingo –
DOMINGO:	I just wanted to congratulate you, that's all, so congratulations- – and I'm getting my business degree; here's the invitation to the graduation party, come or don't come, fine, I don't care, goodbye.
CESAR:	Domingo…how are the kids?
DOMINGO:	Growing up.
CESAR:	One of them is in middle school, right?
DOMINGO:	Yep, we're getting older. I should go now, or the Wicked Witch will have the house come crashing down on me.
CESAR:	He's just trying to protect me.
DOMINGO:	I know, no bimbo eruptions.
CESAR:	I never thought of you that way. You've obviously fulfilled your promise by staying in school and graduating.
DOMINGO:	I – I wouldn't have gotten my degree without your support.
CESAR:	So I wasn't just some stuffy conventional queen giving you a hard time?
DOMINGO:	No. And I'm in rehab now, too, just so you know. Well, gotta go.
CESAR:	Domingo…we had a good time, a wild time, a dangerous time.
DOMINGO:	And now what, celibacy?
CESAR:	Not necessarily.

DOMINGO: Oh, you're seeing someone, not that bitch cow wicked witch cunt, I hope?

CESAR: State senator, gay Republican, he has to be discreet, too, but he likes *Forbidden Games*, the movie, I mean.

DOMINGO: I finally rented that piece of crap.

CESAR: And what did you really think?

DOMINGO: Better than *The Odyssey*. But you know, the Alarcon poetry, the one you recommended long ago –

CESAR: That hit the spot, huh?

DOMINGO: It was boring, too, but hey, I can appreciate boring things now; I liked you, didn't I? I loved you, at one point.

CESAR: Yes…well…now you say that.

DOMINGO: I never really said it, did I? I meant to, I forgot. I…I know I blew it, and blew it big time, but at least I never did it vanilla style. When I raunched, I raunched.

CESAR: Yes, and thank you for not revealing some of our secrets to Mary Ann Dominguez.

DOMINGO: I wanted you to succeed on behalf of all of us.

CESAR: Well, you have your degree now.

DOMINGO: Business degree, boring! But I want to own my own nightclub, and who knows, get into lots of trouble, but that's in the future…

CESAR: There is a future, see? Come here.

(Cesar gives him a hug, a light one at first, but it becomes a more intimate embrace.)

DOMINGO: You're the only one who's touched me everywhere, and I'm not talking only about sex.

CESAR: Thanks…well, I have supporters to thank.

DOMINGO: Good luck to you, Mr. Council Man.

CESAR: Thanks.

DOMINGO: Do us proud.

(They give each other a final wave, Domingo exits. Cesar stands staring. Matt calls for him.)

MATT: Cesar! Cesar!

CESAR: Coming!

(One final look and wave of goodbye and he's out of there as he goes to join the happy supporters.)

End of play